NEW COSMOPOLIS

A BOOK OF IMAGES

INTIMATE NEW YORK. CERTAIN EUROPEAN CITIES BEFORE THE WAR: VIENNA, PRAGUE, LITTLE HOLLAND, BELGIAN ETCHINGS, MADRID, DUBLIN, MARIENBAD. ATLANTIC CITY AND NEWPORT

BY

JAMES HUNEKER

NEW YORK
CHARLES SCRIBNER'S SONS
1915

Published March, 1915

To

VANCE THOMPSON

En Souvenir—"M'LLE NEW YORK"

"Vengo adesso di Cosmopoli."
—*Stendhal.*

INSTEAD OF A PREFACE

ALL my life I have longed to write a preface. Not such tinkling evasions as forewords or introductions, but a full-fledged preface which would render quite superfluous what follows it. Consider the case of Mr. Shaw. His prefaces are such witty masterpieces that they make negligible his plays. But I have never cultivated courage enough to take the first dive into chilly type. Either I have squarely dodged the solemn undertaking or compromised with a *coda;* in one instance I actually fabricated a preface for Egoists (a book that had been printed some years) and placed it in a later one. Even in the present head-line there lurks a meek qualification. However, as brevity may be a pledge of sincerity, I may say this book of sky-lines and perspectives first appeared in the hospitable columns of the New York *Sun*, *Herald*, *Times*, *Puck*, and *Metropolitan Magazine;* that the European notes were written and published before the beginning of the war (from the summer of 1909 to the spring of 1914); and that if silence is preserved as to certain art galleries of Amsterdam, The Hague, Madrid, and elsewhere, it is because these public collections with many others were treated at length in my Promenades of an Impressionist.

That inveterate cosmopolite, Stendhal, wished to be in a city where the people were most like him. Now, Max Stirner, implacable philosopher of egoism, would never have acknowledged there could be a place where his like might be found. As a cosmopolitan by self-election, I agree with both these egoists. The world at large is compounded of rhythmic surprise and charm, as may well be our intimate life; their enjoyment depends upon the vision and sympathy we bring to them. If Stendhal were in New York to-day he could write: Lo, I am at Cosmopolis! The New Cosmopolis. Let me conclude this meagre apology for a preface with the declaration of literary faith made by J.-K. Huysmans: "I record what I see, what I feel, what I have experienced, writing it as well as I can, *et voilà tout!*"

CONTENTS

PART I

Intimate New York

PART II

Certain European Cities Before the War

CONTENTS

PART I

INTIMATE NEW YORK

I

THE FABULOUS EAST SIDE

THE illusions of the middle-aged die hardest. At twenty I discovered, with sorrow, that there was no such enchanted spot as the Latin Quarter. An old Frenchman with whom I dined daily at that time in a luxurious Batignolles gargote informed me that Paris had seen the last of the famous quarter after the Commune, but a still older person who wrote obituary notices for the parish swore the Latin Quarter had not been in existence since 1848; the swelling tide of democracy had swept away the darling superstitions of the students, many of whom became comfortably rich when Napoleon the Little grasped the crown. This I set down as pure legend. Had I not seen young painters, poets, and musicians in baggy velvet trousers walk up and down the Boul' Mich' during the exposition of 1878? And they still pranced about the cafés and brasseries in 1914, their hair as long as their thirst. There may be no Latin Quarter, but the Latin Quarter is ever in a young man's soul who goes to Paris in pursuit of the golden fleece of art.

I recovered from the disillusionment and no more bothered my head about this pasteboard Bohemia than I did at the island of Marken when I was told that its Dutch peasants with their picturesque costumes and head-dress were moonshine manufactured by an enterprising travel bureau to attract tourists. Are there not more Puritans in the West than in New England? But the loss of such a treasured illusion as our own East Side smote me severely. When young and buoyant one illusion crowds out another. After you have crossed the great divide of fifty, with the mountains of the moon behind you, and an increasing waist measurement before you, the annulment of a cherished image wounds the soul.

The East Side with its Arabian Nights entertainment was such an image. Twenty years ago you could play the rôle of the disguised Sultan and with a favourite Vizier sally forth at eve from Park Row in pursuit of strange adventures. What thrilling encounters! What hairbreadth escapes! What hand-to-hand struggles with genii, afrits, imps — bottle-imps, very often — dangerous bandits, perilous policemen and nymphs or thrice dangerous anarchists! To slink down an ill-lighted, sinister alley full of Chinese and American tramps, to hurry by solitary policemen as if engaged in some criminal enterprise, to enter the abode of them that never wash, where bad beer and terrible tobacco filled the air with discordant perfumes — ah! what joys for adventurous souls, what tremendous dawns over Williamsburg, what glorious headaches were ours on awakening the next night!

An East Side there was in those hardy times, and it was still virginal to settlement-workers, sociological cranks, impertinent reformers, self-advertising politicians, billionaire socialists, and the ubiquitous newspaper man. Magazine writers had not topsyturvied the ideas of the tenement dwellers, nor were the street-cleaner, the Board of Health, and other destroyers of the picturesque in evidence. It was the dear old dirty, often disreputable, though never dull East Side; while now the sentimentalist feels a heart pang to see the order, the cleanliness, the wide streets, the playgrounds, the big boulevards, the absence of indigence that have spoiled the most interesting part of New York City.

Well I remember the night, years ago, when finding ourselves in Tompkins Square we went across to Justus Schwab's and joined an anarchist meeting in full swing. There were no bombs, though there was plenty of beer. A more amiable and better-informed man than Schwab never trod carpet slippers. The discussions in German and English betrayed a culture not easily duplicated on the West Side — wherever that mysterious territory really is. Before Nietzsche's and Stirner's names were pronounced in our lecture-rooms they were familiarly quoted at Schwab's. By request I played The Marseillaise and The International Hymn on an old piano — smoke-stained, with rattling keys and a cracked tone — which stood at the rear upon a platform. All was peace and a flow of soul;

yet the place was raided before midnight and a band of indignant, also merry, prisoners marched to the police-station. Naturally no one was detained but Schwab. The police felt called upon to arrest somebody around Tompkins Square about once a month. Anarchist Outrages was the usual newspaper head-line. Why are the Mafia performers never called anarchs? To-day the Black Hand terrorises a region where the bombs in the old times were manufactured of ink for the daily papers. They generally blow themselves up, these anarchists; but there is nothing adventurous in having an eye or a leg blown away by a Sicilian you have never seen. To be arrested twenty years ago for the romantic crime of playing The Marseillaise on a badly tuned piano — is it any wonder I get sentimental when I think of an East Side that is no more? Perhaps the younger generation, which Ibsen described as "knocking," may have its nooks unknown to us, but the old fascination has flown.

Yet like the war-horse that is put out to grass and rears when it hears the tin dinner horn, we pricked ears on learning one summer afternoon that up on First Avenue there was a wonderful brew of beer to be had. Pilsner beer served across genuine Bohemian tables! How the rumour came to my ears I've forgotten, but I was not long in sending its glad import over the telephone. Remember that we now dwell in a city where never before has so much badly kept beer been sold. The show-places are gaudy and Americanised. Fashionable slummers whose fathers wore leathern aprons and drank their beer from tin pails sip champagne at some noisy gilded cabarets or summer gardens to the banging and scraping of fake gipsy orchestras. Where are the small old-fashioned beer saloons of yesteryear with the sanded floor, the pinochle players, and the ripe, pure beverage? Indeed, the German element on the East Side is in the minority. At least it seems so, for your eardrums are pelted by Bohemian, Yiddish, Hun, Italian, Russian, and other tongues. Many speak German, some sort of German, but the original Germans, the Urdeutsch who came to America more than half a century ago, are dead or decaying; their sons and daughters and grandchildren have moved into more fashionable districts and shudder if you mention the name of Goethe.

At first the Professor demurred. He is not timid, but a creature of habit. To tell him the news fraught with significance that you could imbibe foamy nectar while sitting on a high stool in front of a bar, a real, pleasant Bohemian facing you, your elbows occasionally joggled by visiting "growlers," did not appeal to my bookish friend as I had expected. I routed the Painter den, and by combined assault we carried the Professor up-town.

"Get off," I said, "at Seventy-second Street and walk across to First Avenue."

We did so. The prosperity of the neighbourhood after we crossed Third Avenue was positively dispiriting. First Avenue we discovered to be wider than Broadway. Oddly enough, human beings like ourselves passed to and fro. It was the hottest hour of the afternoon. The world in shirt-sleeves sat perched upon steps or chairs, lounged in doorways watching the multitudinous babies that rolled over the sidewalk. The east side of the avenue was deserted, for the sun beat upon the walls and reverberated blinding rays. Of drunkenness we saw none. We were in the Bohemian quarter. At Sokol Hall on Seventy-third Street there were a few pool games in progress; no one stood at the bar. I was the spokesman:

"Isn't there," I said in my choicest Marienbad Bohemian, "isn't there a remarkable Pilsner Urquell somewhere in this neighbourhood?"

"We also sell Pilsner," was the Slavic, evasive answer of a bartender with the mask of a tragic actor.

"Oh, he means Joe's," interrupted a sympathetic bystander. "Of course, Joe keeps the dandy beer."

To this there would be but one reply. We stood treat to the house and went to Kasper's, followed at a discreet distance by several patriots.

By this time the Professor's collar and temper were running a race for the wilting sweepstakes. Joe was pleased to see us. We sat on the celebrated high stools at the bar, and Gambrinus would have been satisfied. It was the essence of Pilsen, Prague, Marienbad, all in a large glass. Joe discoursed. He was proud that we liked his interpretation of the wet blond masterpiece; but not too proud. You can't spoil Joe. He is a wary and travelled man. His son, born here, he tells you with ill-concealed affection, is a violinist, a pupil at Vienna of Sevic, the great teacher of Kubelik, of Kocian! Who knows whether another K may not be added to this group. We drink his health and venture the hope that the triumph of the youthful Kasper will not put into the head of the father any futile notion of retiring. Art is all very well. Violin virtuosi abound; but few men there are who know the subtle science of keeping beer at a proper temperature.

"Look here," cried the Professor, "this is nice, but how about the East Side that you are going to show us, the East Side which is not in existence?"

I suggested that we were on the East Side, up-town, to be sure, nevertheless East Side.

"I want to see the East Side of George Luks, and please spare us your antiquated memories. George Moore knows how to relate memories of his dead life, but you don't. Let's be going." It was the Professor in his most didactic mood.

The Painter who was comfortably anchored, sighed profoundly. He didn't need to leave a snug harbour to see the East Side of George Luks. To my remonstrances and heated assertion that there was no more East Side, that it was only a fable, the Professor bristled up like the Celt he is. "What, then, is the use of writing about a thing that no longer exists? Or, as Israel Zangwill asks in the form of a magnificent pun, 'What's the use of being a countess if you have nothing to count.'" This was too much, and in less than an hour we were threading the intricacies of Grand Street, heading for the region of socialistic rainbows.

"They're off!" chuckled the Painter as he drew forth his sketching pad and pencil.

After a tolerably long tramp we turned south. The street was narrow and not too odorous. High buildings on either side were pierced by numerous windows from which hung frowzy ladies, usually with babies at their bosoms; the fire-escapes were crowded with bedclothes, the middle of the street filled with quarrelling children. The national game on a miniature scale was in progress, and on the sidewalks when the push-cart men permitted, encouraging voices called aloud in Yiddish to the baseball heroes. I don't know what they said, but I caught such phrases as these: "Yakie! Schlemil! machen Sie dot first base! Esel! Oh, du!" And the little Jacob toiled up the street and down again, sprawling over garbage-cans, upsetting two girls dressed in resplendent ribbons for Shabbas, finally touching an old basket and getting full in his smudged features a soft tomato. "Aus!" yelled the umpire who was immediately kicked in the stomach. "Aus! Out!" came in delirious tones from a dancing mass of men — Jewish men with the traditional whiskers, brown straw hats, and alpaca coats. It was startling even to the Professor.

"There is your twentieth-century East Side for you," I began, but the Painter watched other things.

"Yet they think Luks is too realistic, don't they? Just look at those girls." He pointed out a red-headed Irish girl clutching a blonde girl, unmistakably a German blonde, who were both dreamily waltzing to the faded tune of The Merry Widow.

Music which we hurry from across town is near the East River music the conqueror. It mellows the long hours of dry, dusty summer days, and it sets moving in earnest if not graceful rhythms the legs of the little ones. Suddenly the organ began a gallop. Off whisked the girls — Delia and Marike were their names, we were later informed — off they went like two abandoned spielers disguised as children of poverty. What movement! What fire! The blonde with her silvery locks stamped and whirled off her feet the trim Irish girl with the dark red curls.

"Are you chaps never coming along?" asked the Professor. "It will be night soon, and we haven't seen anything yet."

"He's afraid Mouquin's will close before he gets back to civilisation," sardonically whispered the Painter. Luckily the Professor didn't hear.

The café was not well lighted. At the marble tables stooped the bent backs of old men, men who wore curls over their ears, whose hats were only removed at bedtime. They played chess in the dusk and drank coffee at intervals, regarding their neighbours suspiciously. Rembrandt would have admired the dim, misty corners where on musty divans he could have discerned a head, partly in shadow, a high light on the bridge of the nose, or fingers snapping with exultation in a sudden shaft of sunlight that came through a window opening on the west. Groups of two or three hovered about the players. The stillness was punctuated by street cries and the occasional rumbling of that ramshackle horse-car the sight of which sends your wits wool-gathering back to the '80's.

"Wake up," urged the Painter. "I'm going to sketch that table in the corner; the two old birds are watching each other as if plunder were hid somewhere. You know they are afraid to drink beer because a drop too much might lose them a move. So they stick to coffee." He went away, the Professor following.

"Is your friend a painter or only one of those newspaper artists who worry us so much?"

I turned. Beside me sat a mythical old fellow, white-haired, his coat buttoned to his neck, no shirt, evidently, and the hand which plucked his beard as white as a girl's — a girl who has white hands, I mean.

"You look like the Ancient Mariner," I said, "or a Hebraic Walt Whitman."

He smiled. "I may be both for all you know; but you haven't answered my question."

He inclined a benevolent ear. I informed him of our mission and of my disappointment. Again the smile, a smile as ancient as the world and as fresh as to-morrow.

"It is this way," he confided, and his deep-set eyes sparkled. "You are an idealist. Wait until you are seasoned by eighty years. I am eighty, and I've lived on the so-called East Side for sixty of my years. I speak English better than I do Yiddish, yet to earn my bread I write Yiddish plays, stories, love-letters, and would preach if my voice would hold out. I am an ex-rabbi. You know what a rabbi is; you are old enough. An ex-anything is a mistake — particularly an ex-dramatic critic or an ex-president."

"You must have seen many changes in your life over here," I ventured.

"My friend, I have seen many changes, yet nothing changes. We are born, live more or less unhappily, and die. That's all. There are more of my co-religionists now than there were when we first went up the Bowery. Then they pulled my beard and threw stones at us. Now we live in houses built, perhaps, with those very stones; certainly built by our forbearance. We live ——"

He prosed on. He bored me, this octogenarian who resembled both the Ancient Mariner and Walt Whitman. I stopped his rambling by asking: "I suppose the Socialists and settlement-workers have greatly improved the East Side?"

He sat up and roared like an approaching earthquake. The chess-players looked at him, shrugged shoulders, and again tackled their problems. The Professor deserted the Painter and tiptoed out to us. The Painter never budged.

"Socialists! What are they? They have stirred up my people with empty words, fine phrases. Oh, the dreamers of the Ghetto. This idea of an earthly paradise you may trace back to the Persians, to the Babylonians, perhaps to the Sumerians. We are always looking for the coming of him who will rescue us. We are the idealistic leaven in whatever national bakery we find ourselves. You Americans are smarter. When the dollars arrive you are satisfied; it is your heaven on earth; but for the poor, who know nothing, have nothing, golden words fill them with hope. Better prisons than those slimy deceptions of socialism. Yes, our girls marry rich Goyem, rich gentiles — let a woman alone for finding a tub of butter — and then they come down here, some to live and work — their tongue — and tell more lies to dreamers. Ach! it is awful. And your settlement-workers, the white mice, we call them. They mean well, but they are generally misguided busybodies. They pry, pry, pry, and ask insulting questions. Even if we are poor we are humans; we have feelings too. If a Jew is pious they give him a New Testament. They bore or frighten our wives, though they do a lot of good, helping the hungry poor. Yet children go to school hungry. Don't believe altogether in those sights of big new tenements, playgrounds, public schools; there is a lot of misery on your renovated East Side that your philanthropists never reach, that those funny sociological students never see."

I rose.

"Break away!" said the Painter. "I caught the old prophet in my note-book while he was gassing. Let's get out of here."

I bade farewell to the venerable Jeremiah. He looked sadly after us. Not a drink, not a smoke — nothing! And all that wisdom dissipated into thin air, or into ears that heeded not. I was glad when we passed through the narrow doorway obstructed by a wretched rubber plant — or was it a hat-rack?

Without the sky seemed rolled back from the roofs and was a deep blue transfused by the citron-tinted afterglow of a setting sun. On the street were the fuliginous oil-lamps of peddlers. The din was terrific; it mingled with the smell of fish, fruit, and grease. A motley mob jostled us from the pavements; the middle was the safest roadway. An old woman who sat combing her thin grey hair directed us westward; we thought we had lost our bearings. Slatternly females chaffered with the Jewish and Italian push-cart men. Their gestures were not unlike; southern Europe and remotest Russia employ the sign language, a voluble digital language it is. Shrieks of laughter and dismay attracted us farther up. A dwarf with a big head and dressed in the uniform of the Salvation Army was hemmed in by half a hundred teasing children of all nationalities. I assure you that I saw white girls with Chinese slitted eyes, little Irish girls with the Hebraic nose curve, negro boys with straight hair and blue eyes. A vast cauldron — every race bubbles and boils and fuses on the East Side. The children are happy. They are noisy and devilish in their energy. They howled at the dwarf, "Pee Wee!" He was impassive and distributed circulars. In front of a kosher fowl shop another small cyclone was in progress. The place was locked, but in the gaslight we could detect hundreds of chickens hopping over the counter and shelves, and the joy their antics gave the little ones outside was worth a dozen Christmas pantomimes.

"To the Hall of Genius, that's where we are heading, boys!" answered the Painter to a query from the Professor.

I had now become the crusty member of the

crowd. I was tired. The coffee at the chess café had given me a headache; besides, things were not exactly going my way. I came out on this expedition prepared to scoff, and while I had not remained to pray, nevertheless was I disappointed. So I irritably inquired: "What Hall of Genius? What new pipe-dream is this?"

Good-temperedly he returned: "It *is* a pipe-dream, and before we go up Second Avenue I want you to see what you can't see anywhere outside Paris."

"The Latin Quarter?" I sneered.

"No; Montmartre. Now just hustle along, please. It is getting late and I'm hungry."

As we entered the hall the buzzing of voices was almost deafening. At least a hundred tables were crowded with men and women. On the balconies were more tables. Every one was drinking either coffee or beer; the men smoked pipes, cigarettes, with here and there a few cigars. The odour was appalling. I never knew Mother Earth grew such poisonous, weedy tobaccos. We found seats not far from the door.

"It's easier to escape," remarked our guide, philosopher, and friend, "and it's easier to point out the celebrities."

"What celebrities?" faintly inquired the Professor, who was almost a physical wreck.

"Celebrities!" was the response. "Well, I should say so. There's enough brains and genius under this roof at the present moment to burn up our universities, our musical conservatories, our paint-pot academies" — here the Painter paused, I fancied maliciously — "our law courts."

"But why, why haven't we heard of these transcendent individuals?" I interposed.

"Over there," continued the Painter, not heeding my question, "over there is a young fellow who has written the best short story since Edgar Poe. It's so good no one dreams of printing it."

"There are a hundred like him who have written the best story since Poe — only they hug the Great White Way," hinted the Professor cynically.

The Painter gave him a sour look.

"Never mind. I'm telling this story. The fellow I mean is bald. That's why he keeps his hat on. But the remnants of his hair are curly."

"I dare him to remove his hat." The Professor it was who spoke. I kicked him under the table.

"That fat youth yonder," tranquilly resumed the Painter, "is a second Ernest Lawson. He never saw a Lawson landscape because he never got farther than Second Avenue. His clothes, as you see, are not suitable; but if he ever starts in painting as he can ["But won't," cruelly intercalated the Professor] — then he may join the Academy."

"Fudge," said I.

"Fudge or not, he is a genius. He works, when he does work, in a carriage factory. His friend is the grandest dramatist of the age, without a Broadway production. It's a pity he can only write in Bulgarian. The woman sitting near him has Duse, Bernhardt, and Nazimova beaten to a pulp as actresses."

The Professor stood up wearily.

"Now I'm going," he said. "I suppose you will show us next the most extraordinary composer on the planet."

"Precisely," acquiesced the Painter. "To your left is a Russian pianist who has the charm of Paderewski, the magic of Joseffy, the technique of Rosenthal, and the caprice of De Pachmann."

We paid the reckoning. Catching our waiter by his tin badge I asked him as my friends moved streetward: "Who are those folks at the next table? Are they poets or painters or musicians?"

"Nichts! Your friend was having fun with you," answered the waiter. "They are nearly all cloakmakers, and work in the neighbourhood."

"Oh, hollow East Side! Oh, humbug Painter!" I ejaculated when we reached Second Avenue and its cool, well-lighted perspectives. The Painter smiled.

"I faked you a bit of the East Side you writing fellows are always looking for. Now for dinner."

We ate paprika-seasoned food to the clangour

of the usual gipsy band that never saw the Hungarian Putzta. It was at one of the tinsel Bohemias so plentifully scattered along the avenue. I was better satisfied than earlier in the evening, for I had proved that the old East Side was fabulous. I said as much, and was called ungrateful.

"Isn't it interesting, anyhow?" demanded in unison Professor and Painter.

We were about to part at the corner of the street. It was midnight. Suddenly a thin, scared voice asked us to buy flowers. The girl was small. She wore a huge shawl, and on her head was a shapeless hat over which lolled queer plants. But that shawl! It was fit for her fat grandmother and must have weighed heavily upon her frail shoulders. Her features were not easy to distinguish; her eyes seemed mere empty sockets.

The Painter looked at her.

"What you got under that shawl?" he sharply questioned.

The wretched child shifted her feet. "A pussy-cat I found on Second Street. I'm taking it home fer me sisters."

We bought her ridiculous flowers and she disappeared.

"A regular Luks," I observed.

"A Luks all right, all right," chimed in the Painter.

We went home.

II

THE LUNGS

I

A BROAD chest usually means healthy lungs. Now, Manhattan Island is notoriously narrow-chested. Her scanty space across is not redeemed by greater length. Crowded with humans and their houses, there is consequently little space for the expansion of her normal breathing powers. Her lungs, *i. e.*, her parks, are contracted and not enough of them; there never will be. But more than some people think.

New Yorkers, even the most convinced cockneys, know little of their city, or of its lungs. Not only provincial, but parochial, they are only acquainted with the square or little park that adorns — it's a poor park that doesn't bring a sense of adornment — their native ward. Imagine my amazement when I learned after nearly thirty years' residence here that there were one hundred and eighty-two parks in the five boroughs. I read it in a newspaper and couldn't understand why I hadn't discovered the fact, for I've always been a rambler and my happy hunting-ground usually has been the East Side.

However, seeing is believing, and last summer, with my eyes made innocent by several years' residence in Germany, Austria, Holland, Belgium, France, and England, I determined to verify certain vague suspicions that had been assailing my consciousness: that perhaps New York was not inferior in attractiveness to London, Paris, Vienna, Berlin, or Brussels. Perhaps many who go down to the sea in steamers, their pockets filled with letters of credit, might be equally shocked when confronted by the sights and sounds of Manhattan. Perhaps — but let us start on a little tour into intimate New York, without a megaphone or a ready-made enthusiasm; above all, let us be meek and avoid boastful rhetoric; also dodge statistics. Go to the guide-books, thou sluggard, for the latter!

When a writer tackles such a big theme as New York he as a rule fetches a deep breath in the lower bay, steams as far as Staten Island, and then lets loose the flood-gate of adjectives. How the city looks as you enter it is the conventional point of attack. I am sorry to say that whenever I have returned from Europe, the first peep of lower Manhattan, with its craggy battlements, its spires splintering the very firmament, and the horrid Statue of Liberty, all these do so work on my spirit that I feel like repining. Not because I am home again — not, my friend, because the spectacle is an uplifting one, but, shame that I must confess the truth, because my return means back to toil, back to the newspaper forge, there to resume my old job of wordsmith. Why, the very symbol of liberty, that stupid giant female, with her illuminating torch, becomes a monster of hated mien, her torch a club that ominously threatens us: Get to work! Get to work!

Therefore I'll begin at Battery Park, leaving the waterways, the arteries and veins of the city, for a future disquisition.

The image stamped on my memory is the reverse of the immobile. A plastic picture. The elevated roads debouching here are ugly, but characteristic. I'm afraid I can't see in our city anything downright ugly — it is never an absolute for me; as Dostoievsky said, there are no ugly women. The elevated road structure is hideous if æsthetically considered, and that is precisely the way it should not be considered. It rolls thousands daily to this end of the town; they usually take the ferries or subways, a few stroll under the scanty trees, or visit the Aquarium, so we must be critically charitable, too.

Oh, how tired I am of being told that Jenny Lind made her début in this same Castle Garden, "presented" by the late Phineas T. Barnum! Wasn't it a historical fort before it became a hall of immigrants and the abode of the fishes? This much may be said for the latter — it is a real aquarium, and, excepting the absence of an octopus or two, the collection rivals those at Brighton, England (where there are octopi); Naples, Hamburg, and elsewhere.

More exciting than the fish, the seal, or the porpoises are the people. Thousands elbow through the rather narrow aisles and stare as solemnly at the finny inhabitants as they are stared at in return. The sightseeing coaches give their passengers a quarter of an hour's grace to "do" the show, while ragged boys dance about them, obsequiously pilot them, mock them, quite after the manner of the ragged boy on the Marina at Naples.

A veritable boon is this open Battery Park when the gang of wage-earners have fled the lower reaches of the city, when the dishes have been washed, when the janitors and caretakers of the tall buildings bring their wives and children to catch the breeze from the bay. On moonlit nights there are few situations more romantic. Here is freedom for the eye, for the lungs. There are not enough benches, but the walking is good, and to stand on the edge of the "wharf" and watch the bright eyes of ferries, the blazing eyes of the Jersey and Brooklyn shores, and the eyes of Staten Island as the unstable floor of the water mirrors (a cracked mirror) the moonlight and distorts the tiny flames about it, is to enjoy a spectacle fit for men and women who are not afraid to love their birthplace. I like it better when the weather has a nipping freshness and the day is grey-coloured and full of the noises of broken waters, and the cry of birds.

The seamy side of Battery Park is the poor

castaway who has sought its coolness after a hot day of panhandling. But — given a certain amount of leeway — he is harmless. When a woman, the case assumes the pathetic. Begging is semisecretly indulged in. You drop your nickel and escape. If it be daytime you make for South Street to pay that long-deferred visit to Coenties Slip and Jeannette Park.

Perhaps you have seen C. F. W. Mielatz's coloured etching of the slip; if you have, the optical repercussion will be all the stronger when looking at the place itself. The fine old musty flavour of the slip, the canal-boats near the little Jeannette Park — a backwater with its stranded humanity stolidly waiting for something to turn up — and the lofty, lowering warehouses bring memories of London docks; docks where slunk Rogue Riderhood in search of rum after he had landed his dead cargo; docks from which sailed, still sail, wooden ships with real wooden masts, canvas sails, and sailors of flesh and blood, bound on some secret errand to southern seas where under the large few stars they may mutiny and cut the captain's throat; or else return to live immortally in fascinating legends of Joseph Conrad. I almost became sentimental over Coenties Slip, probably because Mielatz had etched it, and also because I had been reading Conrad. Art always reacts on nature, and the reactions may be perfectly sincere.

However, I thought it time to ask a policeman the direction of Corlears Park. He didn't know.

No one knew, until an old chap who smelt of of fish and whisky said: "It's Cor-*lears*, you want?" I had misplaced the accent, and the ear of the average longshoreman in South Street for quantity would please a college professor of Greek.

I went my winding way, finally enlightened. I like the London bobby, for he is obliging and instructive, but I also like our policeman. He is gruffer than his English contemporary — a shy sort of gruffness. I found myself at Canal Street and the Bowery — I don't know why — and was told to continue eastward. If I had taken a Grand Street car to the ferry my journey would have been simplified, but then I should have missed East Broadway and a lot of sights, of which more anon.

I dived into the east. It was a noisy, narrow lane rather than a street, and the inhabitants, mostly babies, were sprawling over the sidewalks. Often I followed the line of the gutter. Then I reached an open space and was disappointed. It was Corlears Park, and the absence of shade was painful. This lack of trees is a fault to be found in the majority of municipal parks and playgrounds. Night, if you don't feel too scared or lonely, is the proper time to enjoy the Hook. The view of the East River is unimpeded. The water is crowded with craft. A breeze always fans one. Women and children, principally Italians and Jews, sit or walk. Cats are friendly. So is the small boy who knocks off your straw tile with his stick. A venerable steamboat, rotting and dismal, the relic of a once proud excursion career, is warped to the wharf. It has flowers on its upper deck, and pale, sick people sit on the lower. You are informed by the inevitable busybody who traipses after strangers that the old boat is now for tuberculosis patients, living or dying, in the neighbourhood. What an ending for man and machine! Hecker's huge structure dominates the upper end of the park, as does Hoe's building over in Grand Street. The chief thing is the cleanliness and spaciousness. The same may be found at Rutgers Park, but without a water-front, always an added attraction.

Tompkins Square stirred memories. It lies between Seventh and Tenth Streets and Avenues A and B. When I first remember it, it was also called the Weisse-Garten, and no foreign nationality but German lived on its arid fringes.

The anarchists of those days gathered at Justus Schwab's, whose saloon was on First Street. There I first became acquainted with Johann Most, an intelligent and stubborn man, if ever there was one, and other "reds," the majority of them now dead. I remember, in 1887, the funeral parade in commemoration of the anarchists executed in Chicago because of the Haymarket affair. A sombre procession of proletarians with muffled drums, black flags, and dense masses of humans. I didn't go home that night. To my surprise I found the old-fashioned bird store — where they once sold folding bird-cages (collapsible) — in the same place, on Avenue A, near Seventh Street. The park is mightily improved. There are more trees, and also playgrounds for boys and girls, a band-stand, and refreshment pavilions.

I entered. On the benches I found "lobbies" of old men, Germans, Israelites for the most part. They were very old, very active, contented, and loquacious. They settled at a "sitzung" the affairs of the nation, keeping all the while a sharp lookout on the antics of their grandchildren, curly-haired, bright-eyed kiddies who rolled on the grass. The boys and girls literally made the welkin ring with their games, in the enclosures. They seemed healthy and happy. There are vice and poverty on the East Side — and the West — but there are also youth and decency and pride. I should say that optimism was the rule. Naturally, in summer, even poverty wears its rue with a difference. I saw little save cheerfulness, and heard much music-making by talented children.

The Tenth Street side of Tompkins Square reminds me of upper Stuyvesant Square. It is positively well-to-do, many doctors and dentists hanging out their shingles on the quaint, pleasant-looking brick houses. A very old German Lutheran meeting-house is at the corner of Ninth Street and Avenue B, and one block lower is St. Bridget's Church. Not afar is a synagogue or "Shool," as they call it, and you may catch a glimpse of the stately Church of the Holy Redeemer on Third Street near Avenue A, with its cartridge-shaped spire (easily seen from Brooklyn Bridge), that suggests shooting the soul to heaven if you are willing.

Time was when the Felsenkeller, at the foot of Fifty-seventh Street, East River, was an agreeable spot of summer nights. It was an open-air café, and while sipping your beverage you could watch the wheels of passing steamboats. It exists no longer. You must go up to East River Park, at Eighty-sixth Street and the river, or to Jefferson Park, opposite Ward's Island, to enjoy the water. There are little grassy hills, with rocks, at the former park that give you the illusion of nature.

I can't say much in favor of Union Square — now hopelessly encumbered with débris — or of Gramercy Park, locked to the public (you are permitted the barren enjoyment of gazing at the bleak enclosure), or of Madison Square, with its wonderful surroundings. These be places familiar. Nor do I care to drag you over to Hudson Park, on the West Side, to Abingdon Square, to Chelsea, De Witt Clinton, Seward, to other parks of another kind duplicated everywhere, even to the scarcity of foliage and benches. Mount Morris Park, at One Hundred and Twenty-fourth Street and Madison Avenue, was, a few decades ago, not so crowded as it is to-day. The hegira up-town has made it as populous as Tompkins Square. And not so pleasant. A little café, with a back garden on the west side of the square, was once a favourite resort years ago. Schmierkäse and pumpernickel, and — Tempus fugit!

II

I positively refuse to sing the praises of Central Park — which was laid out in 1857 (avaunt, statistics!) — simply because that once haughty and always artificial dame is fast becoming an old lady in plain decadence. Who has not sung her praises! Hardly a park, rather a cluster of graceful arboreal arabesques, which surprise and charm, Central Park is, nevertheless, moribund, and all the king's horses and all the king's men can never set her up again in her former estate. The city itself has assassinated her, not by official neglect, but by the proximity of stone, steel, and brick, which is slowly robbing her of her sustenance of earth, air, and moisture.

In the first flush of spring or a few early summer days she wears her old smile of brightness. How welcome the leafy arch of the Mall, how impressive, how "European" the vista of the Bethesda fountain, the terrace, and the lake; how pleasing it is to sit under the arbour of the Casino piazza and watch the golden girls and slim gilt lads arrive in motor-cars!

Then the Ramble, or the numerous bypaths that lead to the reservoir, or that give on the bridle-paths, wherein joyous youth with grooms flit by, or prosperous cits showing lean, crooked shanks painfully bump on horses too wide for them. Ah, yes! Central Park will continue for years to furnish amusement (if that wretched Zoo were only banished to the Bronx!) and deep breathing for the lucky rider who lives on its borders. Also furnish fun for May parties, June walks, and July depredations. It is a miracle of landscape-gardening, notwithstanding its absence of monotony — it abounds in too many twists and turns; it is seldom reposeful, because broad meadows are absent. You can't do much in decoration without flat surfaces. But what mortal could accomplish Frederick Law Olmsted and Calvert Vaux accomplished; the impending ruin is the result of pitiless natural causes.

I once said that one can't be a flâneur in a city without trees. New York is almost treeless, and Central Park soon will be. When not so long ago I saluted the Obelisk on the Thames embankment, that antique and morose stylite sent its regards to its brother in our Park. Some day when the last Yankee (the breed is rapidly running out) will look at the plans of what was once Central Park, hanging in the Metropolitan Museum, his eye will caress the Obelisk across the way. That strange shaft will endure when New York is become an abomination and a desolation.

Arthur Brisbane's notion that the nasty little lakes and water pools be drained and refilled with salt water for bathing purposes is a capital one. Gone at a swoop malaria and evil odours; gone, too, the mosquitoes which make life miserable for nigh dwellers. But the park is doomed; let us enjoy its ancient bravery while we may.

I never skated at Van Cortlandt Park, because I can't skate; but I love the spot, love the old mansion and its relics, love the open feeling about it. Atop of the highest part of the island is Isham Park. To reach it get off at the Two Hundred and Seventh Street Subway station and walk westwardly up the hill, or through Isham Street. On the brow is the little park, looking up and down the Hudson and across Spuyten Duyvil. A rare spot to watch aeroplane races. Not far away is the Billings castle, and across the Fort Washington Road the studio and Gothic cloisters of the sculptor George Grey Barnard.

Often have I enjoyed the Zoological Garden in the Bronx, the Botanical Garden, and the Bronx Park. Our Zoo is easily the largest and most complete in the world. I've visited all the European Zoos, from Amsterdam and Hamburg to Vienna and Budapest. As for the Botanical Garden, I have the famous botanist Hugo de Vries of Amsterdam as a witness, who told me he would be happy to live near it always. The Bronx River is an "intimate" creek and malodorous, but do you remember what cunning little French restaurants were in vogue up there two or three decades ago? F. Hopkinson Smith celebrated one of them in a short story. To-day they charge you more for wine and cookery that are inferior to the old-time establishments. Or has Time intervened with its soft pedal on the gustatory sense? I don't believe it. The enjoyment of the table is the longest surviving of the sociable peccadillos, and nothing can prove to me that either my Burgundy or my Bordeaux palate has deteriorated. But if I get on the subject of food we shall never see Pelham Parkway.

I didn't drive the devil wagon, else I should never have seen what I did — at least not in such brief time and in such a pleasant way. For ten hours my friend wheeled me up Tremont Avenue, the Southern Boulevard — and such boulevards! — to Pelham Parkway, with the park of one thousand seven hundred acres and more (I read this in a guide-book) up from the Harlem River, through magnificent shore and country, the Sound in sight, and a general sense of being in a primeval forest that had been cultivated by super-apes. On grey days the mist along the sedge grass of the water evokes delightful melancholy. We whizzed through towns I had heard of but never visited. Oh, shame! Think of Mount Vernon, Yonkers, Irvington, and Tarrytown! All new to this desperate cockney.

However, it was Pelham Bay that set me shouting. There's a park for you! The entire cityful could go out there, hold a cyclopean picnic, and have plenty of room to turn around in. It is not Fairmount Park, for that is the largest in the East, but it's the nearest thing to it. It is the combination of water and woods that is attractive. The Philadelphia park has the same, but on a vaster scale. Of European parks I can recall none that approaches Pelham — the Boboli Gardens and Cascine at Florence, Hyde, Regent, St. James's, and other London Parks, the Bois, Tuileries, and the Jardin d'Acclimatation, Paris, the Prater, Vienna (a lovely spot), Charlottenburg Chaussée, Berlin — none of these matches Pelham Parkway. The automobiles seem to eat space on the smooth roadbeds. When the projected Bronx Parkway is an accomplished fact, the motorists ought to be forever satisfied.

We crossed from the Sound over to the Hudson on excellent roads. I began to wonder why any one could abide living in Gotham when such a delectable land of milk and honey is so near. I have noticed that when I ride in another man's motor-car I feel optimistic and inclined to see the "slaves of toil" in a rosy mood. And this mood was not banished by our arrival at the Sleepy Hollow Club. From its terraced lawns the Hudson may be viewed in all its majesty. This former home of Elliott F. Shepard is a palace, and, forgetting the joys and woes of Corlears Hook and Tompkins Square, I trained my eyes on the prospect. There is justice in the boast that nowhere may be seen such an extraordinary collocation of the grandiose and the familiar in landscape and waterscape. The Rhine is domestic, colloquial by comparison. Down the Danube at the Iron Gates there is some hint of the dazzling perspectives of Palisades and Hudson, but there again the barbaric note sounds too loud in the symphony of rugged rocks and vegetation. And great Highland Park, Bear's Nose, the new State Park, gift of Mrs. Harriman — what a wealth of natural park lands! When the wicked blasters blast no more, restrained from sinful destruction by the law courts (when?), and there are better travelling facilities, the Palisades side of the river will entertain thousands where to-day it hardly counts its hundreds.

We flew along the riverside. I had renounced all hope of seeing Jerome Park, St. Mary's, Claremont, and Crotona Parks, or even the little Poe Park at Fordham — we had passed High Bridge, Fort Washington, and Macomb's Dam Parks earlier — and farther down I had often visited Morris Heights and Audubon Park, but I was consoled by the sharp contrasts of the shifting landscape. Of course, there was a "panne" on upper Broadway, a burst tire, and the ensuing boredom, but nothing lasts, even impatience, and soon we were through Yonkers, and then across the city line past Palisades Park, with its lights, and, finally, on Riverside Drive, surely vantage-ground from which the ravishing spectacle of down-river may be enjoyed.

It would be unjust to pass City Hall and its park, not because it allures—it does not—but because City Hall is the priceless gem in our architectural tiara. Buried as it is by the patronising bulk and height of its neighbours, it more than holds its own in dignity, simplicity, and pure linear beauty—qualities conspicuous by their absence in the adjacent parvenu structures.

Nor must I miss Prospect Park, Brooklyn, near enough to reach in a half-hour, and from the grassy knolls of which the turrets and pinnacles of Manhattan may be seen. It is far more captivating than Central Park, and the Flatbush Avenue entrance reminds one of some vast plaza in a European capital, upper Brussels, for example. It is imposing with its MacMonnies monument, its spaciousness, and general decorative effect—an effect enhanced by the Italianate water-tower and the Museum farther down, whose vast galleries house so little original art, with the exception of the Sargent water-colours and former Chapman pictures. It is only fair to add that Prospect Park began with natural advantages superior to Central Park, advantages made the most of. This park really makes Brooklyn habitable and not merely an interlude of bricks and mortar before achieving the seashore.

Well, we are not far from Battery Park, whence we started. It is only a swallow's flight this—for I could have dwelt on the special characteristics of each park, on the elevated playgrounds at Williamsburg Bridge, on the various recreation piers — but celerity was my aim, the impression as we skimmed; all the rest is guide-book literature — as Paul Verlaine did not say. I didn't start out to prove anything, yet I think I have suggested that, despite its contracted chest and waist, the lungs of Manhattan are both vigorous and varied.

III

THE WATERWAYS

LIKE the prudent elderly person I am, I arrived at the boat only a half-hour ahead of time. "Better never than early," I remarked — with a certain waggish air — to the ticket-seller, a man of informal manners, who dispensed with a booth and disposed of pasteboards in the open. This lent to the transaction an al fresco character that also smacked of adventure. What an adventure!

I never mounted the gang-plank of an ocean-going steamer with the same trepidation that I crossed the deck of the little yacht on a summer afternoon at the Battery. For one thing I was never, even during a mid-ocean storm, on such a wabbly boat. Every wash from passing craft made it shake like a bowlful of jelly. A sensitive nautical organism. But I was not afraid. It was just two o'clock, and two people were on board. Fifteen minutes later there were eleven first-class passengers, and at three o'clock we received our full complement and lifted anchor for a long and perilous cruise up the East River, through the Harlem, down the Hudson, better known hereabout as the North River, and then into snug harbour at the Battery.

Verily, thrilling prospects and hairbreadth 'scapes were ahead of us. I looked at the captain and crew; both seemed seaworthy. I noted the megaphone of the "lecturer," noted the position of the life-preservers, lighted a fresh cigar, and settled down in my uncomfortable seat to stare and stare and stare.

That fatally fascinating sky-line of lower Manhattan again set me to wondering whether it will ever assume the attribute of stability. The changeless change of New York is discouraging. The eternal characteristics of London or Boston, Vienna or Philadelphia find no counterpart in Gotham. It is but a few years ago and the Singer Building dominated the view from the Narrows; on the Jersey shore, with the City Investing Building it assumed the shape of some fantastic beast, all neck and head.

Now the denticulated battlements of the city cower beneath the terrifying height of the Woolworth Tower. The Municipal Building bulks largely, and already the new Equitable Building threatens to usurp the interest. The eye is caressed by the graceful lines of the Bankers Trust and that Titanic lighthouse on the Seamans' Institute at South Street and Coenties Slip serves as an admirable angle for the gaze to rest upon before it embraces the wide stretch of harbour.

For hours I could sit and compose and recompose — as the painters say — this extraordinary jumble of architectural styles. In the terrific chorus of steel and stone and glass every imaginable tune is chanted, from crazy Renaissance to sombre, savage Gothic, from perverted campaniles to drunken Baroque. The architecture of New York! It is a mad medley of pepper-boxes perched on cigar boxes set on end and pierced by sinister windows. In twilit tunnels beautiful churches are lost like stone needles in metallic haystacks. Consider Trinity Church!

Vain ornamentation that recalls sugar-coated cakes made for festive occasions finish off the spires of bizarre structures which might illustrate an Arabian Nights tale. The top of the Woolworth Tower — is that beautiful or trivial? The peak of the Metropolitan Tower — is that dignified or confectionery? And what of the Municipal Building roof, where curious turrets rob the tower of its meaning? There are no gargoyles in our architecture; the entire structure is usually a gargoyle. But imposing!

Just then the voice through the megaphone announced that Governor's Island was near by, and that the East River passage was about to be achieved. Every one chewed gum, but listened respectfully. The Barge Office faded into the middle distance, and a slight nostalgia overtook me. Here we call it homesickness. Anyhow, it wasn't seasickness, for, while the boat did rock in the wake of ferries and colliers, I experienced little discomfort. Possibly experience on the real ocean may have saved me, for, joking aside, our two rivers can kick up a bobbery when wind and tide are ill-tempered. Our mentor, who had the assured bearing of an actor doubled by a diplomat, was a little given to harping on the statuary of the Custom House. We were under the Brooklyn Bridge before he rather reluctantly let go the subject.

Hurrah! I recognise my old acquaintance Corlears Park, and the battered steamboat in the offing. Around the Hook is Grand Street Ferry, and its street vista. Under Manhattan Bridge, under Williamsburg Bridge, we passed, the navy yard to the right, with several war vessels to be seen.

In summer-time the city might be described as an island surrounded by bathing boys. I never before knew how many contraband plunges were enjoyed by these young rascals. They shrieked at the yacht, and all the passengers immediately became immersed in their maps.

Greenpoint with Newtown Creek did not arouse enthusiasm. It looks just as it smells — unpleasant. As we neared Blackwell's Island and the bridge, our lecturer discoursed on the punishment meted out to wrong-doers, and did not fail to make facetious remarks. The Island looks as neat as a new pin, a very agreeable abode for a summer vacation. As usual, in America all the good things are gobbled up for the wicked. There are Ward's, Randall's, and Blackwell's Islands wasted on the sick and criminal. Why?

Up the Seine the delightful Ile de Puteaux is given over to excursionists, as is our Glen Island. Why must minor malefactors, insane, and diseased humans be awarded the very pick of locations in a fine river so near New York? Couldn't they be handled just as well over in the wilds of Long Island, where they wouldn't damage the arid soil or hurt the monotonous landscape? Some day law-abiding people may come into their own, may enjoy our river fronts, (of wretched wharfs) unequalled anywhere for their views and size.

Opposite, on the city shore, we passed the East River and Jefferson Parks. Both were thronged, for, no matter how hot the day, some breeze circulates at the river. Ward's Island reminded me of St. Petersburg, in the River Neva, where is the charming island called Kamenoi Ostrow. Anton Rubinstein liked it so well that he composed one of his most popular and melodious pianoforte pieces, giving it the above title. But there are no champagne and pretty girls on Ward's; no gipsy orchestras tear passion to tatters as dark-haired beauties kick over the windmill on Kamenoi Island. The Russians know how to enjoy life, and their charity patients and prisoners are never on view — indeed, are sometimes ominously absent from the map of life.

Our guide pointed out the Old Ladies' Home and quoted Meet Me at the Church. No one smiled, for of all the solemn functions I ever participated in this sightseeing trip was the most solemn. The people were visitors from all parts of the State and country. (I overheard invidious criticism made by a man from Los Angeles.) The faculty of attention was in evidence. No laughter, no skylarking, among the young people; all was seriousness that must have gratified the man with the megaphone. They bought his book and post-cards, did those excursionists, and they bought often, for at every twist of the river he had a fresh batch to offer. The resources, oratorical and commercial, of that man were astonishing. I watched his face more than I did the scenery. He was a comedian born, and with a less sedate audience he would have made a hit. Toward eve a resigned look stole over his expressive features, but no complaint escaped his lips. He was one of art's martyrs.

The stunted youth with the flat nose, curly hair, and flow of humour was more of a favourite. He sold opera-glasses, lemonade, tea, and information generally. He assured one timid old lady that with his binoculars she could see the Vaterland coming up the bay (the big boat arrived twenty-four hours later). She hired a pair and looked longingly at the iron steamboats en route to Coney Island. I admired that boy. He would have cracked a joke in the heart of a whirlwind, such his resiliency of temperament.

The yacht no longer rocked. We had reached

the Harlem River, and somnolency reigned aboard. We suffered from a surfeit. This indifference was difficult to arouse. The Harlem water looked crowded after the East River. The bridges piqued us: Willis Avenue, Second Avenue, Third Avenue, New York Central, Lenox Avenue, Central, Putnam, High, Washington, Kings, and the Spuyten Duyvil Bridges — an array which excites your interest because of the diversity. And also that huge railroad bridge across to Long Island, and of the tubes anchored in the stream that are to serve for a subway under the river. Harlem is no longer a suburb. Harlem is the city. The Speedway is superb but solitary. A few Italians mending the road, that's all.

Why does New York empty itself as soon as the sun rides high in the heavens? In London the real season is in progress when the bad weather begins. New York is seasonally the superior of the English metropolis, notwithstanding its occasional torrid heat and humidity. Yet none but visitors fill our motors, sail our waters, or walk our pavements. The resident has slipped away to Newport, or is ambuscaded behind the blinds of his house, ashamed to be seen during the dog-days. Well, he misses a lot. While I don't altogether subscribe to the assertion that our town is the coolest summer resort in the land, nevertheless it is preferable to any other large city that I know of; besides, and this must not be overlooked, time need never hang heavy on your hands; there is so much to be seen that dull care is soon driven away. Think of the dancers!

As we advanced through the canal — we had duly admired the Jumel mansion, with the adjacent pretty Roger Morris Park — the scenes on either bank were mildly entertaining and human — all too human, as Nietzsche puts it — gangs of labourers, bathing youths, large, aggressive boys, rude boys, and coloured; shanties wherein candy and tobacco were sold; canal-boats with the family wash on view, mansions high in air set amid cool arbours, racing crews in frail shells, defiant lads hurling stones — and all the meanness and misery of dirty shore fronts encumbered with offal, garbage, barges standing by, and the inevitable baseball game, with its accompaniment of shouts and swear words and whirling figures, could be seen.

It was a relief to near the Hudson, to glide through its backwaters and finally catch a glimpse of its capacious bosom. The sensation was akin to emerging from a long, sultry corridor into the open sea. Every one awoke — that is, began to take notice. Professor Megaphone fairly trilled out his facts. No one cried, "Thalatta! Thalatta!" After all, your New Yorker is an amphibious human. He is not afraid of the wet, like the majority of our citizens from across the briny. The salt and the savour of the sea are for him a prime necessity. He may not go to the beaches, he may live on

Broadway as far down as Bowling Green, yet never go across to Battery Park; but set him in an inland town and he begins to growl. That saline tang is lacking. He does not miss the clatter and crash of the city as much as the salty air, and when you remind him of this he is quite surprised. He has never analyzed his sensations.

The stagnant waters and stuffy atmosphere of the river that makes New York an island are forgotten when the Hudson is reached. A different humour prevails. We listen to the venerable anecdote of Spuyten Duyvil and we crane our necks to see Island Park, up at the end of Washington Heights. The guide indicates the Magdalen Home, and makes a few quips about the naughty girls therein; this time prunes and persimmons are writ large on every lip. I was relieved when a drizzle began. I lent my umbrella (did you see a large old party who didn't carry an umbrella on a clear day?) to a lady sitting next to me, and her husband held it; thus was a good action rewarded, for I nestled behind his wife and he kept the rain from her. Nothing succeeds like selfishness.

However, it was not a landscape-blurring rain. We easily saw the historic sites and experienced a slight hunger and thirst when the French restaurant on the Palisades side hove into view. The megaphone had reached the premium-with-every-pack-of-post-cards stage. He actually offered free pictures of the great liners. And the rain swept us fore and aft. The stanch little craft dipped her short nose in the foaming billows, the pilot wiped the salt from his eyes, and one of the crew appeared in "slops" and a sou'-wester. Then I knew the captain feared the weather. What he told me later was the truth — he hated the white, thick fog which threatened farther down.

But the voice of the megaphone never faltered. "Ahoy and Avast! This is the last chance to buy at reduced rates views of the noble ocean liners — the Lusitania, Mauretania, Aquitania, Vaterland." Few bought, for what with the rough tide and the impending fog and the misty wind, the passengers were too preoccupied. But the hawker did not miss his chance: "Now, then, the finest remedy for seasickness in the world. A gift in every package." It was chewing-gum.

Claremont was almost passed without comment; luckily, the lecturer caught it with the tail of his eye and we were told in moving accents of the tomb of the amiable child. It was touching, say what you will; this mélange of premature death, chewing-gum, the odour of wet mantles, the persuasive eloquence of the speaker, the giggling under my umbrella — my umbrella, remember! — of the married couple (honeymooners, I'll wager) who were so inconsiderate as to withdraw from my side to their selfish selves and leave me in the zone of wet. No wonder I felt like crying. I thought I did for a moment, but it was only the rain. No lighthouse was in sight. The storm howled. We "peeked" at the cork buoys. The thrill and thrall of shipwreck on a desert canal-boat gripped our fancy.

We swept by that most inexpressive of national monuments, Grant's Tomb, and when we arrived before the Soldiers' and Sailors' Monument, our cicerone spoke of the objection raised by the neighbourhood when the view was obstructed. I confess I sympathised with the dissidents. People, unless they are madly patriotic, don't build mansions to face monuments, and trippers. Everything in its place. As Anacharsis Cloots exclaimed several times during the French Revolution: "I belong to the party of indignation!"

When we neared the city we heard about a famous divorce case that had stirred Riverside Drive. Really, I never enjoyed such a blending of the instructive with picturesque contemporaneous scandal. The lights were showing from Palisades Park, and along the Drive innumerable windows were starry. The palace of Charles M. Schwab once attained, we knew the end approached; with Seventy-second Street Riverside Drive finishes. The cars and tracks that are occasionally concealed on the upper part of the river are here displayed in all their ugliness. Another cause for complaint, and a grave one. Others have made it. I shan't. Our big town is eminently commercial; the æsthetic question is an academic one. If ever New York becomes the City Beautiful, it will be through the operation of causes as yet in the womb of time. Utility first.

And is there a more inviting combination of sea and land anywhere? Not even Rio Janeiro. The Hudson and the Palisades are as romantic as the Rhine; romantic, but not as sentimental. Manhattan Island, thanks to its facility for egress and ingress, can lodge its millions in New Jersey, or over on Long Island — not to mention Staten Island, or up the State. Hasn't the time arrived when the looks of things are as important as the price of things, or even the things themselves? (This is not meant to be metaphysical. I don't mean Kant's Ding an Sich.) When all the piers are steel or stone, when, instead of huddled sheds and dirty wooden docks, the eye will gratefully envisage wide spaces and warehouses, when the shore railroad will have been abolished, when cabbages are kings (they are now; also trumps) and roasted partridges fall from the firmament, oh! what a nice, nice city New York will be! Spotless Town and Phœbe Snow will be consumed with envy, and you and I will be translated to another and, let us hope, a better world. Selah!

The rain had ceased. We were dodging between hooting tugs and lighters. Ferry-boats almost rammed our tender sides, a shaft of sunshine, hot and cross, pierced the clouds. The fog vanished. There was the noise of whistles.

Then we saw the West Street Building, then the Whitehall; soon we rounded the point. The Aquarium was again in the foreground. It was not yet dusk, but we felt the approach of night. The boarders — I mean the passengers — no doubt heard the horns of elfland (or supper) blowing through their memory. And films for the gods made by the eternal scene-shifter were preparing for performance down the harbour. A rosy light broke over Bayonne, the silhouettes of those twin tall chimneys were like unsharpened lead pencils, and a summer sunset, rich, golden, glowing, bathed "mast-hemmed Mannahata." (Alas, Walt Whitman! it is now nearly funnel-encircled.) We had seen the rim of the island, and, even if superficially, the day had proved pleasant. I could repeat the experiment to-morrow with the same joy.

IV

THE MATRIX

I

DURING the cool, rainy streak of weather last July I was in the mood statistical. I heartily dislike figures, which are the most elastic and plastic quantity when manipulated by clever folk, and the most depressing of all combinations is the dubious "science" of statistics, even more than that "dismal science," socialism.

Nevertheless, I was "vastly intrigued," by the statement that the Subway as it now stands has a total length of twenty-one miles. Fabulous! And the enterprise is only in its infancy; the entire island will be honeycombed by swiftly running trains, and there is hope that the ugly "L" roads will be removed and certain broad avenues regain their inalienable but lapsed privileges of light and air — not to mention the cessation of intolerable noise.

If you hear an "L" train starting or stopping — especially in Brooklyn, where the flat wheel is a cult with the B. R. T. — you are reminded of a busy boiler-shop when a lot of orders have come in for Dreadnoughts. The "L" roads are a standing reproach to Greater New York.

It may sound childish, but it is the truth, I confess that I feared to travel in the Subway till a short time ago. I was in Paris some years ago when a catastrophe, a fire, occurred, and the horrors of that accident made me nervous. The Underground in London is gloomy, the cars not inviting — rather dirty, I should say — but the idea of fire never haunts one en route. The masonry is solid, and the dampness would smother any conflagration. The Paris Metropolitan is much more cheerful and better lighted. The service, too, is excellent.

Berlin has only begun experimenting with subways. There is virtually but one. It seems miniature compared to the London or New York subways. The cars are small and light-running. The system is adapted to the shape of the city. You can go from the neighbourhood of the Palace — it is only a few blocks away — to Charlottenburg, with several loops for other districts. The speed is not breakneck, there are no expresses, and every car has a compartment for smokers — from which an overpowering odour of bad tobacco is always present. Our network is colossal in comparison.

The first day I cautiously went down the steps of the Grand Central Station it would not have been a difficult task to send me flying upstairs again. I wasn't exactly frightened, rather nervous. The hustling crowd on the platform didn't give me much chance for reflection, and I entered the first train that I was shoved into

— the magnetism of the mob, as Le Bon would say. I found myself skimming down-town and on a local. It went fast enough for me then; now I avoid locals as much as possible. Who doesn't? Every station stopped at robs us of our precious minutes, although when we arrive at our destination we are apt to waste time staring at a steeplejack, a street altercation, or the baseball returns.

Many years ago I learned to discount the hurry and flurry of New York. We are no busier than Bridgeport or Jersey City, but we pretend we are. It is necessary for our municipal vanity to squeeze and jam and rush and crush. Another vital lie. The conformation of the island has conditioned the transportation problem (Ha! I told you I had been reading the jargon of statistics), hence the "L" roads and the Subway. The more the merrier, say I. Anything that will relieve us of the shameful huddling of humanity during the busy hours, those hours that are a purgatory to decent men and women. May their necessity vanish with the passing of the "L" roads.

But I am not sticking to my story. To be truthful, there isn't much to tell. For a few minutes I was stunned by the roar, disconcerted by the gale that blew backward through the train, and held on to a strap as a sailor hangs on to the main brace in a storm at sea. (I hope it's the main brace.) The roominess of the car, the brilliancy of the lighting, and the absorbed expression of the passengers grew upon my consciousness. Though, so it seemed to me, we were racing with death, no one suggested that such an idea worried his skull. A Subway crowd is typical of the town. Indifference is one prime quality and chewing gum another. Nearly every one chews, the men more volubly — if I may so express myself — than the women.

The lantern-jawed Yankee type is again to the fore. For a generation he had disappeared from our streets, from our illustrations. He is back, shrewd-faced, long upper lip, and salient cheek-bones. But he is the surviving remnant of the once dominant American nation — then a compound of Irish, English, Scotch, with an occasional modicum of German; to-day he is on his last legs, fighting, though he hardly realizes it, against the mastery of the Slav and the Italian. But who cares? We are as yet too young a nation, still in too inchoate a state, to worry about the infusion of more foreign blood. If it is healthy, it is welcome. From the giant amalgam something powerful must emerge even if a sense of continuity is still lacking. But in no American city is the cosmopolitan orchestration so rich, so reverberant and complex.

But the national neurosis of gum chewing is not a promising sign. Are we so nervous, so lacking in self-control, as this St. Vitus's dance of the jaws indicates? To watch human beings feed is never an inspiring spectacle; but this artificial, self-induced labial pleasure — why should it be intruded upon the eye of a neighbour? Animals chew their cud; mankind should not. Æsthetically it disfigures the profiles of pretty girls. If they were only conscious of this! I have seen lovers fondly gazing in each other's eyes, and chewing all the while. Even the police chew. When the Woman Suffrage Party makes a crusade against this minor sin of ill taste I'll have some hope in its utility; this and our vulgar ways of speech, enunciation, and pronunciation are greater evils in the long run than tobacco, alcohol, and racing. They debase the social currency of life, and where there are bad manners, bad morals are not far away.

The correction of these matters is primarily the affair of the women. I really believe that English is spoken nowhere so badly — always excepting Cockney London — as in New York City. Our public schools are the principal poisoners. Ride often in the Subway (on the "L" roads foreigners predominate) and you will hear our noble tongue abominably abused. It's not the general slanginess, for slang has its uses, but the disfiguring twang, the nasal intonation, and the mispronunciation that offend the ear. I had always fancied that only in Brooklyn you heard "Brooklynese," that unpleasant flattening of the vowels, that depressing drawl. But I did Brooklyn an injustice; to-day all New York speaks in the same fashion. Not many young men and women you meet are born here, and their provincial accent has clung to them.

I know the usual philistine will bob up after reading this, crying aloud in righteous wrath: Better our dear old American language with our pure hearts than all the fancy speech of Englishmen! But your hearts are no purer, my misguided but patriotic person, than any other nation's, and the most disagreeable English I ever heard was from the lips of English country people. Really, you can't understand some of their dialects. I am complaining that, with our common-school education, the best in the world, the chiefest thing, our language, is so badly spoken, the art of speech, plain and without frills, the speech that differentiates mankind from the beast world. Chewing gum is a vile habit; at least it keeps silent the raucous New York voice; above all, the voice of the New York woman. Riding in the noisy Subways and gabbling doesn't improve the timbre of the ladies' tone.

However, we are not given to such niceties in the whirl of our daily life. We lack the "faculty of attention," and we lack Sitzfleisch; we can't sit still without twiddling our thumbs, twitching our limbs, or working our jaws. We are without repose, and, much as we may dislike the idea of military service, it turns out well-behaved young men, not a mob of jumping-jacks. Our indifference to the finer shades is the result of our selfishness. It is not a question of men treating women impolitely — though it is exceptional — but of man's impoliteness to man. Perhaps more subways will modify the evil. By that time we shall have lost all our manners.

I know it is the stereotyped thing to say that New York crowds are good-natured. Good-natured is hardly the word — timid, cringing, cowardly are better words. An English or a German or a French crowd wouldn't endure for a minute the slights put upon our crowds by impertinent petty officials. In no country are personal rights less respected. I know the Subway guards are much-suffering, and that as a body they are superior to the "L" road guards, who are dirty as to attire and discourteous to a degree. They tell me that the companies pay starvation wages, but why should the public suffer? I'll tell you why — a whisper, mind you! — in Greater New York the public is a flock of stupid sheep.

II

Pretty girls in our city! Lots of them. In the Subway at morn and eve you can count the plain ones. These girls are of many nationalities. They all dress above their station, wear clothes that are manifestly cheap, in imitation of prevailing fashionable modes. When they cease imitating there is no more hope of social ambition and social ascension. We have no peasant class in America. No self-respecting woman will dress according to her "class" — or her means, either — for she is ever hopeful that her "class" will be a better one, or that her daughters will marry "above" them. This social hopefulness is nation-wide. It is our Bovaryism, our vital lie. The ragpicker's granddaughter marries a duke; the son of a peddler becomes a magnate in the financial world. No other land affords such opportunities in mounting the ladder of life; otherwise the million that annually invade our shore would not be in evidence. When immigration ceases it will mean that the rats are leaving the sinking ship of state. But I can't help wishing the foreign invasion would go elsewhere. New York is full to the brim. A few more plagues of locusts and the entire land will be as bare as a bone.

Yes, pretty girls, a bit too rouged, too flimsily attired, but clean and self-respecting. The old-time chlorotic American type is vanishing; thanks to open-air exercise and increased physical and mental activities, our girls, native or imported, are very vital. Foreigners, accustomed to a more placid and conventional type at home, find them irresistible, chewing-gum and twang included. I find that the brunette, the brown as well as black, is in the ascendant. But there are blondes enough, and the blonde is for the public the high-water mark of beauty. The stage and the vaudeville prove this. Bigger frames are to be seen than a decade ago; the foreign-born women, however, are mostly undersized. On the avenues the shopping women are alike; whether in Brooklyn or the Bronx, the huntress stalks her bargain game like her sister. In the theatre or at home she is more human. They say that only women buy and read books, fill the opera-house and the theatre — also the film shows. But does that account for the present condition of American culture? Is the inside of her pretty head not as distinguished as her gowns? Perish the thought! Let some man more courageous than I answer that question. Max Nordau did, but then the little Doctor never lived in New York.

Emerson says that "steam is almost English." Then electricity must be American. That potentate who, fearing the thunderbolt, built himself a palace underground, and there was slain by the lightning he had tried to evade, would be distrusted if to-day he could revisit the glimpses of the moon. In the bowels of New York he might find immunity from the lightning stroke, but he would find there lightning, though harnessed. What would the Subway be without the electric "juice"? It wouldn't be at all, for we could never have endured so patiently the choking atmosphere of the Underground before Theodore Dreiser's hero, the Titan, gave London electricity instead of steam and smoke.

I am old enough and sentimental enough to miss the locomotive, which man built as an image of himself — puffing, hissing, shrill, and stubborn, and fast-running. A locomotive is very human, not specifically English, as Emerson said. It breathes, it is alive, whereas the electric motor, while more subtle, is also more treacherous. Less noisy, it is less sociable and never greedily consumes coal lumps as does the hungry locomotive. Ruskin loathed steam. Would he have loved electricity? I doubt it. Overhead the electric motor is as noisy as a launch without a muffler. Even in the air man must chatter.

One day I conceived the bold notion of going under the North River by the tubes. I had made the trip to Brooklyn via the tunnel and lived to tell the tale. But New Jersey was a different matter. It was practically foreign soil and farther away. I went from Cortlandt Street, and was disappointed when I got to Jersey City so soon. That spot, like Long Island City, is not to be tarried in. Oblivious of the fact that I could have taken the elevator to the street surface, I toiled up a twisting staircase, as fine a place for sandbagging, garotting, and highway robbery as I ever saw outside of an engraving by the fantastic Piranesi. The day was a rainy one. The lights were dim, the steps many. I was both grateful and disheartened when I reached the open. Why Jersey City? "Vous l'avez voulu, George Dandin," as the saying is in the old Molière comedy. I had disembarked at Jersey City when I wanted to go to Hoboken. The matter was soon readjusted. I asked the advice of the elevator man and he pointed out a ferry-house. But I didn't care to return to my native land. Then he suggested, go down-stairs and take the train to Hoboken. How simple it all sounded. I got into the right car — it goes no farther, I was told — and came up near the Hamburg-American docks; farther up fluttered the flag of the North German Lloyd, and the surroundings looked pleasantly familiar.

By some psychic process of reasoning, which only Hugo Münsterberg could explain, the thought of Hoboken, the sight of "Hapag," made me aware of Meyer's and Naegeli's hotels on another street. Auto-suggestion? Tourists who are unhappy enough to stay overnight in Hoboken during the mosquito season never miss Meyer's hospitable garden, where the cool brew flows. Not to stop there, if only for a drink, is to miss one of the delights of foreign travel. I wasn't dreaming of sailing to Europe, yet did I hurry over to Meyer's later and rested my fatigued organs. Also moistened them as I read *Jugend* and other publications.

I returned by another tube; this time I came out at Fourteenth Street. The cars are the most spacious, clean, and comfortable of all the subways. I paid five cents from the Terminal Building to Jersey City, paid five cents to New York. But why did I have to pay an extra two cents at Fourteenth or Twenty-third or Thirty-third Street? Is this one more McAdoo about nothing? What joy to stamp one's native asphalt! I celebrated by riding down to Herrvater Lüchow and bored him with the recital of my adventure. I noted, in the Hudson tunnels, that I did not suffer from the oppression I always experience crossing under the East River. In the Pennsylvania tunnels the pressure at the temples is also severe. The air is closer than in the Subway tubes.

A mania for movement, a wanderlust seized me after the New Jersey trip. I went to the Bronx via the tunnel, I went to Two Hundred and Forty-second Street and Broadway. It is a pity that the Subway is not altogether an elevated road in those remote parts. The views are wonderful. It was Ernest Lawson who discovered, artistically speaking, the Harlem River and the unknown reaches of the Bronx. His gorgeously rich palette comes happily into play, for there may be seen tender, pigeon-blue skies, splendid, thoughtful trees, capricious, tumbled rocks, and gleaming waterways. His best themes are found near the Harlem River.

For the Bronx I have a weakness, especially the park and the Zoo. When I had ridden in every subway — also in the new Chambers Street to Myrtle Avenue and Ridgewood branch, which crosses the Williamsburg Bridge — I hunted up the Belmont tubes and the old Steinway tunnel. Really, the police of New York are obliging men. At the Queensboro Bridge, Fifty-ninth Street, a sandy-haired officer broke the news to me as gently as if I had been a relative. No, the Belmont tubes at East Forty-second Street were not yet visible, nor the Steinway tunnel. I saw that he looked at me curiously. I must have seemed a greenhorn. "If you want to go to Long Island City," he added, "and I don't see why any one should want to go there" — he paused and I abetted his sly-dog humour with vacant laughter — "just cross the ferry." In thanking him I explained that my mistake had arisen because once in the departed old Grand Union Café I had jumped at a severe blast under the hotel. "Oh, that's nothing," said Simeon Ford to me; "that's the way they send passengers to Astoria." And I had believed him, in the innocence of my metropolitan heart. The sandy-haired one smiled. He knew Simeon.

Then I took to the bridges and ferries. I went to Staten Island and wasn't sorry; crossed to Jersey by several routes and was. The old ferries at Wall, Grand, and Forty-second Streets at first proved picturesque, and soon palled. Brooklyn Bridge, after all, more beautiful than her three sisters (bridge is feminine, isn't it?), the most graceful suspension bridge in the world, is become too familiar. We cross it, and seldom afoot, thus missing that magnificent panorama of architecture, bay, islands, and distant Jersey shore. Besides, its Brooklyn side lacks the dignity and space of the Flatbush Avenue approach to Manhattan Bridge. That, indeed, is most impressive. On Sunday mornings the Jewish market is one of the sights of the town.

I like the Williamsburg Bridge, with its long perspective of Delancey Street, now giving us a European vista, and its big playground atop. The view is puzzling. You look for the two adjacent bridges and your glance collides with the sugar-refinery across the river, which at this part is all askew. You must twist your head to see the other bridges. Returning, you note the Queensboro Bridge, and decide to visit it. It is a strange structure and a cantalever; as it is, I feel safer on Brooklyn Bridge. The best part of the Queensboro is just over Blackwell's Island.

There is material for observation that takes days to exhaust. The various bridges spanning the Harlem become more attractive the farther one goes westward. Several are excellent for suicidal purposes. They all look like Ernest Lawsons, so strangely does nature pattern after art. As for the possible bridges to cross the lordly Hudson, I hope never to see them. As a spectacle those waters need no bridging. Tunnels are always more expeditious. Doubtless some day both rivers will make of Greater New York greatest New York, for they will be solidly bridged; anyhow, the East River. So mote it be!

III

New York, intimately seen in the summer, its family wash on the line, all its linen not spotless—ah, the lure of the hanging gardens!—make us forget Babylon, and its millions are as ghosts.

I said something of the sort to the man with the megaphone — the dry-land Don Quixote who whispers information atop of one of the sightseeing coaches. His answer was characteristic: "If I never saw Babylon again I shouldn't be sorry. What with hanging on a bumping coach, talking through my hat, and dodging banana peels and dead cats on Rivington Street, I yearn for the old farm at La Mancha." He was playing up to me, for he knew I had compared him to the Knight of the Rueful Countenance. So the Don let me see that he was familiar with the topography of a Spanish city. He also said Dulcinea and Rozinante with clear, firm articulation. Evidently a man of superior parts. Needless to add, that Sancho Panza was the chauffeur.

But unless you only care to scratch the surface, those sightseeing tours are far from satisfactory, though excellent experience for a budding novelist. Naturally Chinatown is only a sham and the much-vaunted Bowery a bore. On a warm afternoon the up-town ride along Riverside Drive — barring the ducking of tree branches — is agreeable; but going southward you are bumped on the abominable Broadway with its rude wooden roadway, and to see only the basements of high buildings is not exactly seeing them from afar. Besides, you are stared at, sometimes jeered. The offensive "Hayseed!" is flung at you, and you really must be alert on some of the crowded East Side streets to avoid rotten fruit meant for your head by some malicious youngster.

I fancy the idea of the coach doesn't please many people in that district. It seems an impertinent intrusion, and then there is always the chance of an accident. The chauffeur is cautious, Don Quixote diplomatic. Nevertheless I held my breath several times near Mulberry Bend; children there are as plentiful as that fruit in season, and they are both careless and reckless. We were held up by a street-car (there is still one in operation) on a particularly narrow street. A well-dressed man, an artisan or a barber, cursed us: "You rich think you can come down here and kill our children!" he cried in excellent English, shaking his fist all the while. His hands, I noted, were clean.

Don Quixote shook his head mournfully. "Rich?" he muttered. "Rich?" we echoed. There wasn't a man in the excursion who didn't carry a cheap silver watch. We were glad to start. That accusation was too much for our bank-accounts. We blushed at the very imputation of wealth.

I'm sure I shall be accused of inconsistency when I say I'm not shamed by the East Side. I know that the poverty there is appalling, that people are packed as in a pickle jar, that crime and disease stalk in company with hunger and dirt, yet these horrible conditions are not on view for the casual spectator. I never had the courage to explore one of the old-fashioned crowded tenement-houses. If he has been in London he knows that the East End is the last word in revolting conditions. Or Paris, or the Berlin North Side, or the Ghetto in Vienna. Over some of these places is written: "All hope abandon ye who enter here!" None of these spots is as cheerful, as clean, or as prosperous as the East Side of New York. It is more crowded than it was ten years ago, and more attractive. Take Rivington, or Hester, or Essex, or any street in the network of that congested district, and while you make slow progress through the mob of children, women, peddlers' carts, vegetable and fish shops, men and babies, this crowd doesn't seem in the last gasp of poverty. It is noisy, dirty, chattering, chaffering, and good-tempered. It is the air of New York, that electric ozone which makes for optimism.

Where there is so much smoke there is sure to be fire; and the fire is the money spent on food and fruit and at the "movies." The smell of fish is never absent. As for the types, they are marked. The old division of Little Italy, New Jerusalem, Bohemia, Germany, Servia, Greece, and other nationalities no longer holds. The Jews are everywhere; so are the Italians and Czechs. Some predominate in certain quarters; for example, you will find many Bohemians along First Avenue, Avenue A, and Avenue B above Fifty-ninth Street; Italians still congregate about the Bend, and there are many Poles hard by Tompkins Square.

If I had a friend who was desirous of seeing certain parts of southeastern European cities — of Lemberg, where cluster Galician Jews; of Vienna, Prague, St. Petersburg, Warsaw, Cracow, even of Berlin and Naples — I would invite him for a week's cruise on our East Side. There is no necessity of going across the water to hear foreign tongues, see odd costumes or study strange physiognomies. They are all on view day and night in New York, the only New Cosmopolis on the globe. Every nation is represented; each has its café, its newspaper, its church, its theatre. Optimism rules the roast. The "unwritten law" over there is: Crescite et multiplicamini! Maternity hospitals are everywhere, so are baby carriages. This huge ant-hill is the matrix of New York, its nursery, its refutation of race suicide.

If you cross Canal Street eastward from Third Avenue you will emerge in Rutgers Square and East Broadway. The entire district might be called a show-place, not as an evil example, but as a normal East Side neighbourhood. With a schoolhouse, a public library, a park, and a big newspaper office, this square is typically civilised. Free from dirt, full of busy, bustling humanity and contented, romping children, for me it is representative of present conditions in the life of the New York poor. Not that these people consider themselves the poorest — they do not; but they are not rich, though some are fairly well to do.

At Maisel's bookstore on East Grand Street you will find the best literature of the world; indeed, more good literature than you can find at similar establishments farther west. The East Side is an omnivorous reader. Stupendous is the amount of books studied and digested; books of solid worth, not "best sellers" or other flimflam alleged "literature." As a nation we are becoming as superficial in our reading as we are in our taste for the theatre. Our native theatre has nearly touched low-water mark, and the film theatre — that twin brother to dime novels — is only a degree lower; stupidity and vulgarity in two instead of three dimensions.

You would smile if I told you that there is not much drinking in this quarter; they are not addicted to alcohol and they do love sweetmeats. I can count the places on the East Side where good Pilsner is on tap. The Russians, Poles, Ruthenians, Greeks, and Servians are not beer drinkers, though the Bohemians are. As a matter of record there is less drunkenness in New York than in, say, Glasgow—that is in proportion to their respective populations. London is infinitely more intemperate.

I went through Broome Street and saw its solitary tree — it is there yet, near Attorney Street, or some such street. I thought of the Ancient Mariner when I saw that tree, lonely but tough-minded, as William James would have said.

Two decades ago Mr. Howells wrote that if

any American novelist struck a note as profoundly tragic as Dostoievsky it would be false to our social conditions. But since then the temperament of the country has changed, owing to immigration. There is tragic chaos and the hurly-burly of the deracinated about us.

It would demand the resources of a Dostoievsky to paint our East Side in all its exotic, variegated, and bewildering colours. No genius of less calibre than that of Fyodor Mihailovitch's could essay the giant task. Where is he? Here is the raw, rich material for the great American novel. But where is the novelist? Let me suggest that only an American of Celtic brilliancy, Teutonic profundity, English intellectuality, French art, and the idealism of the Slavic Hebrew could compass the theme.

In Europe there is room for race prejudice, but not in America. Here it is self-stultifying, self-contradicting, and utterly abhorrent to democratic principles. We freed the black race, we must free ourselves of all race prejudice. We need the Jewish blood as spiritual leaven; the race is art-loving and will prove a barrier to the rapidly growing wave of fanatical puritanism. Nevertheless, at the expense of seeming inconsistent, let me suggest that one of the burdens of life would be lightened if our passenger transportation system were otherwise. The greedy and not too tidy bandits who run the wretched public automobiles are only the servants of their employers. But these miserably kept machines are too high-priced for the masses. In Subway and surface, on "L" cars the people you meet are not always clean: some because of ingrained hatred of bathing; others, decent working men who can't help themselves. I've frequently seen them embarrassed when they crowded against well-dressed ladies. What do you expect for a nickel? But if they did as they so sensibly do in Europe — have two or three classes at a slight increase of fare — we could snap our fingers at the hired automobile tyrants.

Theoretically, we all love our fellow man; but you like him better if he is clean, don't you? I do. And now, don't imagine this suggestion is a covert attack on our immortal principle of equality. It is not. The motor-cars might be judged from the same standpoint. I can't afford a motor-car, but I could scrape together ten cents for a seat in a clean, sweet-smelling car, where the filthiest sort of humans would not sprawl over me. One man is as good as another — politically; but if a man won't wash, that is the objection to his presence. But what Mayor, what Board of Aldermen wouldn't veto a bill to have separate cars! Class against mass would be the slogan, when the only issue in question is soap versus dirt.

I know I'm voicing the opinion of a civilised minority. But there, again, come into play the timid tactics of our local sheepfold. At first jeered, these separate cars would become a necessity, like the ten-cent stages on Fifth Avenue. Has anybody denounced as "enemies of the people" these coaches? No, because the "people" ride in them and like them. Until New York follows London, Paris, and Berlin and maintains an efficient and cheap taxicab service we must clamour for the next best thing — ten-cent surface and Subway cars. They would soon pay. But I suppose the great god Graft must be appeased by the usual burnt-offerings and what we demand must be deferred to the Greek Kalends. *Avos!*

New York has been called a calamity, a freight yard, a boiler-shop, an open trench, a mining gulch — with its manners and tastes; in reality it is the most aggressively noisy city on earth. Mostly unnecessary noise. It was Schopenhauer, annoyed by the whip-cracking of Frankfort carters, who denounced noise as a prime enemy of the intellect, denounced as lacking in finer sensibility a nation or city that endured noise. In our town he would have gone mad. And little relief in sight for us.

As to the increasing horrors of ugly loft building in the very centre of the residential section, that is a subject for sorrow to old New Yorkers. No law can keep off these pernicious flocks of locusts who ruin, æsthetically speaking, wherever they alight. Entire Manhattan Island will in not so many years become a vulgar Tophet of industrialism. I doubt if even the present rush to Long Island by manufacturers will long avert the time when belching chimneys will be so closely built as to swap smoke, and the narrow streets crowded with chaffering strangers. *Ichabod!*

But I'm tiring you with all this futile talk, and I'm tired myself of the East Side. When I left the book-shop I went over to the Vienna Café on Broadway, a sort of alimentary modulation from east to west, and as I crossed Second Avenue at Tenth Street I saw the coach with Don Quixote on the sidestep, the machine quietly resting, the passengers as solemn as owls. The megaphone man sardonically smiled at me as he dusted from his coat some yellow particles: "The highly civilised East Side! I got this dose of insect-powder on Essex Street." After all, it depends on the point of view, doesn't it? "Back to La Mancha!" I called out. In reply he waved his long ironic hand. He looked more like Henry Irving than ever as the coach slowly went northward. "Ladies and gentlemen this was once the famous Boulevard Café," I overheard, as the rubberneck wagon faded from view up the avenue.

V

THE MAW OF THE MONSTER

I

THE mighty maw of New York! Even Zola might have handled the Brobdingnagian theme inadequately. The avalanche of food that is swallowed in twenty-four hours and the river of liquid that disappears down parched gullets on this island — decidedly, several Zolas would have their hands full in dealing with the story.

Statisticians give you rows of figures, but to interpret the huge crude symbol is another matter. You remember how Zola treated in Le Ventre de Paris (The Stomach of Paris) his Cheese Symphony! Truly a Rabelaisian performance.

But New York is double the size of the Paris of those days (1873), and instead of one national cuisine it boasts half a hundred. I am at the outset trying to show the magnitude of the task, a task I decline to undertake. But I may succeed, after a fashion, in indicating the resources of a city wherein even Pantagruel could line his monstrous paunch and slake his magnificent thirst.

THE MAW OF THE MONSTER

With the possible exception of London, there is no place like New York for versatility in eating and drinking. Nearly all cuisines are represented. You can eat kosher or munch birds'-nests in the Chinese style; while French, Russian, German, Dutch, Italian, Spanish, Hungarian, Polish, Austrian, Turkish, Syrian, Rumanian, Greek, Portuguese, Cuban, Mexican, Liberian — why drag out the list? — are to be found; everything from everywhere may be had in our city — everything but fried oysters as they cook them in Philadelphia. And that important fact will be clearly set forth during the course of this solemn sermon on gluttony.

It is only natural when a man's hair begins to thin and he has gout in the gums that he sadly turns to the "pleasures" of memory, a bitter-sweet game, the shadow of a vanished substance (this is a Celtic bull, but it is what I mean), and one which always sets the teeth on edge. Just why the man of the "lonesome latter years" should recall the feastings of his youth, I leave to psychologists.

He may have written at least one sonnet or story, he may have painted a row of brilliant portraits or landscapes, yet set him down before a fire and straightway he falls to musing about the girls of yesteryear or that particular night when the wine-cup was not red, but champagne-coloured. Or Finelli's fried oysters. Or the terrapin of Augustin (both in Philadelphia). Or the salads and burgundies at Delmonico's. Or

— and this happens, too — the taste of those oysters eaten fresh from the shell at a cart-tail coram publico, say, on Fulton Street three decades ago. The miserable sinner should be thinking of his soul and lo! his belly is still his god — that is not in reality, for he is a dyspeptic and almost toothless, and Uncle Uric a daily visitor, so it needs must be only memory images, and poor entertainment such recollections usually are. Mother Church, who has minutely catalogued every nuance of transgression, calls such a perverse mental operation "morose delectation."

But it is not of such sour stuff that my dreams are made. Contrariwise, I recall with intense amusement the New York restaurants and cafés of a quarter of a century ago. Were they any better then than now? is the inevitable question.

The answer is that we were younger then, our appetites and teeth unafraid; nevertheless, there are many changes and not all for the better. The young folk nowadays are not epicures. Wine palates they have not; cocktails and the common consumption of spirits have banished all sense of taste values. They are in too much of a hurry to dance or to ride, to sit long at table and dine with discrimination.

The number of cheap, quick-fire food hells is appalling. One understands during the midday rush that a glass of milk and a slice of pie suffice, but when the day's toil is over and the upper town achieved, then we expect leisure and elegance, taste in the evening menu. They are seldom to be found. Noisy bands of music-makers, ill-cooked food and hastily gobbled, shrieking instead of conversation, and then — dancing. This is the order of the evening. The theatre is rapidly disappearing, I mean the real theatre, and only in a few choice spots is the cult and ritual of dining observed and performed.

However, these few do exist, and there you will find the remnant of a once-powerful congregation, members of the Church of the Holy Epicure. But they are doomed. Eating and drinking are rapidly entering the category of the lost fine arts. Bolting, guzzling, gum chewing, and film pictures have driven them away.

Some day, say hopeful prophets, they will return. I doubt it. Our age is too materialistic. The noble ideals of the gourmets are forgotten, and, as Matthew Arnold would ask — in the eloquent phrases — slightly altered — of Maurice de Guérin: "The jealous gods have buried somewhere proofs of the origins of all good things to eat, but upon the shores of what ocean have they rolled the stone that hides them, O Macareus?"

When I first drifted into town from Paris, about 1886, I was taken by the late Hugh Craig, a cultivated literary man — the genre still existed in those days — to the café of "Billy" Moulds, in University Place, a centre for actors, writers, artists, musicians, as well as business and professional men. There I met the poet Francis Saltus, truly a brilliant raconteur; there I ate — on off days, financially speaking — the magical decoction of the Moulds chef, a bean soup without compare. And free! There I met about all the friends I now possess.

I have seen editors of trade weeklies, who abused each other with a vituperation that was vitriolic, forget the ardours of inky bottles and drink harmoniously. Such was the atmosphere of the establishment — also the persuasive personality of Mr. Moulds. I once watched the famous Wagnerian tenor, Albert Niemann, swallowing cocktails from a beer-glass. He "lived to tell the tale" the next night as Siegmund at the opera.

While I was faithful to this first hospitable house I soon found mettle more to my taste in and around Union Square. Opposite Steinway Hall, then the very hub of musical New York and America, were Lienau's and Maurer's, and, best of all, there was a certain place presided over by a blue-eyed, rosy-cheeked young German, whose amiability was proverbial, whose beer was perfection. Need I add that the elect saluted him as "Gus," or that to-day he is August Lüchow, millionaire importer and, despite a few ounces extra of flesh, the same hospitable soul he ever was.

At Lienau's there gathered such people as William Steinway, then a power in the political and musical world, the Anton Seidls, Theodore Thomas, Wilhelmj, Mr. and Mrs. C. F. Tretbar, the Nahum Stetsons, Scharwenka, Joseffy, Lilli Lehmann, Frank Van der Stucken, the Victor Herberts, Constantine von Sternberg, Rosenthal, Max Heinrich, Mr. and Mrs. Von Inten — the very cream of the musical aristocracy. If you tired of Lienau's — with the celebrated fat barman "Schorch," you could go over to Brubacher's or the Hotel Hungaria. And then there was "Andy" Dam, host at the Union Square Hotel, or Webber's wine-house in Third Avenue. A genuine atmosphere of Teutonic "Gemüthlichkeit" existed in those times that are no more.

The German theatres throve, both at the Thalia in the Bowery and Amberg's in Irving Place — afterward Conried's, now Rudolph Christian's. The old-fashioned German lager-beer saloon was still to be found, comfortable havens with sand on the floor, pinochle on the table, and even a pure brew. Do you recall Eckstein's, Grambow's—he was in East Tenth Street then — "Peter," in University Place; "Pat" Schmenger, Theiss, Hubel, Goerwitz — now Allaire's — Oscar Pusch — afterward Louis Singer — Greitner, with the high-tenor voice; Koster & Bial's, Mock's in Forty-second Street, and Terrace Garden when Michael Heumann was in charge? Or the old Moñico!

Some of these places still exist, but there is one that does not. Where Proctor's Theatre now stands in East Fifty-eighth Street was a small brewery operated by Peter Buckel. Big trees pierced the floors of the piazza, and under them you could sit and enjoy yourself; opposite was Terrace Garden — it is still the same old Terrace Garden — always filled with people. The street then reminded me of a street in Vienna.

The old Café Boulevard was worth while in the beginning, before it became a fashionable "slumming" attraction, and the old Fleischmann Vienna Café, next to Grace Church, was a centre for Conductor Anton Seidl, Antonin Dvořák, the Bohemian composer — I am forced to explain who these celebrated musicians are, for the horde of philistines that invade our city know nothing of art, little of manners, but much of money-getting — and many visiting virtuosi; the excellent coffee was the magnet.

Where is the Grapevine? Where is the spirit of Philip Brod? Instead one may go to Janssen's Hofbraü on Broadway or to Sokol Hall on the upper East Side, or to Kaspar's old place for Pilsner; or, best of all, to Dr. Knirim of sanitarium fame in Pearl Street, where your thirst is studied and prescribed for and where you get beer at a healthy temperature, not forgetting the privilege of capital conversation with the worthy doctor.

I have a friend who devised on paper a Pilsner route thirty years ago, starting from the Widow's in Atlantic Avenue, Brooklyn, and ending at the West End in One Hundred and

Twenty-fifth Street. There were not so many of these life-saving stations then as now, but their paucity wet your expectation, not to say your whistle.

Another peculiarity of the long ago was the morning "bracer." Fancy champagne cocktails, a drink of doubtful virtue, consumed by the young bloods and old bucks. To-day it would be considered criminal to drink champagne at 9 A. M. But they did it, those copper-lined stomachs. Now at the worst they consume beer — a wise change. Men seemed more vigorous to us then, and seem more fidgety and nervous in this year of grace. Perhaps it is an illusion.

There is not so much drunkenness in public or private to-day; social opinion is hostile to it. The phenomenal "tanks" of the eighties have disappeared, dead or converted. I remember at the Everett House, since demolished, an old codger, rich enough to own a carryall, in which day by day he transported his thirst from tavern to tavern, winding up at the Everett. A quaint, venerable party, indeed, who grunted, rather than spoke. What an existence — riding from "jag to jag" and growing in wickedness with the years! A character for a novelist, his.

The more aristocratic never went to ordinary bars, but to the bar of the Fifth Avenue Hotel or the Hoffman House or the old Brunswick or the Victoria, where notabilities, chiefly political, were as cheap as nuts. We went to the St.

James when Dorval was there, or to Reisenweber's at the Circle when genial John was all over his establishment. Really, personality counted then. Now you rush in as you would to a drug store, gulp and away. For little cafés like Philip Brod's, near the New York Athletic Club, the personality of the host was its mainstay. Think of the old Arena when William Muschenheim was on deck. What a joyful spot it was! Probably one of the reasons that "Jack's" (John Dunstan's) café is liked so much is the promenading between tables nightly of its stately host. Personality still counts in an age of "canned music" and automatic lunch taverns. However, no one need suffer for a drink in New York, despite the puritanical antics of the prohibitionists (for revenue).

II

By a decided negative must be answered the question: Are the chop-houses as good as of yore? (Have you ever noticed when people begin to talk of English cookery they say "yore" or "anent," as they say "oui" at Mouquin's, or "ausgezeichnet" at Lüchow's?) No, they are not, and you may point out a lot of places and I'll say: These are gorgeous establishments, but where are the fat English mutton-chops, the musty old ale, and, don't let us forget it, the peaceful atmosphere?

At Browne's, then in a side street off Broadway, you were at your ease. In Adam Engel's it was the same. Or at the Studio in Sixth Avenue, or Stewart's, or Wallace's, Martin's, or numerous places in the lower part of the town whose very names I've forgotten. And where has gone Parker's, which stood in Sixth Avenue near Thirty-fourth Street? In Fourth Avenue, at Twenty-first Street, was a chop-house kept by a German named Eschbach. It was small, but delightful. There, once upon a time, I listened an entire evening to the muted conversation of Rudyard Kipling, who was piloted to the house by his brother-in-law, Wolcott Balestier. Here assembled nightly actors, mostly from the Lyceum Theatre, in the palmy days of Daniel Frohman, and there came the prince of talkers, Maurice Barrymore.

I was sorry to see Eschbach's go, though I 've no doubt "Jack's," Healey's, Browne's — now in Broadway — are just as good. But I'm not as good, and that is the pith of all rambling memories by old blades with a grudge against present conditions. (Grouch is a more fashionable word.) You would if you could, but you can't! Anyhow, in my prime — and I'm not yet precisely tottering — they didn't call a Welsh rabbit a "rarebit." (That's a knockout for pot-house æsthetics!)

One oyster house at least shows but little change, except in its increased clientèle. I mean Dorlon's. I think there was a Dorlon's down-town somewhere. Fulton Market, wasn't it? I only frequented the Madison Square restaurant with the oyster clock outside. What jokes have been made by men (a trifle how come ye so!) about that clock. "I was up to 'Y' minutes past 'O,'" cries one chap, and is convulsed at his own nimble wit. Alas! the pathos of distant humour. Silsbe's is still in existence in Brooklyn, near John Ryan's famous Pilsner station (wireless).

Do they still eat macaroni and consume Chianti in New York? If they do, show me a Moretti — like the old Moretti in Fourteenth and in Twenty-first Streets — a Martinelli (in Fifth Avenue), a Solari — in University Place — a Riccadonna in Union Square, or even a Pedro's, in Centre Street. The truth is that there are hundreds of Italian restaurants where the spaghetti and the wine (Californian) are as good as at Moretti's. Ah! but the old man could cook. Those veal-chops, the spaghetti, rich and abundant, and the oily salad! Exclamation-points fail to express the gustatory sensations at Moretti's. Another restaurant where personality was a heavy asset.

At Pedro's, down-town, discovered by newspaper men, the surroundings were simple to the point of dusty napkins and faded wall-paper, but all was forgiven because of the flavour. Now we eat to the accompaniment of delirious tango music, pay tips to greedy Greeks, and go to bed hungry for a savoury dish.

Cockroach Hall, so nicknamed, was farther

up-town, and it was well patronised till the rumour got out that cockroaches were seen floating in the soup à menestrone. After that I went over to Maria del Prato's in West Twelfth Street, where "Mickey Finn" threw bread at you and you liked the poetic attention. (Maria retired in affluent circumstances and was last seen by Vance Thompson in Venice, healthy and homesick for Gotham.)

Both the Mouquins' restaurants, up and down town, are about the same as they ever were. But a pure French cuisine in New York is not possible. The "custom of the country" intervenes, meaning the palate, and imperceptibly a chef adapts himself to his environment. Nevertheless we have here a true cosmopolitan cuisine, from green corn to caviare, from snails to clams.

In the old days you singled out certain restaurants for certain dishes. At Sieghortner's, in Lafayette Place (now Street), or at Heim's, in Twenty-seventh Street (near the old Browne chop-house), you were served with German dishes of the rarest, also the most expensive. Lüchow's, where delicacies gathered from the four quarters of the globe may be had, has not a cheap tariff; indeed, it is a costly one, but the two Germans I mention were very dear for those days.

One item was the Rhine and Moselle wine — the best bouquets, together with imported hare — a luxury then — and Canada mutton — another luxury, but not now — and you paid a pretty reckoning. I recall Theodore Thomas, the great conductor, and his concert-master, Max Bendix, as frequent visitors at Heim's. (Thomas was an epicure; Seidl ate what was set before him, but craved strong black Havanas.)

At the Sinclair House, also a memory, you ordered "angels on horseback" — in other words, fish-cakes with poached eggs atop. Its tomato soup was capital. The old Astor House had its "specialties," as had Smith & McNell's, now vanished; as had Lyons's, on the Bowery — they gave you better beefsteak than you could get in a restaurant of a higher class. Oyster-patties were better made, and raw oysters at ten cents a dozen (no napkins) seemed celestial. And the hot-corn Mammy, with her turban and far, clear cry at midnight (in Third Avenue, too) "Hot corn! Hot corn!" Cobweb Hall is still in existence, though I believe the old proprietor is dead. Even the salt was saltier, and the butter more buttery than the sandy substitute and oleomargarine in contemporary usage.

What's become of the little withered Italian who sold matches from Fourteenth to Forty-second Streets every night, with his comical farewell: "Gooda nighta, Boss"? There be men still living and in full possession of their strength who not only frequented Andy Horn's at the Bridge (there was only one bridge in those remote days), and also "Doc" Perry's drug store, there to absorb editorial culture and "reportorial" quinine (slightly disguised). Of course, they were newspaper men, not journalists, of whom the late "Joe" Howard always said: "It's the money of newspaper men that pays the funeral expenses of journalists."

III

The Grand Union Hotel, which is no longer on the map of life, was for years my pet hostelry — was truly a landmark, and Simeon Ford and Samuel Shaw national figures.

The "holy of holies" in my time was Delmonico's. To-day it has a hundred rivals. Nevertheless it remains Delmonico's, the unique. Sherry's is very attractive — the name is an aperitive — and such gorgeous hostleries as the Gotham and the St. Regis have menus to match. But being a democratic person, I prefer down-town Haan's, Bustanoby's, the Brevoort, or the Lafayette — the oldest and the best of Martin's restaurants. I never cared for his Delmonico undertaking; it was neither good Martin nor real Delmonico. At Shanley's — the original Shanley's was on Broadway below Thirtieth Street — Rector's, Churchill's, or the cafés of the Plaza, Savoy, Netherland, Biltmore, Vanderbilt, or Ritz you can order what you wish and get it. I find little change in the Savoy Café, and I am still fond of the al fresco character of down-town Delmonico's, in Beaver Street.

On that street there are two or three Italian and French restaurants — "Frank's," for instance — which for wine, cuisine, and service have no superior up-town. Then there is Angelo's in Pearl Street, and Farrish's chop-house in John Street. When James Breslin conducted the Gilsey House it was a hotel of the first magnitude. And there are Billy the oysterman's, Pontin's in Franklin Street, and other resorts still in existence.

As for eating around and about New York, the road-houses are legion since the advent of the motor-car, and they have hurt the business of the New York restaurants. Over on Long Island, up in Connecticut, down on Staten Island, you are royally fed at royal prices. You can stop in Central Park at the Casino (Dorval) or at McGown's Pass Tavern, and then make a dash for Claremont, the most picturesquely situated of all the river houses. There is the Abbey, or Ben Riley's — which evokes the old Arrow-head Inn, Saratoga Lake — or some pleasant French cafés on both sides of the Hudson. The old Hudson Inn farther down Fifth Avenue still holds the fort as a solitary survival. But when in pursuit of the Amber Witch out of town, I don't waste time at any of the beaches — where they torture beer into the semblance of discoloured ice-water — nor do I go up the river, but simply get on the Brighton line, dismount at Consumers' Park, don't even look at the ball game at Ebbets Field, and march into Fred Winter's garden, where the herculean proprietor — he is a prize-winning athlete — holds gentle sway, where the view of either Prospect Park or the Brooklyn Institute consoles the eye, and where — but why continue? The crickets are booming in Flatbush, the hunters are up at Sheepshead Bay, God's in his heaven and all's well with Tammany. This mixture of Walt Whitman, good old Sir Thomas Browne, Robert Browning, and Plato (all Tammany braves are Platonists) must be set down to the heady nature of my discourse. But the greater the truth the greater the caricature.

I promised as a sort of a coda to tell you of the absence in New York of the fried oyster. Your cockney-bred New Yorker looks askance at you if you mention fried oysters. No wonder. The leaden, lumpy, greasy, tasteless wad of flabby batter and hard, shrivelled oyster that masks in Manhattan as a fried oyster is enough to revolt the maw of a Patagonian.

I well remember Charles Delmonico telling me years ago, and with a gesture of despair, that he had sent a chef to Finelli's in Philadelphia; that said chef, a man of imagination and technique, ate himself bilious at Finelli's trying to solve the secret of the magical batter; that he returned home with this secret — olive-oil, the pan spluttering red-hot, and the oysters quickly dropped in and harpooned at once — and the first day he served the oysters at the Broadway restaurant he lost his job. He had absolutely failed.

But, strange to relate, in Philadelphia there were others besides Finelli who knew how to serve a fried oyster so that it tasted like a cross between a poem and a croquette. Both Philadelphia and Baltimore are renowned for their terrapin, red snapper, ducks, pepper-pot, deviled crabs, lobsters, and oysters — better oysters than Cape May coves, about the middle of September, there are nowhere. McGowan's, in Sansom Street in Philadelphia, can give you the best of terrapin and fried oysters, and even in Finelli's time there was a certain "Billy" Van Hook, who was celebrated for his fried oysters — his wife really cooked them. (Here is a potent reason why woman should have the vote.) She is still alive at her restaurant on Library Street, where the oysters are as poetic as ever.

But New York never imported the dish; in fact, I don't mind confessing that in the matter of sea food and its preparation New York still lags in the rear of Baltimore and Philadelphia.

However, on this rather pessimistic note I shan't end; after all, sea food is not the only reason for a good kitchen. The maw of New York is the most capacious in the world, and it is also the best-filled.

VI

THE NIGHT HATH A THOUSAND EYES

I

In New York "the night hath a thousand eyes." That is why all cats are not grey by night. The Great White Way, pleasure-ground of the world, is the incandescent oven of the metropolis, and under its fierce glare all felines appear alike. But grey, never.

The sad-coloured procession that slowly moves through Piccadilly, the merry crush of the Friedrichstrasse, and the gayer swirl on the Grand Boulevard are not so cosmopolitan as Broadway on a summer's night. Every nationality swells the stream of petticoats; "As the rill that runs from Bulicamé to be portioned out among the sinful women," sang Dante, and one exclaims: Lo! this is the city of Dis, when in the maelstrom of faces; faces blanched by regret, sunned by crime, beaming with sin; faces rusted by vain virtue, wan, weary faces, and the triumphant regard of them that are loved. You think of Bill Sykes and his cry of terror: "The eyes, the eyes!"

NIGHT HATH A THOUSAND EYES

The city has begun its nocturnal carnival, and like all organised orgies the spectacle is of a consuming melancholy. No need to moralise; cause and effect speak with an appalling clarity. Through this tohubohu of noise a sinister medley of farce and flame, the Will-to-Enjoy, winds like a stream of red-hot resistless lava. In describing it your pen makes melodramatic twists or else hops deliriously.

The day birds have gone to bed, the night fowl are afield. The owl is a denizen of the dark and Minerva's counsel, for all that wisdom is not in the air. Even veritable cats as they slink or race across the highway are bathed in the blaze of a New York night with its thousands of eyes. No, all cats are not grey by night in Gotham.

But from the heights, what a different picture! Then the magic of the city begins to operate; that missing soul of New York shyly peeps forth in the nocturnal transfiguration. Not, however, in Broadway, with its thousand lies and lights, not in opera-houses, theatres, restaurants, or roof-gardens, but on some perch of vantage from which the scene in all its mysterious beauty may be studied. You see a cluster of lights on the West Side Circle, a ladder of fire the pivot. Farther down, theatreland dazzles with its tongues of flame. Across in the cool shadows are the level lines of twinkling points of the bridges. There is always the sense of waters not afar.

NIGHT HATH A THOUSAND EYES

All the hotels, from the Majestic to the Plaza, from the Biltmore to the Vanderbilt, are tier upon tier starry with illumination. Beyond the coppery gleam of the great erect synagogue in Fifth Avenue is the placid toy lake in the park. Fifth and Madison Avenues are long shafts of bluish-white electric globes. The monoliths burn to a fire-god, votive offerings. The park, as if liquefied, flows in plastic rhythms, a lake of velvety foliage, a mezzotint of dark green dividing the east from the west. The dim, scattered plains of granite housetops are like a cemetery of titans. At night New York loses its New World aspect. Sudden furnace fires from tall chimneys leap from the Brooklyn or New Jersey shores; they are of purely commercial origin, yet you look for Whistler's rockets. Battery Park and the bay are positively operatic, the setting for some thrilling fairy spectacle. A lyric moonlight paves a path of tremulous silver along the water. From Morningside Drive you gaze across a sunken country of myriad lamps; on Riverside the panorama exalts. We are in a city exotic, semibarbaric, the fantasy of an Eastern sorcerer mad enough to evoke from immemorial seas a lost Atlantis.

Below in the theatres are the moving pictures, those tantalising ocular spasms, or optical shadow for dramatic substance. Let us go to one of these mute entertainments (barring the clattering orchestra), and to the best, "Cabiria," manufactured by a man of genius, Gabriele d'Annunzio, out of shreds and patches and fragments from Flaubert's "Salammbô," "The Last Days of Pompeii," "Samson and Delilah," and a dozen dime novels; a monstrous olla podrida of incidents, a jumble of movements, all without sense or relevance, nevertheless so filled with action that the eye is rapt by the sheer velocity of the film. No story can ever be definitely related, for the essence of photography is the arrest of motion, and despite the ingenious mimicry of movement, there is no narration, only poses.

The very faults of photography are exaggerated; the figures in the foreground are giant-like, in the middle distance or distant perspective they are those of pygmies, so that in a room a woman's figure at the edge of the picture suggests a giantess, while her maid, supposed to be a few feet away, is a miniature. And then the wavering, swimming, flickering of sharp points of light — the eye is more fatigued than at a dramatic performance. Why music if the films suffice? The truth is that the moving pictures are a remarkable mechanical device, but never for a moment can be considered in the category of art.

Those mountains belching sparks and fire are sensational, but not artistic pictures; pantomimes with tableaux is a better description. One scene had an element of vraisemblance; it depicted a sweeping foreground, such as Daubigny was fond of in his rare, larger canvases; a troop of savage horsemen appear on the ridge of the hill, silhouettes in strong relief against a clear sky. If these figures hadn't cavorted down the slope, the picture would have been an impressive one, but the movement, paradoxical as it may seem, killed the illusion.

Great art can suggest the rhythm of multitude on a flat surface, but the public, like Mr. Crummles, demands its real pump. The swimming episode with the splashing water is "real" enough, but there is no art in it. I mean no illusion. Those Salammbô tableaux in temples, particularly the scaling of the citadel — Spendius, you may remember in Flaubert's immortal romance, got into Carthage with the barbarian chief Matho by way of the aqueducts — are duly exciting; but one phase of Flaubert and the picture lives, isn't a shaky simulacrum.

When it was all over, when the last strident blast of the brass, the last howl of the chorus, and and the last absurd printed "plot" on the curtain had ceased, I felt as if I had been at a banquet where the food and drink were whisked off the table before I could touch them.

Of what mental and emotional calibre are the audiences that frequent such shows? The world has been seized by a craze for them. They demand the minimum of thought from their spectators — who, incidentally, chew gum — and give to the eye the maximum of sensation. The attitude is purely receptive. You watch untouched by emotion the most "thrilling" spectacles and hairbreadth escapes. Anything like simplicity is a bore.

I've tried to sit through so-called plays; I've heard certain film actors and actresses — God save the mark! — called "great," and their gestures gave me the same impression one gets before a cageful of monkeys. Only the monkeys are more amusing.

This shadowland is never dramatic, never poetically suggestive, never human. The absence of the human voice, a marvellous instrument that bridges the space between us and our neighbour, is depressing, as depressing as the enforced silence in a hospital ward. The substitute, usually vulgar, noisy music, is an impertinence. A diversion for children, an aid to science, an entertainment for deaf-mutes, but not an art for intelligent people.

What has become of our taste these latter years? "Canned" music, mechanical pianos, moving pictures, dancing, these be thy gods, Philistia!

I suppose the time predicted by H. G. Wells is at hand, a time when reading shall have vanished, and with it the other arts; huge gramophones will furnish the public its news and bring to the parlour the muse of the mud gutter — and literature — and the moving pictures will be so extraordinary that all the world will be a film. Truly, a millennium of vulgarity and intellectual darkness, the glorious results of universal education! The second coming of the Huns and Tartars of ignorance is overwhelming us.

II

Years ago I wrote a story of a musical composer whose advent sets singing and dancing the entire world, so potent is the appeal of his rhythmic and magical art. In Italy his progress was that of a trailing comet. The feminine madness first manifested itself there and swept the countryside with epidemical fury. Wherever he played the dancing mania set in and the soldiery could not put it down by force of arms.

Nietzsche's dancing philosopher, Zarathustra, was incarnated in Illowski's compositions. Like the nervous obsessions of mediæval times, this music set howling, leaping, and writhing volatile Italians, until it began to assume the proportions of a new evangel, a hysterical hallucination that bade defiance to law, doctors, even the decencies of life.

For women his music was the moth's desire. Wherever he went were women — women and children. Old legends of the ancient gods were revived. The great god Pan was said to be abroad. Rustling in the night air set blushing young folk. Like a torrid simoon, an emotional renascence traversed Europe. The fountains of the great deeps of democracy were breaking up. Music was become ruler and the world and his wife danced on the pinions of song. Likewise on their heads and heels. The very earth was shaken at its axis. The dance was triumphant.

Well, some such fantastical nonsense I wrote, but after I laid down Rupert Hughes's brilliant book, What Will People Say? I realised the seriousness of the present situation. But Tango, instead of my Russian composer, Illowski, is king.

I determined to investigate. I haunted roof-gardens (so-called, though some of them are subterranean), I jostled the common people, my own kind, in nickel dance pavilions; on glassy floors I saw with wide-open eyes couples ill-assorted but whirling, and amid tropical shrubbery on sultry nights I sweated for my sins, that I might satisfy the meanest of all venial vices, curiosity.

I became a regular Paul Pry. I edged my way through panting humans to catch some gleam in their fever-sunken eyes which would betray the psychology of their obsession. I went to palm gardens and cabarets, I saw people lifting their legs at ice-cream dancing "parlours"; Sunday-school dancing did not scandalise me, for I remembered that David danced before the ark (or was it Noah? I know that Noah, too, had his ark); and at a church picnic the dominie danced, and there were film pictures.

At the Astor, the Vanderbilt, atop of the Strand, in the Biltmore, at the Jardin de Danse, the McAlpin, the New Amsterdam, at the Ritz, at Rector's, on Madison Square Tower, at a half-hundred other places I sought and did not find. The novel I mention had inflamed my imagination as the dancing had evidently inflamed the imagination of its author. But Mr. Hughes was luckier than I.

This is what I saw everywhere — a composite picture. Let me select the Biltmore, whose floor next to the roof, with its approaches, deserves the appellation palatial. A vast dinner salle, an oblong dancing floor, the general scheme of decoration a muddle of Japanese and various discordant elements, a high estrade in which a weary orchestra always played in one tonality, the placid key of F; towering above was a tall statue of Neptune, hence the title of the floor, "Les Cascades." Why Neptune and his trident (he looked like Bernard Shaw fresh from the bath) in a dancing salon I can't say.

A water-god, his presence had a decidedly temperate effect — I saw little if any drinking. The Herr Oberkellner seemed shocked when I asked for plain hops. I argued with him that in the entire room there wasn't any one drinking champagne.

"Ah, non!" he replied, "the war, you know!" "It's Neptune, you mean," I retorted. Then the band began to play, and in the tepid key of F I forgot the beverage, my eyes agog.

Ah! where was the orgastic fury, where the exotic abandon of these dancers? No spoor of delirium, and absolutely nothing bacchanalian. Intoxicated by the ice-water that they so recklessly absorbed, I saw middle-aged, bald business men with their mature partners (their wives, of course; your "Go up, thou baldhead!" doesn't dance with maturity unless it is a matrimonial obligation), slide and slip and twist and twirl in such a decorous fashion that I shuddered.

I remember that when I arrived in Paris for the first time — it was October, 1878 — the Jardin Mabille did not close its doors till later. I have participated in the Bal Bullier on the "other side of the river," and I knew Montmartre when it was Montmartre and not a Parisian Chautauqua. I've seen all the cancans worth mentioning — rather, unmentionable — and while I did not expect in our staid Quakerish old New York any such license, I did yearn for a little more animation. Why, it was a Brooklyn sociable on a larger scale!

Occasionally a little pot-bellied fellow tried to clutch his massive partner, but in vain. It was a living picture of the old woodcut by Rowlandson, "Thou art so near and yet so far," in sober terms. The portentous gravity of the entire function impressed me. Perhaps these very middle-class-appearing persons were overcome by the magnificence of their surroundings; perhaps the jarring decoration oppressed them, or it may have been the Turkish-bath atmosphere. I was afraid to ask the head waiter, for I saw that I was under the ban. The key of F, damnable iteration, struck up a valse rhythm, and then the dancers, one and all, essayed a two-step. The cross rhythms, so piquant in Chopin's A flat valse, were translated from the psychical to the physical plane, and fearing for my morals I sneaked away, wondering if there were such dances as the Tango, Maxixe, or Gummy Grip, the Lame Duck, Fox Trot, or Honey Bug — perhaps I should say, Bunny Hug. After paying my bill at the hat-check department I found I had just enough money left to go home, and home I went. I had eaten my peck of dirt that day, and I should have been satisfied. But I was not.

The next night found me on the roof of the New Amsterdam, said to be the true home of twinkling heels. Also the spot favoured by the Mayor and his official family; ours is a dancing administration. Anything Ziegfeldian ought to be edifying, and I found myself between two musical fires — an orchestra of coloured men and a band of Spanish-looking gents who plucked guitars, or balalaikas, and made music of a more exotic but less rhythmic character than their dark-skinned rivals.

These rival organisations hammered away at one another, and there was some zest in their performance. The dancers, too, displayed fire. But the men, the men, why will they dance? Good and bad, they all look so stupid in their dinner jackets (a costume devised for waiters), their legs like stovepipes, their thick-soled shoes clumping about. Even if a woman is clumsy, her drapery attenuates her lack of grace. In costume a man is barely endurable as a dancer — say in the opera or Russian ballet — but in our ugly daily dress he is simply absurd.

There were several young chaps who danced lightly enough, but grace they knew not. The girls made a more pleasing impression. They exhibited all the new steps, most of them idiotic in their simian distortion of natural rhythms, and they gyrated with a certain degree of recklessness. But at Steeplechase the dancing is heartier, more clever, and at any negro ball the coloured lassies outpoint their white sisters in elasticity, in swaying rhythms, and diabolic abandon. Compared with the dancing I saw at Madrid and Seville of Spanish gipsies, sometimes on table tops, all that I've witnessed thus far in New York is tame and so respectable.

Did you ever watch a Polish woman dance the Mazourka? Or a Hungarian the Czardas — I don't mean the mock-turtle paprika of our dance palaces? These so-called "fashionable" fakers who wriggle to the admiration of a heavy-footed crowd are caricatures. The dance is not in their nerves, it's in their pocketbooks. I understand the success of the moving pictures — it's a lot of gaudy nonsense for little money, but the meaning of the dancing mania has taken me much time to solve. An excellent custom for young and old it is, a foe to the use of medicine, and generally provocative to the appetite, yet the search for health does not account for its popularity.

My notion is this, and I may be mistaken: In the dance the world, instead of playing spectator, is itself the chief actor in the pageant. On this popular stage every one may star. They can have all the pleasures of professional artistic life without its penalties. The ego has found its own (shade of Max Stirner !) — and theatres, moving pictures, even motor-cars, must bow low to the victorious dancing dervishes. I am looking forward to the aeroplane as the next avatar of pleasure. Till then America will be satisfied with perfectly proper dancing capers, films, and chewing-gum. However, we outlived the roller-skating and the rinks thirty-five years ago; so let us not despair. But the incredible abuse that was lavished upon poor, respectable Salome of Strauss and Wilde is, like the proverbial curse, coming home to roost—more's the pity.

III

The room is long and narrow, its walls mirrored; the ceiling is too low for the good of the lungs, because every one was smoking the night I went in after leaving the Strand. It was too early for "Jack's," too late for the vaudeville at Hammerstein's Victoria, so I thought of the Canary Cage, the most popular of resorts given over to Bohemians and other rainbows. Half-cabaret — where the solo performers are the guests — half bird bathtub, where the wines do not prompt to a fall, the Cage is the most engaging of all the nightly spectacles in Gotham.

Naturally for the "highbrow," the "lowbrow," or "bonehead" is not made free of this republic of arts, letters, and canaries; I did not arrive too soon. The band up-stairs was playing at its top notch, the diners had descended to the ground floor, and the windmills were agitating their arms and theories in every corner.

There sat the professor who nightly demonstrates how the Japanese could have captured Berlin in three moves: move one, with the salt-cellar; move two, with a teaspoon; the third, with the fork; positively, the table is worn with ruts because of this continuous war strategy. When he isn't warring, the professor whispers to you — confidentially, of course — about the young genius he has discovered, a painter who can give points to Cézanne. But at bottom, he is conservative. He never favoured the "extreme left" of crazy cubists and concubinism, expressivists, zonists, futurists, vorticists, and post-impressionists who make their drinks warm with their oaths and rantings. Indeed, he shivered every time a shriek of "Nietzsche" or "Marinetti" came from across the room. There sat the choice cénacle at a long table, putting away everything from absinthe to zoolak. (I am sorry to state that the man who drank the latter was a nuisance.)

A Matisse-versus-Picasso controversy was in full sway when I joined the party — not without audible dissent from some boys who called me "that antiquated bric-à-brac who thinks

Chopin wrote music." I knew these admirers of Arnold Schoenberg, and I knew that they had never heard a note of the Vienna composer, and when they did they wouldn't be able to distinguish it from Yankee Doodle.

But the name! Ha! a musical iconoclast! Down with the old fogies! Down with Richard Strauss, the reactionary! They smashed reputations. They sneered at the major gods, also the minor. One person (he wasn't over twenty), attacked Walt Whitman as the type of the perfect classicist, and after the noise of broken glass had ceased and the head waiter had separated the combatants, the table was cleared of broken bottles, and the argument began anew. A genius trumpeted like an elephant, and the cock-crowing evoked memories of the Latin Quarter.

I was captivated. My youth was renewed by the battle, the sound of cannon, and the neighing of the steeds; I, too, said "Ha! ha!" to the mules — at least they were as stubborn — but I was ruled out. No nineteenth century, back-number æsthetics! Give us futurism or give us oblivion; and they sought the latter at the very spigot.

I was not disconcerted. It was only natural for the younger generation to kick in the panels of the door. Grandfathers and other antiquated relatives should submit to curfew. And the tolling of young bells is the tolling of their knell. So I listened, remembering it did not seem so many years ago that I had helped in the same sacred cause of "knock your neighbours while you live; else get knocked." How this gang of painters, sculptors, poets, etchers, philosophers, writers, and pudding-heads did hit every head that moved on the contemporary map of literature or art!

In my time critics quarrelled over the emotional quality and technical merits of poets. I discovered that to-day in America a poet is a joke. Let us wrangle over the rights of interesting criminals, the ethics of sewer-pipes, or the sentimental social rehabilitation of moral lame ducks (not drakes); but poetry — fudge! Marinetti writes poetry. (So does a telegraph operator.) The leader, who is a prose rhapsodist doubled by a vaudevillist, challenged me to duel, the weapons to be Velasquez and Matisse. I selected Bach, and the matter was dropped. An Irishman always knows the trick of splitting the difference, and I think Johann Sebastian Bach a greater painter than either the Spaniard or the Frenchman in dispute.

A Scandinavian made us roar at the yarn, a new one, about the son of Björnstjerne Björnson, the Norwegian poet, who had intruded himself uninvited on the bridge of an ocean steamship. When politely asked by the captain to go to the lower deck he haughtily responded: "Do you know to whom you are speaking? Do you know you are addressing the son of Norway's greatest poet?"

"No matter," replied the captain softly. "You must leave the bridge, Mr. Ibsen." The poor man must have fallen overboard at the icy irony of the answer.

A minute later a fresh conflict was in progress. Some one cried: "Ibsen! Oh, the Land of the Midnight Whiskers! Why not drag in some other mouldy dramatist, like Molière or Shakespeare?"

"Or Bernard Shaw?" came in a flash, and the air was thick with war-cries. "Nietzsche!" "Schoenberg!" "Wedekind!" "Marinetti!" "Matisse!" "Picasso!" "George Luks can smash the slats of the whole crowd for pure paint." The professor shook both fists at the ceiling, groaning with Celtic emphasis: "Ah! Les ratés." The band which had come downstairs, intoned the Marseillaise, and the house vibrated with the refrain, "Marchons; marchons!" "This is not a 'Canary Cage,'" I ruminated, "but a cage of young eagles. The name of the place should be changed to the 'Café of To-Morrow.'" Here the sun never sets, but always rises, though it never seems to attain the meridian — possibly because these brilliant midnight sons go to bed every day before noon.

I made my retreat from this covert of vandals behind the cloud of a thunderous chorus, in which verbal splinters floated: "Marinetti!" "Encore de bière!" "Matisse!" "Imbécile!" "Schoenberg!" "Hund!" "Nietzsche!" "Let's all go up to Jack's!"

I quickly melted in the mist as the band moved up the avenue, chanting and praying.

From his attic of dreams, from his tower of ivory and spleen, the morose impressionist saw unrolling beneath him a double lane of light, tall poles, bearing twy-electric lamps, either side of nocturnal Madison Avenue, throwing patches of metallic blue upon the glistening damp pave — veritable fragments of shivering luminosity; saw the interminable stretch of humid asphalt stippled by rare notes of dull crimson; exigent lanterns of some fat citizen contractor. Occasional trolley-cars, projecting vivid shafts of canary colour into the mist, traversed with vertiginous speed and hollow thunder the dreary roadway. It was now midnight. On the street were buttresses of granite; at unryhthmic intervals gloomy apartment-houses reared to the clouds their oblong ugliness, attracting by their magnetism the vagrom winds which tease, agitate, and buffet unfortunate ones afoot in this melancholy cañon of marble, steam, and steel. A huge, belated, bug-like motor-car, its antennæ vibrating with fire, slipped tremulously through the casual pools of shadowed cross-lights; swam and hummed so softly that it might have been mistaken for a novel, timorous, amphibian monster, neither boat nor machine. To the faded nerves of the fantastic impressionist aloft in his ineluctable cage this undulating blur of blue and grey and frosty white, these ebon silhouettes of hushed brassy palaces, and the shimmering wet night did but evoke the exasperating tableau of a petrified Venice. Venice overtaken by a drought eternal; an aerial Venice with cliff-dwellers in lieu of harmonious gondoliers; a Venice of tarnished twilights, in which canals were transposed to the key of stone; across which trailed and dripped superficial rain from dusk and implacable skies; rain upright and scowling. And the soul of the poet ironically posed its own acid pessimism in the presence of this salty, chill, and cruel city — a Venice of receded seas, a spun-iron Venice, *sans* hope, *sans* faith, *sans* vision.

VII

BRAIN AND SOUL AND POCKETBOOK

I

There is no escaping the spirit of pragmatism which circulates about Columbia University. It is in the air, and you encounter it as soon as you reach Broadway at the One Hundred and Sixteenth Street Subway.

Here, you say to yourself, is the very cortex of the city; it represents its intellectual ideals, and with the unfailing mimicry of nature, it seems to be what it represents — I mean its simulacrum gives one the impression of a very busy centre of study: above all a practical one.

No mooning on these sunlit heights as you would at Harvard or Oxford. The sternly pragmatic ideal of New York is reflected in its chief seat of learning. The wooded walks and solitude-haunted spots of certain European universities have no counterparts here. Even the George Grey Barnard statue Pan looks askance at his own pagan nudity. Business first, dreaming afterward — if at all — might be the motto blazoned at Columbia.

The bustle even during the summer session

is highly gratifying. Groups of young women may be seen going into commons or standing at the hall of philosophy. The hard, unromantic aspect of the various buildings — magnificent, some of them — coupled with the encroachment of the town, robs our university of all provincial colour; not even the green campus, where they play everything from Maeterlinck to croquet, disturbs the hard, self-assured picture of scholastic success.

One need not fear that at Columbia any useless art will be found encumbering the curriculum. The æsthetic note is absent, but it is more than compensated by the presence of the cheerful pragmatic or the powerful materialistic. And yet — and yet I think that huge doses of Ralph Waldo Emerson should be daily administered to offset the deadening of lofty ideals; above all, to stifle the pernicious belief in majorities, in quantity instead of quality, in the mob in place of the man. There are no types; there is only the individual. But what is pragmatism to one man, to another may be poison.

I could wish for more æsthetic "atmosphere" about Alma Mater. The equipment is of an eminent order. I don't know how many students are annually turned out bright and shining and bursting with knowledge upon the community, but the number must be great. That they make "culture hum" may be rated in the high standard of our theatres and literature.

And the teachers — how many there must be!—none with "dandruff on their coat collars," for they are all paid huge salaries and can afford such luxuries as clothes-brushes and trips to Europe. I saw some of them lounging on the grass in dignified attitudes, some who earn as much as poor bank presidents slaving below in the heart of the city.

They impressed me. Little wonder New York is the very hub of the universe in the matter of culture. Columbia is a vast asset in the intellectual life of the city. To be sure, we never hear of any extraordinary idea, book, or work of art emanating from its cloistered shades, but only consider the amount of bright young wits it unleashes to do business in "our midst."

Pragmatic! Why shouldn't it be pragmatic? Business men, not poets or symmetrical characters, is the modern need, and this university is prime in its manufactory of practical youth.

For the girls I can't say as much. Barnard has its statistics. The specimens I saw were admirably ambitious, plain, and preoccupied with their studies.

You don't saunter at Columbia; there is too much intellectual ozone in the air, even on hot days. The spick-and-span condition of the colleges and their approaches finally gets on your nerves and you escape either to Morningside Drive or over to Claremont.

In and around Morningside may be the coming new "Fifth Avenue." The old can't long resist the attacks of the commercial philistines. Why shouldn't this part of the town be the home of our "aristocracy"? There is space, commanding views, the air is pure, and there is the absence of the crowd. Spaciousness is the key-note.

From the top terrace of Morningside Park the scene is fascinating — a tremendous city lies spread below you. Its chief quality is its variety (and gas reservoirs). Now, from Riverside Drive the landscape is monistic — if I dare employ such a term; from Morningside it is pluralistic. The perspective of Broadway — up here of stately width — with the Subway cars emerging into the sunlight is very attractive. You have the feeling that another New York could be housed on these heights; and will be — the march upward is unmistakable.

I crossed through One Hundred and Twenty-second Street and reached the Drive, near Grant's Tomb. At Claremont I again saw the tomb of the "amiable child" and again nearly wept at the thought of this, the last amiable child, dying too soon. Since then he has had no successors in our city.

I always admire the far-away Tudor-like towers of the College of the City of New York, dark field stone and white terra-cotta, and under their shadow there are pleasant walks. The unfinished Cathedral of St. John the Divine is imposing at a distance, and Fordham College is attractive because of its leafy surroundings.

As for the New York University, thereby hangs a tale. I had seen the Hall of Fame from the Harlem River and found other view-points, and I determined to visit the place, a daring enough proposition for a New Yorker.

I made tentative inquiries, as I wished to avoid notoriety — the mere notion of a native visiting the Hall of Fame might lead to international complications. A Subway guard, after consulting the map of his memory, counselled me to take the Broadway train and alight at One Hundred and Eighty-first Street. This I did on the hottest day of August. Then a newsman told me to catch the University Avenue car.

I did so, my wonderment momentarily increasing. I knew I wasn't quite in Albany or Poughkeepsie, for I saw the legend: "Amsterdam Avenue" when I came out of the Subway "lift" (it is as deep at One Hundred and Eighty-first Street as in the London Underground). But University Avenue and the various viaducts, the glorious sweep of the valleys and hills — the coolness, the purity of the air. Where was I? Was it Sunium's Heights? The conductor of the swift trolley-car told me the neighbourhood was known as "Kike's Peak." He said this soberly and I could see he meant no offense: he but recorded a simple fact, so I told him in return that God was ever good to the Irish and to his own.

After that diplomatic stroke we got on famously, for he was Irish himself.

I was dropped at the Hall of Fame terrace about ten minutes of a too short ride from Amsterdam Avenue. Everywhere open country, with avenues of comfortable houses, mansions, and cottages. The stroll up a quickly ascending hill was reassuring.

The college buildings came into view. One, with a cupola, I recognised as the Hall of Fame — as I had supposed, but it was the library with its large rotunda and excellent appointments. I asked a man who was operating a lawn-mower the whereabouts of the hall. "There!" he said, indicating a colonnade that wound about the college halls and faced the Harlem River. A handsome, ornamental granite loggia led me from one end of the terrace to the other.

There is a museum where there are portraits and other memorials. I didn't visit it. It was the bronze tablets that interested me. Only two portrait busts were to be seen. All the names of the celebrities are not yet in bronze. I found Longfellow, but not Poe; then it occurred to me that perhaps his name would never figure among the mediocrities of the hall; perhaps also pious prohibitionists had headed off the inclusion of the name of a notorious drunkard, and thus evaded a painful scandal.

I was further convinced when I discovered in the Women's Hall the name of a temperance advocate. What a charming idea! By sheer negation you may become famous, while Poe, poet and "alcoholic," might prove the contrary, and thus be a dangerous precedent. Poor Poe! Far better is he in his last resting-place at Baltimore. I know I slightly annoyed an attendant in the library by asking foolish questions. However, if you wish to secure a niche in the Hall of Fame call early and register with your urn. The only disqualification is the possession of genius, and as that is a rare quality in any land we have all a chance for immortality. How the celestial convicts in heaven, as they execute their matutinal rhythmic lock-step, must envy their neighbours who happen to be in the Hall of Fame. A mounted policeman showed me the homeward route. But of all the prospects that from the colonnade of the New York University is the most arresting. Even the chimneys of an electric-light plant can't quite spoil the view. Why more people don't make this pilgrimage instead of crowding the dirty beaches at Coney Island must be set down to perversity. There are no peanuts on this "Pike's Peak" of the Brain of New York.

II

When I first made known my plan I was scoffed at, then commiserated, and finally admired for my audacity. Never, I was warned, would I survive the shock. But I persisted. I had seen the basement of a department store from the Subway and the outside of another in Brooklyn, why shouldn't I venture within? Once I attended a suffrage meeting and I still live. Why is a bargain day at a department store more dangerous to a man? Besides, I had read Zola's Au Bonheur des Dames, and could reality be more gigantic than that particular fiction? In Berlin a visit to Wertheim's, on the Leipzigerstrasse, hadn't daunted me, nor the stores of Tietz, nor had the Grands Magasins du Louvre or Au Printemps in Paris ruffled me; indeed, I found some of these establishments diverting though disappointing, after their American rivals.

In London, Selfridge's, Peter Robinson's, Snelgrove's, or any of the other smart shops in Regent or Oxford Streets did not convince me that imitation is always the sincerest form of flattery. Certainly the London big stores are modelled after ours, and their imitation is far from the original. I am not boasting, only stating a hard fact known to every New York woman who shops abroad.

But could I stand a bargain day in New York? That was the rub. After praying to escape battle, murder, and sudden death and inspecting my life-insurance policy I placed myself in the custody of one who knew the ropes, and, closing my eyes, entered one of the biggest. I was at once whirled to the top of the palace and shown a spotless kitchen. I saw people eating in large, airy dining-rooms, from the balconies and windows of which the city might be enjoyed. The quality of the cooking amazed me, but not as much as the tariff. That's why men were present. A man dearly loves a "bargain" luncheon. I dived down to the cellar in an express elevator and inspected acres of things. Each floor I repeated the same experience. I thought of the once-celebrated French conjurer and prestidigitator, Robert Houdin, the first to apply electricity to clocks, the clever magician who invented "second sight."

I remembered how he had, in company with his son, his "accomplice," so trained his eye and faculty of attention that, after passing a shop-window heaped up with a hundred articles he could remember them all and write down the list for verification. I wondered if his shrewd and embracing vision could have captured the distracting number of objects on a single floor here. In a multicoloured dream I wandered through a maze of matter, labyrinths of glittering shapes. As in a nightmare I saw carpets that courteously saluted me and grand pianos in company with tin pails that gossiped together.

Haughty damsels regarded me icily. "Going up!" became a Leitmotiv at every landing. With admiration I registered the memory of the coloured gentlemen who manipulated the elevators. Ladies, hot, cool, fat, and slender, entered at every stop. They didn't seem dangerous. I passed vast rooms all white, or red, in a mysterious half-light. I looked the other way when we encountered oceans of lingerie.

Finally, a slight hubbub told me that we were

near the seat of war. Yet everybody stood. Seats, an army of them! I saw a mass of females in an inextricable tangle, and I thought of the Stock Exchange. Nothing was different except the absence of shouting.

But in lieu thereof a serried battalion of determined feminine warriors swept the bastions, and the enemy was theirs. The only wounded, strange to say, was a thin, tall floor-walker. He limped away in the direction of the wholesale perfume department.

I timidly asked what was the booty of war, and promptly received a snub: "Didn't you read this morning that gimp was marked down one-half?" Bon Dieu! What is gimp, and why should it be "marked down"? "What songs the sirens sing!" once wrote Sir Thomas Browne.

Elsewhere we experienced no bargain rushes, only plain bargains without battle. The basement positively intimidated me. People really go to these shops unafraid and unarmed. Think of the miles and miles of material spread before you! Think of the tax on eyes and legs involved in a day's shopping! Yet women, day after day, thus put in their time walking and bargaining and staring. On Sundays they devour the advertising pages of the newspapers in search of the particular article they long to procure at a bargain. Little surprise that we are a nation of idealists when womankind "uplifts" us through the subtle "marking down" of values.

I traversed, not without grumbling — the pace was beginning to tell — such stores as I had read about. Arriving at the most palatial rather fagged but still determined, I found there an air of classic restraint. The open centre to the roof is refreshing after some oppressive ceilings I had passed under.

Nowhere on the globe are there shops like ours. If people say Paris or London or Berlin, simply reply — New York! You may buy anything from an elephant skin to a needle. But so lacking in the "bargain" sense are men that when I finally escaped, about five o'clock, to the park I found that I had not bought a penny's worth except some luncheon and an ice.

In other words, I was an impostor. But there are thousands such, chiefly women, who pass the day agreeably in pricing goods they never purchase. It is their substitute for alcohol, and a less dangerous one. (Ahem!) As I watched some who really bought after much chaffering for the sake of chaffering, I recalled Rabelais's description of a dog with a marrow-bone: "If you have seen him you might have remarked with what devotion and circumspection he watches and wards it; with what care he keeps it; how fervently he holds it; how prudently he gobbets it; with what affection he breaks it; with diligence he sucks it." Bargain day is a marrow-bone sweet to woman; sweeter even than the Votiform Appendix.

III

When I began this series of studies devoted to intimate New York I had no intention of describing the town at large, only the corners that appealed to me; but as you are carried against your will in a human maelstrom, so I find myself far from my original plan.

I have, for myself, rediscovered New York. Its vastness almost appals. No fear of over-populating, if the East Side congestion could be tapped. There is room enough for millions north of us, and without crossing the rivers.

On the libraries I shan't dwell. They are at your elbow if you choose to visit them. I still regret the old Lenox Library, possibly because of its position. Certainly no structure will duplicate its dignity and massiveness. With the New York Library I am not yet well acquainted. I have dropped in to some excellent exhibitions of Frank Weitenkampf, curator of the print department, but I feel strange in the library proper, possibly because I miss the homely atmosphere of the Astor Library.

Of the clubs and hospitals there is naught to be said here, and it would be superfluous to find fault with the ugly Metropolitan Opera House when so much beautiful music is made within; or with the Metropolitan Museum of Art, so beautiful without.

I wonder who would read literature in our public libraries or visit the Metropolitan Museum of Art if there was no East Side! Isn't it odd that these "foreigners" are in the majority among the visitors of our art institution in Central Park? To be sure, there are warmer places in town on a June Sunday afternoon. This fact is appreciated by a large number of folk hailing from the East Side. You meet them there any time after the dinner-hour — German mode — and in any of the side streets from Sixtieth to One Hundredth, starting from Avenue A. They wear holiday clothes, and they beam with satisfaction. A treat is ahead of them. To wander in the cool twilight of the lower galleries; to flirt in the face of the Egyptian mummies; to giggle and gossip among the monster plaster casts; to stare at the marbles or sit placidly before bright-coloured pictures — what joy for the "uncultured" classes of the far East Side! You see them streaming up Fifth Avenue. Their faces are shiny. It is hot. Fathers and mothers with families, sometimes numbering eight or ten — ask the doorkeepers, who groan and growl as the entire "mishpogah" attempt to push through the turnstile at the same moment — Russians, Italians, Poles, Hungarians, Bohemians, Serbs, Croats, Greeks, Roumanians — Hebrews many of them — file by and ramble about, content to be reminded of some European or semi-Asiatic city, where, on their native heath, they once looked at pictures with the same appreciation.

A Walt Whitman catalogue alone could sum up the ethnical and kaleidoscopic variety of the mob that besieges the museum gate on summer Sunday afternoons. Yet a decorous, on occasion even a reverent, crowd, especially before sacred subjects, and a mob startlingly garbed. The children prefer the ground floor. It is of stone and cooler, there are "queerer" things to be seen than up-stairs. Sleighs shaped like boats, and dead men and women in marble on tombs, and churches, too; above all, Notre-Dame and the Pantheon. How delightful would it be if there were such toys at home. How the babies would crawl in and out of the big doors! Perhaps they might make a big bonfire if straw and matches could be gathered! The mummies — what a jolly set of ugly mugs in painted, canoe-like coverings! What a glorious ride on that Colleoni horse, whose feet must wear invisible seven-league boots, so magnificent the possibility of their stride! The George Grey Barnard group always elicits puzzled remarks; a wrestling-match, with the under man down and out for ever, is the usual verdict.

But before Borglum's Mares of Diomedes there are no doubts expressed. "A good run for your money!" says a sporty youth, with hair plastered on forehead. His girl nods. It is an object-lesson in the psychology of sex to watch the procession passing Makart's monster panel, with its riot of women in dazzling nudity. The girls always gaze unaffectedly at the explosive colour and large-limbed creatures. Their masculine escorts look carefully in the opposite direction. Why? It may not be amiss to state that the museum authorities displayed admirable judgment in their refusal to fig-leaf modern statuary. At the Louvre, at the Vatican, at a dozen other galleries in Europe, this needlessly offensive custom prevails. New York, with all its infernal prudery and prurience, has not thus defaced Rodin's superb bronze, l'Age d'Airain. It is Rodin at his best; nervous the touch, sinewy the figure, the planes of which melt into the ambient atmosphere no matter from which point you approach. It is as good, if not better, than the original at the Luxembourg. Its stark power, however, carries no message for the Sunday guests, though you note an occasional look of awe; but to the multitude it is one naked man the more; therefore to be warily circled.

What charm lurks in the bronzes by Jules Dalou! Mother's Love is a centre of attraction. As for the lace collections — they are ever difficult to reach, because of the women. The merits of Manet, Monet, and Whistler may be left to critical mankind; but every woman who enters the building, whether she wears a shawl on her head or rides there in a motor-car, is an authority on lace. Go and judge for yourself. Mrs. W. K. Vanderbilt has donated a "creation" in Brussels appliqué, once the property of Isabella, late Queen of Spain (a lace-like lady in her diaphanous day). As it is a baptism dress with veil, the women are literally mad over it. But let us fight our way up-stairs. On the main staircase we stumbled over a family party comfortably settled for an impromptu luncheon; the cold eggs were being tapped when an attendant, on the verge of a righteous apoplexy, came to the rescue, and wails of indignation arose from the lungs of six hungry children. "Art be hanged!" is what the father muttered in Czech, as he piloted his crew to the green and more hospitable park. The museum men have their troubles.

The Morgan collection is a Mecca for the majority. They make for these galleries — as a rule the hottest in the museum — with a unanimity that spells for the curious the colossal attraction in the name of J. Pierpont Morgan. This loan collection includes some beautiful pictures, but not the best in the museum. However, the crowds flock to Georgiana, Duchess of Devonshire, because of her legend as well as her hat. The name of Gainsborough you hear last. A favourite is Miss Farren, by Lawrence. The Raphael is not a big drawing card. It leaves the multitude untouched — seemingly; I can only judge by appearances. Nor are the Hobbema or the Van Dycks much admired; but Reynolds — Lady Betty and Her Children — the Greuze, the Hoppner, and other canvases of the ilk never miss an audience. Subject, not art, is the lodestone. It was ever thus, and ever will be, let critics scold as they may. A little girl playing with a kitten would swerve the attention of the public from such a masterpiece as The Maids of Honor, by Velasquez. Naturally, the furniture and porcelains in this section come in for their due share of homage.

Though we have no Salon Carré, no Tribuna, in the museum, there is a certain gallery, with its priceless works of art, that would be a paradise to live in. With the two small Rodins for company regard the old lady of Frans Hals and her sober-faced husband. There in the Rembrandt Sibyl, or the well-fed gentleman wearing a turban, you may see the self-portrait of Rembrandt. The Goya is flauntingly brilliant in comparison. But it is rather disconcerting to observe the blank air of non-recognition with which the collection in this gallery is observed. The same is the case with the new Vincent Van Gogh, or the wonderful sketch by Manet of a Montmartre funeral. The mob presses through to the adjoining room, there to admire pink sunsets, silly flower girls, glazed marines — a conglomeration of the most indigestible pictures in the building. It is the subject that attracts the throngs. All the afternoon you hear the babble, and if you are a linguist you may remark the similarity of the questions and exclamations before the Winslow Homer canvas, which dramatically depicts a sea scene: "Oh, my! Look at the black man! He's dead. No, he isn't, but he soon expects to be swallowed up by those sharks. What sharks? Isn't he fishing?

There's his line, that coloured rope. Unsinn! It's a devil-fish, see it wriggle its eight arms! Yes, eight, just count 'em. There's a water-spout! The ship! the ship! Ain't the water wet and green?"

About a half dozen keepers succumb of a Sunday in answering the questions put to them. No wonder. Homer has painted better pictures than this framed melodrama of piratical horrors, but none so popular. The Renoir group is comparatively neglected, the Manets absolutely neglected, with the possible exception of the Boy with a Sword. Possibly the rich harmonies of the Renoir-Charpentier family portrait do not appeal. I saw several persons study the little girl sitting on the large dog, but whether it is the child is not pretty enough — as a matter of fact, she is adorable — or because the bluish tone distracts, only a shrug of the shoulder happened before this work. It probably denotes suspended opinion; no such shrugs occur in the face of the two Claude Monets, which hang hard by — frank grinning is often accompanied by laughter. The vivid beach scene with the choppy waves and lovely sky are too much for many. Because it evokes nature this marine offends or tickles the risible rib. If the water had been pink, the sand inky, and the sky full of woolen clouds, and the human figures carved out — oh! what cries of amazement and joy. Meissonier! That's the chap for us. His soldiers, his horses (hair, hoof, hide), you can see them all — count the hairs — clear as glass or brass. Besides, he tells a story.

So does Detaille. What good is that ugly guitarist of Edouard Manet? Why, he looks like a little old Spaniard in Houston Street who plunks out Iberian melodies for you, and is glad to earn a copper. That's the trouble. He is too lifelike, this Manet, even for the Academy Signori — extremes meet, the East Side and learned academicians. His silhouette may be as masterful as if executed by Goya; his eyes, they burn with a hard fire; and look at his hat, his costume — no! all this is mere imitation. The proletarians are idealists, as are our academic painters. They all want to dream; they long for the unreal; their ice-cream is pink of hue. They sigh for Marble Halls by Lord Leighton and Alma-Tadema. Life is dull, drab, cruel — at times, vile; in art let us get away from life as far as possible! Thus do Laura Jean Libbey, Marie Corelli, Hall Caine, and the East Side touch hands with our immortal academy. A little touch of pink paint makes all the world kin.

With or without his note-book, a likely reporter could glean columns of Sunday afternoon stories at the museum. I notice that the "popular" guide, in the guise of a young lady, has already begun. Students of character after "human interest" anecdotes, and sociological sleuths, would be embarrassed by the richness of the soil. There are girls enough there on Sundays to people our barren moon; they are, for the major part, broad of girth, squat of figure, bright-eyed, and often possess a pretty wit. Said one, before that too voluptuous Cabanel, The Birth of Venus (a capital soap advertisement): "Sadie, what's she called?" "The Bath of Venus," replied the other. No one smiled, for the improvised title fitted. Whistler's Falling Rocket is not popular. "It's too dark to see the sparks," said a man who had sneered the Monets off the map of his acquaintance. But one painter's — I've forgotten his name — picture of the forging of a shaft, with its glow of molten metal, is a perpetual object of interest.

No one stops in front of the portrait of a Spanish Lady, by Mariano Fortuny. Why not replace it by an Eastman Johnson "coon" subject? There's a popular idea for you! The Vanderbilt gallery is always crowded; the variety of themes and its painters make it beloved. Nor should the supercilious critic wave ineffectual flags of protest. Deeply implanted in the human consciousness there is a craving for the tale simply told. The Vanderbilt gallery supplies many examples. The Millets, Daubignys, Meissoniers, De Neuvilles, Detailles, Benjamin Constant, and the Oriental subjects of Fromentin, Gérôme, Decamps, and others are always the centre for admiring visitors. And who shall gainsay their taste? This mid-century art was once the shibboleth of our fathers, to whom misty impressionism, angular cubism, and imbecile futurism was, and is, a riddle and an eyesore. Take them, by and large, the East Side crowds that fill the Metropolitan Museum on Sunday afternoons are as excellent judges as the visitors on pay-days. At least they know what they dislike.

A more gracious form of public benefaction is hardly conceivable than the Benjamin Altman donation of art treasures to the Metropolitan Museum. Mr. Altman loved pictures and porcelains and sculptures, and, while not a man with a fixed idea or belief in any one school, still he knew what he wanted and procured it. His picture-gallery was not the result of long years of meditation and collecting, though his china was. He had certain preferences, notably the quaint old Dutch school, some Flemish primitives, and the noble Spaniard, Velasquez. Yet that did not prevent him from admiring the Italian primitives, and, while his magnificent gift to the museum is in no sense a representative gathering of any particular school, nevertheless it reveals the catholic tastes of its donor. But we must guard against the prevalent opinion that the Altman collection is faultless, is above criticism; indiscriminate admiration naturally enough expressed just now in the first flush of gratitude at the magnitude of the gift may prove a stumbling-block to both student and amateur; in a word, all the pictures and art objects in this collection are not masterpieces. Far from it. There are private collections in America that excel at every point, quality and quantity, the Altman; furthermore, there is bound to be a slump in critical values if the key is pitched too high at the outset. Consider the case of the Morgan collection and the now openly expressed disappointment of connoisseurs who had expected something faultless, whereas, setting aside the Raphael, the Fragonards, and the Gainsborough Duchess, there are some pessimistic people who assert that the gem of the collection in the museum is the portrait of a little Dutch baby, and that by an unknown master, for masterly it is.

Therefore, it is well to guard against uncritical enthusiasm. All Rembrandts are not masterpieces — especially when his pupils painted them; and Frans Hals painted unequally, as the Altman examples prove up to the hilt. Nor must the rather reckless use of such sacred names as Giorgione and Titian be accepted without protest. But the Rembrandt Gallery is a handsome one, a baker's dozen of the masters, and, while it cannot be compared en masse with the Cassel Gallery assemblage — what gallery can outside of the Rijks Museum? — the Altman Rembrandts are his trump-cards. Several, at least, are masterpieces; all are of interest, though not equal in artistic merit. The Old Woman Cutting Her Nails is a magisterial, almost monumental, work, and is already the lodestone for visitors. Yet, after two or three visits it ceased to make the profound appeal it should have done, because it is obviously not

Rembrandt at his mightiest. For one thing, the figure is overmodelled; the bulk is sculptural rather than pictorial; there is more than a suggestion of pose, of a self-consciousness that robs the composition of pristine simplicity, of the effortless art of which Rembrandt knew so well the secret. Dramatic is this old woman with the untrimmed nails, but she is also out of, and not in, the frame — like an operatic primadonna she faces the footlights ready for her exalted aria. Of the paint quality there is no doubt — it is beautiful in its easy sweep and fat richness. The imagination of the Seer of Amsterdam is greatly daring, and the head is sibylline, but not altogether in the clear-obscure of the painter. Simplicity is the quality least in evidence. If this sounds like hypercriticism, please remember I've lived with the Rembrandts of the Louvre, National Gallery, at Cassel, and in Holland. Still, what a piece of luck for Mr. Altman to have secured this rare specimen, for it is unlike any Rembrandt I've ever seen in its rhetorical quality. From the sombre heart of darkness the master plucked mystery, and, except in his etchings — after all, the man at his best — he seldom touches earth with his august feet; touches reality, as did, say, Vermeer.

But this old woman like her neighbour, also an old lady, is far from being the Elizabeth Bas of the Rijks. More characteristic is the Toilet of Bathsheba, on another wall. This lovely dream in gloom and old gold I studied for years in the back room of Count Steengracht's mansion on the Vyverberg, at The Hague. How many visitors to that fascinating Dutch city have admired this woman who tempted the royal psalmodist! She is not subtle or comely as are the Titian women, but she is compelling enough, and she is placed in an enchanting glow which Rembrandt alone could evoke. For me, Bathsheba is the Rembrandt of the Altman collection, and after the first imperious pull of The Old Woman Cutting Her Nails relaxes, you will find yourself returning to the magnetic portrait of the unfaithful wife, which has the true visionary aspect of Rembrandt. Why the Rijks Museum authorities allowed this masterpiece to escape may be set down to the fact that too much money had been spent on the new Vermeers from the Six collections. And a Vermeer is always worth a dozen Rembrandts on the sheer score of rarity.

The Lady with a Pink is attractive, as is the portrait of The Auctioneer. The Pilate did not intrigue me; it seems rather vague or empty. The Man with a Magnifying Glass is psychologically strong. The others are more or less negligible. Hendrickje Stoffels is distinctly inferior to the portraits of the same lady in the Louvre and the Kaiser Friedrich Museum, Berlin. The so-called Little Masters were a disappointment, the Vermeer — Holland's master colourist — being an early effort, the so-called Drunken Servant Asleep, said to be from the historical sale of 1696; though Burger-Thoré believes Mr. Widener's picture with the same name, but differently treated, is the original of that sale. Certainly it is better painted than the Altman example, which latter is a rather dull, heavy performance — its edges are too soft for the master — lacking the magic atmosphere, spacing, and exquisite touch of Vermeer. Some of the still-life shows his touch, and there are passages of paint in the rug that are superb; the wall, too, is very swell; but, as a Vermeer, this does not rank with Mr. Widener's Woman Weighing Pearls, Mrs. Gardner's, Mr. Frick's, or Mr. J. G. Johnson's, in Philadelphia. Go, after studying it, into the Marquand room at the Metropolitan Museum, and look at the thrice-lovely girl with the pitcher, sometimes called The Girl Opening the Casement. That is beautiful Vermeer, with its blue, yellow, and silvery-grey tonalities, much more so than the Morgan Vermeer, which hangs hard by. I confess that the De Hooch, Nicholas Maes, the Gerard Dou, the Terburg (or Terborch) did not interest me; like the three Frans Halses, they are mediocre. The Wheatfields, by Jacob Van Ruisdael, is fine and better than the Hobbema. Of the three examples by Frans Hals, two of them are in his bacchanalian, bombastic vein — a Jan Steen vein. I recall The Merry Company from the Hudson-Fulton Exhibition. Its pattern is ingenious, its colour scheme hot and flamboyant. None of the three display the virtuoso brush work of the brilliant Dutchman. I like better the Marquand Halses, not to mention the Rembrandts; but not the so-called Hille Bobbe, or The Smoker, which are both unhappy attributions; the original of Hille is in the Kaiser Friedrich Museum, Berlin. It wouldn't surprise me to learn that several of these Halses are by Dirk, not Frans.

The Christ of Velasquez is, as De Beruete relates, an early work. It is hot and heavy in colour, as heavy as Caravaggio. A Velasquez for the student of his various manners it is, but not very convincing. The Philip IV is a pale, feeble school piece, possibly by his son-in-law, Mazo. At the Prado, and in the National Gallery, the real Philip IV may be seen; not here — above all, not in the Boston Museum, where the Philip might be a replica of the Altman, or t'other way about. The two Van Dycks are nice, though hardly significant; nor by the same token is the Titian. Giorgione and Vermeer are such rare birds that it is arrant blasphemy to place their names in a catalogue unless the picture ascribed to either of them is unmistakable. Mr. Berenson believes this Altman portrait to be an unquestionable Giorgione, and there is no disputing Berenson. Nor Bode, either. But even if it is a Giorgione, does that say much for this particular canvas? It is the Venetian of his period, and exhales a certain charm, as do many Venetian artists of Big George of Castelfranco's days.

BRAIN AND SOUL AND POCKETBOOK

A few years ago I happened to be in Hamburg, and reading the advertisement of Consul Weber's pictures, I visited his house, and there found a few good pictures, also a profusion of junk and wholly worthless attributions. A small Rembrandt, the head of a boy, was capital, and at the sale later eagerly snapped up. Down on the dismal cellar-like first floör were about a half acre of Flemish, German, and Italian primitives. Among them The Holy Family, by Andrea Mantegna, which Mr. Altman was happy in capturing. It is the treasure of his Italian section, a work of exceeding charm and nobility. Mantegna is not often encountered in European galleries, and now artistic Europe may visit our museum to see this Mantegna. I wish I could become as enthusiastic over the Memlings — of which one at least betrays German origin (all these Memlings are doubtful), or the Albrecht Dürer — once known as Our Lady of the Gumboil, and full of poisonously acid paint; or over the Botticelli (?), or Memling's Betrothal. Whosoever has tarried in Bruges will not long delay before this well-executed composition, devoid though it be of spiritual atmosphere. The Diereck Bouts is excellent, and the Cosma Tura very attractive, attribution correct or not. That's precisely the verdict that may be passed on the majority of the Altman collection. Many of its pictures are beautiful without their resounding names. So why worry over precision in attribution? What could be lovelier than the Gerard David, The Christ of the Miniature (in case B)? One must go to Bruges to better it. The Mainardi, the Barend Von Orley, the Lippi (?), the Fra Angelico (?), the Verrocchio (?) are all of moment, aside from their ascriptions. The portrait of a Lady by Bartolommeo Montagna is a specimen of Venetian art that, notwithstanding its modest position, is engaging. The Hans Maler I've seen elsewhere; like the Holbeins, it is characteristic. The latter are as hard as nails, with wiry silhouettes. The Francia and Messina portraits are vital.

The porcelains, enamels, furniture, tapestries, and miscellaneous art objects would take a year to describe. The sculpture is generally impressive. There is the Houdon Bather, a splendid marble, full of elusive, slippery modelling, with enough accents to redeem the figure from suspicion of prettiness. The Clodion terra-cotta was formerly entitled The Triumph of Pan, instead of the conventional Intoxication of Wine. (I remember it at the Doucet collection sale in Paris.) It represents in plastic perfection the culmination of ecstasy, the very apotheosis of passion, withal, in terms of idealised art. The facture is marvellous. Only think of such a gathering of names as Mina da Fiesole, Germain Pilon, Verrocchio (?), Sansovino, Rossellino, Benedetto da Majano, Luca della Robbia, John of Bologna, Alessandro Vittoria, and Donatello. I am not sure but that when the authoritative critical appraisement of the Altman collection is finally made, his sculptures will rank the rest. The Donatello Madonna, the Mino Head of St. John — in the round and the youthful charm of which is irresistible — the Sansovino Charity, and the Madonna of Robbia, not forgetting the delicious relief of the Madonna and Child of Rossellino, these, with Pigalle's Mercury and the Houdon and Clodion examples linger longer in my memory than the pictures — the provenance of which need concern us less than the consideration of their intrinsic artistic merit.

If you alight at the One Hundred and Fifty-seventh Street Subway station, west side, and walk down a block you will come upon a structure of Indiana limestone, of an architectural type that is a happy compromise of classic and romantic. It is not more than one hundred feet in length, and in depth seventy feet. The building stands in One Hundred and Fifty-sixth Street, west of Broadway, in Audubon Park; air and sunshine have plenty of space to play about its severe and graceful lines. It is the Hispanic Museum. Mr. Archer M. Huntington, a profound student of Spanish archæology, literature, and art, has brought together an extraordinary collection of antiques, manuscripts, marbles, bronzes, books, Hispano-Moresque ware, medals, coins, letters. In Europe — Madrid for example — this house beautiful would be an objective shrine for passionate pilgrims. New York is so interested in dancing that it has little time to visit the Hispanic Museum unless a sensation is provided such as the impressionistic pictures of Sorolla.

A tiled space after you have entered by the big iron gates on the granite stairs gives an imposing perspective. The attention is first caught by two gigantic repoussé bronze doors from Egypt, of the fourteenth century. They were found by Mr. Huntington at Cairo, and were formerly the wings of a door on the mosque of the Mameluke Sultan, Barkuf, whose name is inscribed in Arabic. Tiles and mosaics on the walls and halls evoke dreams of the Alhambra, of Spain when it was most beautiful — Moorish Spain. If one may dare say it, the interior of the museum is of a cosy magnificence. It is not large, nor yet is it cramped. The spacing and arrangement of the various objects of art have been planned by a master hand. You have a sense of intimacy. You wish to linger, to "loaf and invite your soul" under that glassed patio, from which you may peep over into the reading-room with its fifty thousand volumes. A small boy in buttons, who is not even half Spanish, offers you a leather plaque, upon which are inscribed the names of the masters whose pictures adorn the walls — some thirty odd. It is a moment to rejoice. New York has never seen, in a public place, such a gathering of Goyas and El Grecos, while the two Velasquezes, wonderful examples, are claimed by certain experts to be the only genuine ones in America by the great Spaniard.

One portrait is supposed by those whose judgment is worthy of credence to be that of a certain Cardinal Pamfili, or Pamphili, spoken of by Palomino. (What visions of cool bosks and sweet meadows are evoked by the old name, the Pamphili gardens at Rome!) Velasquez painted the heads of many churchly dignitaries while in Rome — the Pope and several cardinals. His Innocent X in the Doria Palace once seen will never vanish from the secret chambers of the brain. The present portrait is that of a man in the flower of his age. Though wearing scarlet cope and biretta he still preserves a youthful air. He sports, as did many a noble priest of those days, a little moustache. His is a sleek face. The eyes suggest a shrewd nature, not easily fathomed. Its depth and lustre, the solid modelling of the head, the planes of the face, to assess a few values, are all masterly. The expression is both powerful and delicate. The figure swims in space. Viewed from the opposite end of the gallery, you feel as some one alive were looking at you through an aperture framed in gold. Vitality, nobility in characterisation, and superb paint are displayed in this portrait. If Velasquez did not paint it — and such authorities as the late Señor de Beruete and Professor Venturi assert that without the peradventure of a doubt he is its author — then who in the name of El Cid was its creator? Certainly a glorious artist. It would be too cruel to compare it with the alleged Velasquezes I have seen here. It has quality, that indefinable quality, like unto the golden, floating tone of a Stradivarius violin (or its richly varnished belly).

The Granddaughter Portrait by Velasquez comes from the collection of the late Edouard Kann, of Paris, and is a life-size bust portrait of a sweetly grave little girl. Señor Beruete believes her to represent the daughter of the painter Mazo and his wife Francisca Velasquez, therefore a granddaughter of Velasquez. The tonalities of the picture are subtly beautiful, the modelling mysterious, the expression vital and singularly child-like. It is a fitting companion to the aristocratic cardinal. Of the Grecos there is a brilliantly coloured Holy Family; a St. Joseph, said to be the portrait of the painter, and a large canvas showing Christ with several of his disciples. The most magisterial of the El Grecos is the portrait of Cardinal de Guevara, from the former Kann collection. A notable work. The Goyas are unequal but interesting. One depicts the horrors of war, and is probably a sketch for the picture at the Prado, Madrid. We know it through the etched series, entitled The Horrors of War, a companion set to the Caprichos. Cruel, violent, exuberant, it is truly Goyaesque. So is its neighbour, a bucolic bit. The portrait of the Duchess of Alva, a large canvas, shows us that coquettish dame pointing to her feet, where the artist has scrawled his signature in the dust. It is modern in feeling, as modern as Zuloaga, though a trifle wooden in the articulation of the wrists and ankles. The Duke of Alva (The Bloody Duke), is by Antonio Moro — strongly masculine in feeling. In dull-coloured armour, carrying across his arm a truncheon, this sinister nobleman does not belie his fierce reputation. What power, what painting! Note the tactile values in that sceptre, not of iron but of wood; one has the sense of lesser weight as it reposes on the steel-clad left arm — not to mention the justness of the rendered texture. General Forastero, by Goya, hangs on the same wall, and also a man's portrait by Murillo. The general effect at the other end of the gallery is brilliant. Carreño de Miranda's Assumption of the Virgin hangs in the centre. On either side are two Morales, a Valdes Real, and a rich-toned Murillo. The Miranda might have been painted yesterday, so clear and fresh is the body of its paint. On the two long walls, south and north, there are portraits by Spanish artists — an excellent one of Philip IV — and altar-pieces and ecclesiastical subjects, Hispano-Moresque lustre ware, sacred vessels, gold, silver, precious stones, bronzes, door-knockers, iron-work, coins of rare value. Moorish, Roman, Carthaginian, and Spanish coins may be seen and wondered over, a wonderment that finally modulates into the theme of the collector's indomitable patience and sagacity. Mr. Huntington is an authority on Spanish and Moorish coins. Hê has written a history concerning them. And the collection of old books, unique maps, and manuscripts! It will be the work of a lifetime to catalogue the riches of this museum, which, excepting the British Museum, has no rival. Francis Lathrop painted in monochrome the heads that are ranged under the galleries; also two capital copies of the Velasquez masterpieces in the Prado, The Maids of Honor (Las Meninas) and The Spinners (Las Hilanderas). The decorations throughout are warm in tone, the various carvings tasteful. Medallions adorn the outer walls with appropriate names of great Spanish artists and thinkers. Loyola is one, a significant indication of the donor's catholicity. Flanking the Hispanic Museum is the Numismatist Society's home.

IV

Of the theatres there is no end. Nevertheless true drama is not yet lodged here. The heterogeneous elements that make up our theatre-going public demand amusement of the most elementary variety and get what they ask for.

With music the case is different. We have an extraordinary conductor, an Italian born, and only one orchestra that vies with the Vienna Philharmonic Society orchestra; of course, I refer to Toscanini and to the band from Boston, the Higginson veterans; but there are several capital orchestras in the city and plenty of minor organisations. America still imports its music and music-makers. Thus far our musical genius has found fullest expression in the invention or the development of mechanical toys, pianos, and the like; such as the soulless phonograph with its diabolical concatenation of sounds and the malignant "records" of famous singers, whose voices, because of this sinister "sea change," become colourless, rasping, pinched, metallic, a very caricature of the original. Edison is better known now than Beethoven.

The most characteristic example of American music is, thus far, Edward A. MacDowell's Indian Suite, and not Antonin Dvořák's so-called New World Symphony, which latter, despite its occasional utilisation of negro tunes, is a composition more Bohemian in colour and character than American. (Why go to the negro for "American" melody: he is not an aboriginal, the Indian is; besides, the negro in America, be it understood, never created native music. And has the so-called "African" music exerted anything but a debasing influence?) If you insist on the African element then Stephen Foster and Louis Moreau Gottschalk are the greatest American composers, for both invented "negro" tunes, the latter, so-called creole music.

Our greatest American novelist still lives in England, and the "great" American novel will never be written because art is not a question of magnitude, but of intensity. The average conception of the "great" American novel is a bundle of dialects. But the human soul has no dialect.

With painting and sculpture the case is brighter. We have a native school of landscape, and if our figure-painters do not lead in the world's procession our sculptors make a showing. New York is full of hideous public statuary, as it is full of horrible architecture, but the Sherman, Nathan Hale, Farragut, Hunt Memorial, Ward's Pilgrim, Browne's Washington in Union Square should make us forget the Dodge, the Cox, and other attempts.

I confess that in the Mall of Central Park there is a nerve-destroying aggregation. But how about the marble abominations of the Siegesallee, Berlin! To every city its municipal bad taste. Paris is alone the home of outdoor statuary that does not offend the taste.

On the other hand, some of our churches soothe the eye. St. Patrick's Cathedral makes perfect Gothic music in moonlight nights, and the very bulk of the St. John Cathedral on the Heights is imposing. The new St. Thomas, despite its newness, pleases the eye with its harmonious lines, as Trinity does by its age. St. Paul's Chapel, Grace Church, old St. Mark's, to mention a few classic examples, are show-places.

If you search for the soul of New York you must not go to its market-place, but to its churches; therein its still small voice may be overheard. Without the roar is mundane.

I might have included the newspaper buildings under the caption of "The Brain of New York," but just now there seems to exist such a prejudice against "highbrows" that it is more prudent not to place "journalists" in that category. But the newspaper buildings belong to the "sights" of the town. Anything more architecturally charming than the Herald, dwarfed as it is by its giant neighbours, does not exist here, and of the Times I once wrote — having a vantage-point then in upper Madison Avenue: "To enjoy the delicate and massive drawing of the Times Building as etched against a southern sky — now ardent, now fire-tipped, jewelled, or swimming in the bewitching breath of a summer's day — one must study it from the north. A silhouette in the evening, and often like a child's church of chalk lighted at Christmas, it flushes rosy in the morning, and during the afternoon the repercussion of the sun waves drowns it in an incandescent haze. The fronds of stone ranging below it support this bell-tower — for it is of the true Campanile order from afar — as if it were an integral part of them. It, too, spires northward, where the park blooms, an emerald oblong. On its pinnacle the city below wears the precise, mapped-out look and checkered image it has from a balloon, or pinned on a surveyor's chart."

As to the Stock Exchange, Custom House, Clearing House, Sub-Treasury, and Chamber of Commerce — their beauties are perennial.

BRAIN AND SOUL AND POCKETBOOK

Of the little things to be seen in our intimate New York I might make a book. Not always the wide waterways or vast spaces bring to the eye such ravishing impressions as those caught at the corner of some alley or through the arch of one of the big bridges. There is Baxter Street. There is Edgar Street, the shortest street in the city. Or there is Dutch Street. And there is Fletcher Street. Go find it and see the Singer Building from its coign; or Brooklyn Bridge from Frankfort Street; or Coenties Slip; or that ever delightful part of New Street where it ends at Marketfield Street and the Produce Exchange.

There's an intimate corner for you, and another is just off the narrowest and highest street of all (I hope this is so!), Exchange Place, east of Broadway. On the hottest days Exchange Place seems cooler than the street, as you crane your neck to see the slit of blue sky.

Then, if craving magnificent dimensions, there is the Grand Central Station, the largest in the world, and the end is not yet. Wonderful as are its proportions, the façade in Forty-second Street is disfigured by the little shops beneath; nor does it convey the majestic power of the Pennsylvania Railroad Station, to my mind the most beautiful without of all railway stations and the most imposing within. It is a unicum; the Grand Central Station a complex of buildings.

I have seen strange sights. An American flag flying from the gilded dome of an East Side synagogue; a man blocking the way in a sudden little street, yet a shaft of sunshine and a bit of landscape showing through him so bow-legged was he; a cat raising a litter of chickens — in a Brooklyn back yard as seen from a train; a hen in Flatbush that crows before laying eggs. I once saw a crowd so dense that City Hall Park was impassable. It was at the beginning of the war when the city was charged with anticipation as if by electricity. I tried to push by, but vainly. It was in front of the *Evening Sun* office, and finally I asked the policeman the latest news from Belgium. I thought he spied me curiously. "Look for yourself," he laconically replied. I did and saw by the baseball score that the Giants were not in the lead.

It was a typical summer-afternoon crowd. I hadn't realised the happy fund of indifference possessed by the crowd. Truly happy thus to forget — in a game — the tragedy across the water. A meeting of street salvationists farther down the street made uncouth sounds like savages pacifying their idol — all alike in their worship of ugliness.

The old saying, "See Naples and die!" may be replaced by "See New York first!" She may be enormously vulgar, and the genius of her is enormous, and never suggests mediocrity. You may hate or love her, but you cannot pass her by; and if Stendhal were alive to-day he would rechristen the city Cosmopolis, the noisiest Cosmopolis that ever existed, but also the New Cosmopolis, the most versatile city on our globe.

VIII

CONEY ISLAND

I

BY DAY

It was a poster that sent me to Coney Island again, although I had sworn never to tread again that avenue of hideous sights and sounds, had taken a solemn oath to that effect years ago. But that poster! Ah! if these advertising men only knew how their signs and symbols arouse human passions they would be more prudent in giving artists full swing with their suggestion-breeding brushes.

This is what I saw on the poster: A tall, energetic band conductor waving his baton over a succulent symphony of crabs, lobsters, fruit, fish, corn, cantaloups, clams, and water-melons — truly a pretty combination, for the overtones are Afro-American, the undertones Asiatic cholera. Nevertheless, an appealing orchestra to palates jaded by city restaurant fare and the hot, humid streets. I was in haste to be off. I mentally saw that gustatory symphony. I heard its colicky music. I tasted its clambake instrumentation. I must take the boat at once.

As the tall, architectural chimneys at the lower end of the Island slowly receded I noted the waffle-like effect of the myriad windows set in their staring walls. Waffles! Yes, that is the new note in American architecture; it is the very soul of the art. Waffles! This discovery comforted me somewhat, and I began to enjoy life and sought for a fresh thrill by gazing steadily at the Brooklyn shorescape.

Perhaps the first definite impression made amid the thousands of confusing, beckoning, and mutually destructive sights as one comes up the harbour is Brooklyn Bridge, seen across the green of Governor's Island. The woven wires of the structure seem to float; no water, except that in the immediate foreground of the spectator, suggests the notion that this is a bridge; rather is it a fantastic apparition strung across an emerald prairie, a huge harp ready for the fingers of some monstrous musician, whose melodies would be hurricane-like, not æolian. The illusion vanishes the farther down or up one sails; it is trapped at its best near Staten Island.

The coast-line of Brooklyn does not lend itself to optical enchantment. But it is not more depressing than, say, the docks of London after you leave Blackfriars Bridge going down Greenwich way. Brooklyn is more cheerful because of the greater spaces of waterway, because of more diversity as to sky-line. In London the heavens seem closer to earth, the sky not as far away as ours. High buildings are rare along the Thames, while Brooklyn boasts many. The time is not long since the Hotel Margaret was the proud monarch of all it surveyed across the harbour. Now it has numerous rivals. They are beginning to string down the shore and run a race with the church spires that gave to the town of Beecher and Talmage its nickname. With the picturesque villas and the old fort, the interest merges into the strand, into the superior beauties of Bath Beach and Norton Point.

The same old iron steamboats, with the same old band of itinerant musicians, arouse memories. They still play Non è ver, as they did a quarter of a century ago. And more memories when the Grand Republic passes cityward, its flags and pennants flying, the venerable steamer as attractive-looking as ever; dwarfed, to be sure, since the advent of ocean leviathans, she still makes a gallant showing.

Is our river-excursion service commensurate with the volume of its business? It far outshines in efficiency and in the size of its craft the Thames or the tiny boats on the Seine. Nevertheless, our steamers are not equal to the strain put upon them; they are old-fashioned, cramped, and with mediocre accommodations. They are crowded, too, beyond the danger-line. A fire, a panic, a collision, and the inherent unworthiness of most of the excursion boats in our harbour would be revealed in a moment. The great god Chance is the patron saint of pilots and owners. Votive candles in abundance should be burned before his image by grateful worshippers, for it is due to his graces that we somehow or other muddle through season after season without serious accidents. But when one arrives it is usually in the category of the catastrophic.

As I first recall Coney Island, one could walk on a wide, clean, shining space of sand from the Point to the Oriental Hotel. No vile barracks and booths snouted their noisome features to the water's edge. There was no Sea Gate in those days, and the top of the Island was practically barren and given over to fishermen. To-day the villas and hotels at Sea Gate have improved matters; but go up the beach a bit, and what disillusionment follows!

From where the Brighton bathing pavilion stands, down as far as Ravenhall's, is the craziest collection of tumble-down hovels — you can't dignify them with any other term — that ever disgraced a beautiful sea-view. There are exceptions: the Oriental Hotel, — which hasn't changed, — the Brighton Beach Hotel, the several large casinos and restaurants clustering about the end of the ocean boulevard, and also the municipal bath-house, a building worthy of its purpose. I may have omitted a few others, and I'm duly sorry in advance; yet do I cling to my belief that if the whole horrible aggregation of shanties, low resorts, shacks masquerading as hotels, and the rest were swept off the earth by some beneficent visitation of Providence, the thanksgivings of the community would be in order.

This sounds selfish, but it's not a question of personal feeling; it is a pestilential fact that the municipal authorities tolerate such a plague — for it is a centre of moral and physical infection — on the very heels of the city. This rings of humbug "uplift," but it is the naked truth. Privileges usurped from the public are granted to a lot of greedy money-muckers who bamboozle the people. The poor, more than the rich, rob the poor.

But the people, the poor people! Must they be deprived of their day's outing, of the innocent, idiotic joys of dear, dear old Coney? You know the sentimental cant of the East Side sociologist and the friend of the "peepul." No, this is no attempt to depreciate the enjoyment of the masses and classes (the latter are much given to visiting the Island as a sort of vicious open-air slumming spot), there is more than one centre of amusement — unlike Sodom, Coney Island can boast at least ten good inhabitants — but they only serve to set off the repulsive qualities of their neighbours.

I know that you can't make the public enjoy the more refined pleasures of a beach free from vulgarity and rapacious beach-combers, male and female, unless it so wishes. Even mules will not drink unless thirsty. The Montessori method applied to an army of excursionists would be ludicrous; it's a sufficient infliction on children. In a word, it is not a question of restriction but of regulation; decency, good taste, and semibarbarism should not be allowed to go unchecked. Coney Island to-day, despite the efficiency of the police, is a disgrace to our civilisation. It should be abolished and something else substituted.

And now, having abolished the eyesore by a mere waving of my wish-wand, let me tell you of the joys I experienced after I had landed at the Steeplechase Park pier in company with some hundreds of fellow lunatics of all ages and conditions, for when you are at Coney you cast aside your hampering reason and become a plain lunatic. It was a great French writer who advised his readers to make of themselves beasts from time to time, to kick over the slow and painful step-ladder of moral restraint and revert to the normal animal from which we evolved. It is never a difficult precept to follow, although the writer didn't mean his text to be exactly interpreted as I am now doing.

After the species of straitjacket that we wear in every-day life is removed at such Saturnalia as Coney Island, the human animal emerges in a not precisely winning guise. He and she and the brats are a mixture that sets you thinking over the idle boast that our century is the flowering of culture. As Gustave Flaubert says: "The patriot doesn't always smell nice."

Again you think — cleanliness is greater than godliness, and if mankind were friendlier to soap this old globe of ours would be a sweeter place to live on. But where can they keep cleaner than at the seaside, and what seaside is so cheap, so near by as Coney? Sound and unanswerable arguments. The man with the Brobdingnagian mouth who salutes you from the signs as you enter the portal of Steeplechase would smile still wider if you attempted to answer them. So let us throw logic to the dogs and simply be happy because we are alive, because the wind is not only in the heather, brother, but because the smell of the frankfurter "dog" as it sizzles over the fire ascends to eager nostrils on the dock.

The fisherman sits line in hand as we pass; a sign informs that there are twenty-five thousand bathing-suits to hire, and we listlessly gaze at the hulk of the only American vessel captured in the war with Spain. The barkers arouse us. We buy a string of parti-coloured tickets. They are so many keys that unlock to us the magic chambers of this paradise of secular joys and terrors. You may swim or guzzle; on the hard backs of iron steeds, to the accompaniment of bedlam music, you may caracole or go plunging down perilous declivities, swinging into the gloom of sinister tunnels or, perched aloft, be the envy of small boys.

There is an Italian garden where basket parties are forbidden — the only spot in the establishment — and a vast hall where, as if practising the attitudes and steps of some strange religious cult, youths and maidens indulge in simian gestures and in native buffoonery. Food, mountains of it, is cooking. The odour ascends to the stars; but you forget as in a monster wheel human beings are swung in a giant circle. Coasting parties clatter by or else are shot down a chute into irritated water. Every device imaginable by which man may be separated from his dimes without adequate return is in operation. You weigh yourself or get it guessed; you go into funny houses — oh, the mockery of the title! — and later are tumbled into the open, insulted, mortified, disgusted, angry, and — laughing. What sights you have seen in that prison-house, what gentlewomen — with shrill voices — desperately holding on to their skirts and their chewing-gum.

What I can't understand is the lure of the Island for the people who come. Why, after the hot, narrow, noisy, dirty streets of the city, do these same people crowd into the narrower, hotter, noisier, dirtier, wooden alleys of Coney? Is the wretched, Cheap John fair, with the ghastly rubbish for a sale, the magnet? Or is it just the gregariousness of the human animal? They leave dirt and disorder to go to greater disorder and dirt. The sky is bluer, but they don't look at the sky; clam chowder is a more agreeable spectacle; and the smacking of a thousand lips as throats gurgle with the suspicious compound is welcome to the ears of them that pocket the cash.

How's that for a rhythmic cadence after the manner of Flaubert?

The late Jacob Riis once told me that many times he despaired at the apparent hopelessness of his efforts to instil the love of cleanliness among his poor. To their ancient habits these people revert, like the beast-folk in H. G. Wells's The Island of Doctor Moreau. And at Coney Island where the mob is thickest, where your ear-drums are shattered by steam-organs, sheet-iron bands, and the yelling of barkers, the "people" hurry. I looked, as others before me have looked, for Walt Whitman's "powerful uneducated persons," but in vain. By way of compensation every one seemed content.

But the joylessness of it all! The miserable children, sick from their tenements, sit on dirty newspapers spread on the dirty sand and in the poisonous blaze of the sun — for some reason this sun is supposed to kill in town but will work wonders at the beach. What kind of food is swallowed I leave to your imagination. The place should be called Ptomaines Beach. Family parties with baskets (ever welcome) are better off; they know what they swallow.

I looked up my orchestra of sea food and found it. I confess I enjoyed its crabbed music. Once indoors, away from the glare and roar, your nerves begin to simmer and your throat craves the cool of an element not washing the front door of the hotel. Then you try to think. Impossible. It is a world of screams and hootings.

Farther up at Brighton matters improve, though wooden sheds disgrace the beach and bar people from its use. I sighed over — I always do — the thought of 1888 and the pavilion at Brighton Beach where Anton Seidl gave us ambrosial music. Coney Island was as bad as it is to-day, but the Seidl music furnished an oasis in a dreary desert of vulgarity. There were some New Yorkers alive in those dear but distant days. New York was not yet an open, noisy trench; nor was it then the dumping-ground of the cosmos. However, I am not a pessimist, and if I rail at the plague spot, Coney Island, it is with the hope that some day it will vanish and be succeeded by pleasant parks, trees, sea-walls, and stone walks. This madland of lunatics, who must go up in the air, down in the earth, who must have clatter and dirt, might be relegated elsewhither. Certainly people don't go to Coney for the sea or the air or the view.

If the worthy ladies and "uplifters" of indeterminate sex (chiefly old women in trousers) would turn their attention to making the seaside beautiful, or if not beautiful then decent, they would justify their civic existence. Here is where the busy female, with or without a ballot, can come in. A new and attractive Coney Island should be their slogan. But the public likes to be fooled, swindled — alas!

Where stood the old Manhattan Hotel is now a comely terrace which, when the trees have grown, will be a garden by the sea. The bathing pavilion is still there — too small for its clientèle, yet cleaner than Brighton and less populated. As I no longer bathe at the beach, I hold no brief for any particular location. I am stating the bald, unflattering facts.

There is Brighton, England, as an example to emulate. What a beautiful boulevard by the water it has built, so satisfying in its solidity and spaciousness. The hotels are massive, the view unobstructed. Ostend and Scheveningen, two other European resorts, are also examples for the heedless and conceited public administrators who let our beaches go to rack and ruin or evade the issue by erecting temporary structures. That's why so many Americans go to Europe in the summer. They get something for their money.

But if you want to experience the "emotion of multitude," there is no spot on earth for the purpose like Coney Island.

II

AT NIGHT

It was the hottest night of the summer at Coney Island. All day a steaming curtain of mist hid the sun from the eyes of men and women and children; yet proved no shield against the blasting heat. Humidity and not the sun-rays had been the enemy. And when a claret-coloured disk showed dully through the nacreous vapours just before setting we knew that the night would bring little respite from the horror of the waking hours. It was a time to try men's nerves. The average obligations of life had faded into the abyss of general indifference, one that had absorbed the exactions of daily behaviour — politeness, order, sobriety, and decency. Add a few notches upward on the thermometer, and mankind soon reverts to the habits and conditions of his primitive ancestors. The ape, the tiger, and the jackal in all of us come to the surface with shocking rapidity. We are, in a reasonable analysis, the victims of our environment, the slaves of temperature. Heat and cold have produced the African and the Laplander. At Coney Island during a torrid spell we are very near the soil; we cast to the winds modesty, prudence, and dignity. Then, life is worth living only when stripped to the skin.

Three seasons had I passed without a visit to this astonishing bedlam, yet I found the place well-nigh unrecognisable. Knowing old Coney Island, the magnitude of its changes did not so much amaze and terrify me. One should never be amazed in America. After an hour's hasty survey, Atlantic City seemed a normal spot. Broad stretches of board walk, long, sweeping beaches, space to turn about — these and other items might be added. But at Coney Island the cramped positions one must assume to stand or move, the fierce warfare of humanity as it forces its way along the streets or into the crazy shows — surely conceived by madmen for madmen — the indescribable and hideous symphony of noise running the gamut from shrill steam-whistles to the diapasonic roar of machinery; decidedly the entire place produced the sensation of abnormality, of horrible joys grabbed at by a savage horde of barbarians, incapable of repose even in their moments of leisure. Some one has said that the Englishman takes his pleasures sadly; then we must take ours by rude assault. All Coney Island reminded me of a disturbed ant-heap, the human ants ferocious in their efforts to make confusion thrice confounded, to heap up horrors of sound and of sight.

There must be in every one, no matter how phlegmatic, a residuum of energy which may boil over when some exciting event knocks at the door of our being. It is, psychologists assure us, the play-instinct of the animal in us that delights in games innocent and dangerous. If forty thousand people assemble to see a game of baseball, how many more would gather with feverish gaiety if there were a surety of the umpire's death at every game? The Romans daily witnessed men and women destroyed in the arena of their circus — witnessed it with a satisfaction æsthetic and profound. The reason was not that they were less civilised than the moderns, but only more frank. Their play-instinct was more fully developed and the classical world was not hampered by our moral prejudices.

As cruelty is proscribed among highly civilised nations to-day — the game of life being so vilely cruel that the arena with its bulls and tigers is unnecessary — our play-instinct finds vent in a species of diversion that must not be examined too closely, as it verges perilously on idiocy. Coney Island is only another name for topsyturvydom. There the true becomes the grotesque, the vision of a maniac. Else why those nerve-racking entertainments, ends of the world, creations, hells, heavens, fantastic trips to ugly lands, panoramas of sheer madness, flights through the air in boats, through water in sleds, on the earth in toy trains! Unreality is as greedily craved by the mob as alcohol by the dipsomaniac; indeed, the jumbled nightmares of a morphine eater are actually realised at Luna Park. Every angle reveals some new horror. Mechanical waterfalls, with women and children racing around curving, tumbling floods; elephants tramping ponderously through streets that are a bewildering muddle of many nations, many architectures; deeds of Western violence and robbery, illustrated with a realism that is positively enthralling; Japanese and Irish, Germans and Indians, Hindus and Italians, cats and girls and ponies and — the list sets whirring the wheels of the biggest of dictionaries.

CONEY ISLAND

In Dreamland there is a white tower that might rear itself in Seville and cause no comment. (This was so before fire destroyed the place.) Hemming it about are walls of monstrosities — laughable, shocking, sinister, and desperately depressing. In the centre flying boats cleave the air; from the top of a crimson lighthouse flat, sled-like barges plunge down a liquid railroad, while from every cavern issue screams of tortured and delighted humans and the hoarse barking of men with megaphones. They assault your ears with their invitations, protestations, and blasphemies. You are conjured to "go to Hell — gate"; you are singled out by some brawny individual with threatening intonations and bade enter the animal show where a lion or a tiger is warranted to claw a keeper at least once a day. The glare is appalling, the sky a metallic blue, the sun a slayer.

And then the innumerable distractions of the animated walks, the dwarfs and the dogs, the horses and the miniature railway. Inside the various buildings you may see the cosmos in the act of formation, or San Francisco destroyed by fire and quake; the end of life, organic and inorganic, is displayed for a modest pittance; you may sleigh in Switzerland or take a lulling ride in Venetian gondolas. But nothing is real. Doubtless the crowd would be disappointed by a glimpse of the real Venice, the real Switzerland, the real hell, the real heaven. Everything is the reflection of a cracked mirror held in the hand of the clever showman, who, knowing us as children of a larger growth, compounds his mess, bizarre and ridiculous, accordingly. There is little need to ponder the whys and wherefores of our aberrancy. Once en masse, humanity sheds its civilisation and becomes half child, half savage. In the theatres the gentlest are swayed by a sort of mob mania and delight in scenes of cruelty and bloodshed — though at home the sight of a canary with a broken wing sets stirring in us tender sympathy. A crowd seldom reasons. It will lynch an innocent man or glorify a scamp politician with equal facility. Hence the monstrous debauch of the fancy at Coney Island, where New York chases its chimera of pleasure.

Nevertheless, with all its perversion, its oblique image of life, is Coney Island much madder than the Stock Exchange, the prize-ring, roller-skating, a fashionable cotillion, a political mass-meeting, or some theatrical performances? Again I must bid you to remember that everything is relative; that the morals of one age are the crimes of another; that I am, comparatively speaking, a stranger to our summer cities and perhaps not peculiarly well fitted to judge of such an astounding institution as Coney Island.

The madness converges below Brighton, reaching its apex on Surf Avenue, jammed with pleasure-seekers, fringed by "fakers" and their utterly abominable wares. Farther up the beach order reigns, men and women are clothed in their right mind, walk, talk, and act rationally. At the Oriental dignity prevails. Few people are to be seen. The place slumbers. You feel that in such a hotel you may live as you wish. Manhattan, no longer queen of the beaches, has its interest. The bathing attracts. The wide porches and the dining couples are pleasing to see. A theatre there is for those to whom the ocean is not a stimulating spectacle. Walk farther. We reach Brighton. There the pot begins to bubble. A smaller Coney confronts you. You pass on. Stopping before what was once Anton Seidl's music pavilion, you indulge, more sadly than sentimentally, in memories of those evenings, over two decades ago, when the sound of the waves formed a background for the dead master's music-making — Beethoven and Wagner and Liszt.

Instead of Brünnhilde and her sisters' wild ride, we hear the wooden horse orchestrion screeching "Meet Me at the Church." Move on? Has public musical taste moved with the years? Meet me at the madhouse! We reach the Boulevard and note its agreeable vastness. The sun has set and the world is become suddenly afire.

Then Coney Island, with its vulgarity, its babble and tumult, is a glorified city of flame. But don't go too near it; your wings will easily singe on the broad avenue where beer, sausage, fruit, pop-corn, candy, flapjacks, green corn, and again beer, rule the appetites of the multitude.

After seeing the aerial magic of that great pyrotechnic artist Pain, a man who could, if he so desired, create a new species of art, and his nocturnes of jewelled fire, you wonder why the entire beach is not called Fire Island. The view of Luna Park from Sheepshead Bay suggests a cemetery of fire, the tombs, turrets, and towers illuminated, and mortuary shafts of flame. At Dreamland the little lighthouse is a scarlet incandescence. The big building stands a dazzling apparition for men on ships and steamers out at sea. Everything is fretted with fire. Fire delicately etches some fairy structure; fire outlines an Oriental gateway; fire runs like a musical scale through many octaves, the darkness crowding it, the mist blurring it. Fire is the god of Coney Island after sundown, and fire was its god this night, the hottest of the summer.

At ten o'clock the crowds had not abated. Noise still reigned over the Bowery, and the cafés, restaurants, dens, and shows were full of gabbling, eating, drinking, cursing, and laughing folk. I had intended to return either to my hotel or to New York, but the heat pinioned my will. In company with thousands, I strolled the beach near the Boulevard. An amiable policeman told me that few people would go back to the city, that, hot as it was at Coney, the East Side was more stifling. The sight of cars coming down crowded at eleven o'clock and returning half-full at midnight determined my plan of action. I went to my hotel, put on a sweater and a cap, changed a bill into silver, and with a stick for company I returned to the West End. There were more people than before, though it was nearly one o'clock and the lights were beginning to dim. I searched for the friendly policeman, but instead found a surly one, who warned me that it would be a risk to venture upon the beach if I had a watch or money. I longed for a Josiah Flynt who would pilot me through this jungle of humanity. The heat was depressing and mosquitoes made us miserable. They knew me for a fresh comer and exacted a sorry toll from my hands, neck, and face. I wavered in my resolution to spend the night on the beach. I had left my rake at home, and as I am not a socialist I could not emulate the performances of the "white mice," as the East Side names the good, well-dressed young men and women of means who make sociological calls on them, note-books in their hands, curiosity in their eyes, and burning enthusiasm in their hearts.

All the lights of the pleasure palaces were extinguished. Across at Riccadonna's there was still a light, and peering over the Brighton pavilion there was a pillar of luminosity that looked a cross between a corn-cob and a thermometer afire. I sat down on the sand. I would stay out the night. And then I began to look about me. In Hyde Park, London, I had seen hundreds of vagabonds huddled in the grass, their clothes mere rags, their attitudes those of death, but nothing in England or America can match what I saw this particular night. While the poorer classes predominated, there was little suggestion of abject pauperism. Many seemed gay. The white dresses of the women and children relieved the sombre masses of black men, who, though coatless for the most part, made black splotches on the sand. In serried array they lay; there was no order in their position, yet a short distance away they gave the impression of an army at rest. The entire beach was thick with humanity. At close range it resolved itself in groups, sweethearts in pairs, families of three or four, six or seven, planted close together. With care, hesitation, and difficulty I navigated around these islets of flesh and blood. Sometimes I stumbled over a foot or an arm. Once I kicked a head, and I was cursed many times and vigorously cursed. But I persisted. Like the "white mice," I was there to see. Policemen plodded through the crowds, and if there was undue hilarity warned the offenders in a low voice. But it was impossible for such a large body of people to be more orderly, more decent. I determined to prowl down the lower beach, between the Boulevard and Sea Gate.

My sporting instinct came to the surface. Here was game. Not in the immemorial mob, joking and snoring, shrieking and buzzing, would I find what I sought. I tried to pass under the bathing-houses, but so densely packed were the paths that I was threatened by a dozen harsh voices. So I pursued a safer way, down Surf Avenue. It was still filled with people — men and women, battered, bleary, drunk or tired, dragged their weary paces, regarding each other as do wolves, ready to spring. We all felt like sticky August salt. Reaching the beach again, I was too fatigued to walk farther. I propped my head against the wooden pillar of an old bath-house and my eyes began to droop. I heard without a quiver of interest the sudden scream of a woman followed by ominous bass laughter. Some one plucked a banjo. Dogs barked. A hymn rose on the hot air. Around me it was like a battle-field of the slain. A curious drone was in the air; it was the monster breathing. A muggy moon shone intermittently over us, its bleached rays painting in one ghastly tone the upturned faces of the sleepers. The stale, sour, rank smell of wretched mankind poisoned the atmosphere, thick with sultry vapours. I wished myself home.

Then a gentle voice said — the accent was slightly foreign:

"What a sight the poor make in the moonlight!" I did not turn, but answered that I had thought that same thing. The voice proceeded. It was not strong, though a resonant barytone:

"You are alone, good sir; but look at my brood, and don't wonder at people dying without asking the world's permission."

I half arose, expecting that it was a beggar who addressed me. A child began whimpering. I saw a woman on her side holding with relaxed grasp this crying infant — the wail was hardly perceptible above the swish of the surf. Near her were two older children. The man who had spoken to me was sitting, his head plunged almost between his knees, his skinny hands supporting his head. He was exceedingly poor, wearing only a ragged shirt and trousers. His head was large and curly with thick hair. He could not have been more than forty. When he lifted his head his eyes in the moonshine were like two red cinders. A wild beast — and with a gentle, even cultivated, voice. I went over to him. The child still moaned as the fingers of the exhausted woman opened farther. I forgot sociology and wondered if here was a case of starvation — a hungry family in all the Gargantuan feast of Coney Island. The idea was horrible.

"What's the matter, Batiushka?" I asked, adopting a familiar form of Russian salutation. He fell on his knees.

"Brother," he panted, "are you a Russian? A Jew? Help us. We have not eaten since yesterday morning." I confess I shuddered. I confess also that I didn't believe him. A man, a Jewish man with a family, in New York and starving! New York, with its rich charitable institutions! And this fellow tried to make me think that he needed food; that his wife and children needed food! I had eaten my dinner at the Manhattan, and I enjoyed that selfish credulity which an able-bodied gourmand feels when he is approached by some one who has tasted no food for days.

And this miserable being came nearer to me, feebly, supplicatingly. His eyes were like red dots in the head of a famished animal. His hot breath issued as from an open grave. The child sobbed louder, and the mother, half awake, clutched it. She sat up. The other two children arose, alarmed, silent. It was too much for my pampered nerves. Bidding the man remain where he was, I ran across the beach to the Bowery and into a little saloon full of half-drunken, vicious people. Ten minutes later we sat at an improvised supper of pretzels, cold fish, and beer. I knew this family wouldn't touch anything else. Starvation itself would not force them to break their tribal law. I have an idea that I was thirsty myself, for I enjoyed the flat beer and I enjoyed the subdued ferocity with which the family ate and drank. The baby did not stir. It had fallen asleep. The mother, a worn-out woman, still young, mechanically put the food into her mouth, not looking at us, not speaking to the two girls. She was numbed by hunger and heat.

"See here, what's your name?" I asked. "My name," he stammered, "is Hyman." "I mean your family name," I demanded; "Hyman is your first name." He gave me a keen glance. Then he quietly replied: "You are right. My full name is Hyman Levin." "Have you a home?" I pursued. I felt my importance. I was playing the rôle of benefactor, and what philanthropist, great or small, does not desire the worth of his money? Besides, it is good policy to cross-examine a starving man. He appreciates your interest at such a time. (Oh, what smiling villains are we all!)

"I live in an alley near Oliver Street. Usually we go to the recreation pier near Peck Slip, but the child was so sick that I came down here last night." "Last night?" "Yes, I pawned my coat to get the car fare."

This is a truthful report of the man's conversation. He was out of work — sickness — and he had pawned, piece by piece, bit by bit, everything in the house. His wife went to the pawnhouse, while he, scarcely able to hold up his head, watched the baby. The children lived in the streets, feeding at the garbage cans, thankful for such a chance. Is this exaggeration? If you think so, then you don't know your own city. Such things happen every day. The neighbours were kind, especially the Irish. But they, too, could scarcely boast more than one meal a day. Hyman coughed; he evidently was marked for the death of a consumptive. Yet he fought on. The charities were available — for a time. But funds ran low; public interest also ran low. The Levins found themselves within five days of rent time in their room, a musty, dirty garret. Life from heat and insufficient food became intolerable, and, half crazed with fever, on that hot Monday, they contrived to reach the seashore. With only a few pennies, yet they were happier; they could at least breathe fresh air, see the water. But so forbidding was the appearance of this unhappy family that they were warned off the board walk and frightened away from the crowd of pleasure-seekers. We do not care to see these death's-heads at our feasts. Finally they found refuge under the bath-house, and there I met them.

Worse remains. When the dawn came up softly like the vanguard of an army without banners I shook the sleeping Hyman. I awoke the woman. I had heard queer sounds in the throat of the child, noises like water slowly dripping into a well. Why should I go on? The child was dead, and I was not surprised. Nor were the parents. They made no outcry, but covered the little thing with the mother's old pelisse. Stunned by their cumulative misfortunes, this death was accepted with the fatalism of a Russian. I told a policeman the story, and a half-hour later the entire family was carted away with the promise that they would be given food and shelter.

There was a bitter taste in my mouth. If a poor devil of a tramp or a working man had met me then I should not have been able to look either one in the eye. Oh, how cheap is charity!

The silver I spent did not relieve the Levins. They had scarcely bade me good-bye, so oppressed were they by their sorrow, their shame. They must have hated me. The man was not ignorant. His English betrayed a reader. He had conversed well about Gorky and Tolstoy, had read Karl Marx, and knew the names of all his saints of anarchy. A socialist? I do not know. I only know that your bookish theories go to smash when you hear a man's voice thrill with anguish. A pauper, you say, a lazy, good-for-nothing? Ay, perhaps he was — perhaps they all are; but drunkard, thief, even murderer, must they starve? Anarchs and infidels? So were the Americans of 1776, according to the English.

Remember what Richard Jeffries wrote: "Food and drink, roof and clothes are the inalienable right of every child born into the light. If the world does not provide it freely — not as a grudging gift, but as a right, as a son of the house sits down to breakfast — then is the world mad. . . . I verily believe that the earth in one year produces enough food to last for thirty. Why, then, have we not enough? . . . It is not the pauper — oh, inexpressibly wicked word! — it is the well-to-do who are the criminal classes." Grant Allen said that all men are born free and unequal. True. But should they be allowed to want for bread?

Don't ask me the remedy. I am neither a professional prophet nor a socialist. Don't throw socialism at my head. Ready-made prophylactics smell suspiciously. The "dismal science" scares me. Before the fatal words "unearned increment" I retreat. And the socialist's conception of the state approaches singularly close to the old conception of monarchy. I know that there are many Levins in New York, of many nationalities. Starve in New York, the abundant city, where "God's in the world to-day"? Impossible! cry the sentimentalists. I didn't believe it, either, until I met the Levins. That adventure has cured me of all foolish optimistic boasting. I have told the story plainly. I realised of how little account to people in such awful straits is the clangour of contending political parties. Of what interest to a man, his belly pinched by starvation, whether one Jack in office is ousted by another Jack who desires the place; whether this one is President, that one is governor? A flare of fireworks, a river of beer, on the East Side for a night, and the people are forgotten by their masters. It has been so always; for eternity it will endure. Does not Campanella's sonnet sing:

The people is a beast of muddy brain
That knows not its own strength, and therefore stands
Loaded with wood and stone;

. . . .

Its own are all things between earth and Heaven;
But this it knows not, and if one arise
To tell this truth it kills him unforgiven.

Grunting, growling, spitting, coughing, the huge army of thousands began in maelstrom fashion to move cityward. Some stopped at the half-way house of whisky; many breakfasted, but the main body made a dash for the cars. The night had been a trying one, the new day did not promise; yet it was a new day, and with it a flock of fresh hopes was born. The crowd seemed rested; in its eyes was the lust of life, and it was absolutely good-humoured. I heard a vague tale about a man-hunt during the night — how a thief had been chased with stones and clubs until, reaching Sea Gate, he had boldly plunged into the water and disappeared. His hawk-like features, the colour of clay from fright, had impressed the old man who related the story. In return I told the Levins' heart-breaking tale, and he did not appear much interested. What signified to all those strong, bustling men and women the death of a tiny girl baby — dead and hardly clad in a wisp of blackened canvas?

"Better dead!" The mobs thickened. Policemen fought them into line. The hot sun arose, in company with the penetrating odours of bad coffee and greasy crullers. Another day's labour was arrived. Soon would appear the first detachment of women and children sick from the night in the city. Soon would be heard the howling of the fakers: "Go to Hell, go to Hell — gate!"

I felt that I had been very near it, that I had

seen a new Coney Island. I went home, after this, the most miserable night of my life — miserable because my nerves were out of gear. I was once more the normal, selfish man, thinking of his bed, of his breakfast. I had, of course, quite forgotten the Levins.

PART II

CERTAIN EUROPEAN CITIES BEFORE THE WAR

I

VIENNA

I

I ALWAYS know when I am in Austria; the coffee is much better than the watery, flavourless compound you are offered in Germany. Perhaps the sharper accents of the Viennese cuisine may not appeal to you — the German cookery by comparison is colourless — but the superiority of the coffee and pastry is manifest.

I am sure this is not a happy way of beginning to sing the praises of Vienna, the magnificent; but, after all, sufficient for the day is the Baedeker thereof. Open that invaluable volume penned by a man and brother, and you will find sound advice as to seeing Vienna and its environs in three days, more or less. Now I submit that is not the way to do it; ten years in the Austrian capital wouldn't exhaust its charms, yet as most travellers allow themselves about a week or ten days, it is best to follow the advice of good old Br'er Baedeker. And here I leave him, for I am essentially a rambler, a prowler, lazy, leisurely curious, and seldom sorry when it's dinner time. (Mrs. Ralph Waldo Emerson once remarked that Thoreau never went beyond the sound of the dinner horn, and who am I to be ashamed of a similar weakness?)

Of course, the proper manner of writing on such a resounding theme as Vienna would be to begin, as do all the guides and guide-books, with St. Stephen's Cathedral (old "Steffel," as it is called by the natives) for the central point of departure, trailing around the churches, trapesing through the art galleries, and finally going to the Prater.

You recall the popular lecturer, the spot-light, the "ladies and gentlemen, this evening we propose to visit the city on the blue Danube. To the right you may notice the spire of the wondrously beautiful cathedral erected in the year" — click, and the screen shows you the church! The stomach of Vienna first interested me, not its soul, and after a ride around the city in the "saloon carriage" of the Municipal Street Railway line I started out to investigate the places wherein Vienna eats and drinks. Please pardon this unconventional method. Doesn't a traveller when arriving in a city eat and drink before he goes sightseeing?

Let me hasten to tell you that I have been in Vienna both winter and summer. The latter season is incomparably the better time to enjoy the town, but if you haven't been there in winter you only know Vienna one-half.

June is lovely. December more brilliant, more stimulating. I confess at the outset I like the Austrian kitchen better than the German.

Hungary lends her paprika, her paprika-chicken, her gulyas, her Esterhazy roast, and Vienna has her bread, her real Schnitzel, various stews, risi-bisi (rice and peas), suckling pig, splendid fish, sausages, rich soups — Minestra, an Italian variety — and dumplings in a dozen shapes. And Apfelstrudel! And Kaiserschmarn! A half hundred delicious desserts, with the aroma of coffee as an aureole at the close of the meal (or at five in the afternoon). Nevertheless, there is seldom repletion; you are satisfied with the flavouring and do not, as in Germany, eat, eat, eat, as if in search of something you seldom find.

If I whispered that the difference between German and Austrian cookery depended upon butter and the judicious use of the humble onion you would, perhaps, smile. Yet is it so. The onion and its more athletic relative, garlic, is the foundational base of not only Austrian but the best cuisines in the world. I see you hold up hands of horror, nevertheless a nuance of garlic lends many a meal its flavour. (I said a nuance!) It is the chromatic scale in the harmonies of taste. Viennese cooks know this, and without your leave employ that so-called offensive vegetable, the onion, so skilfully that you eat and admire.

Naturally no one will admit this, tourists are so scared of the health-giving product. But my mouth still waters over my memories. The noble art of glutting is cultivated in all Austria.

I strolled from Sacher's on the Augustinerstrasse, where the menu is first-class, high in price, the wines impeccable, over to Hartmann's on the Ring. It is across the street from the Grand Hotel, and I'll wager there is no restaurant in Vienna where one hears so much English (usually American-English) as in this comfortable, comparatively cheap establishment. Its cuisine is Austrian mixed with French. The cooking is excellent and sets a pace. Meissl and Schadn's on the Kärntnerstrasse is typical Viennese, with its suckling pig, risi-bisi, pickled veal, and sauerkraut (such sublimated sauerkraut), to be had at far from high prices. The Stephankeller (Café de l'Europe) is another meeting-ground for good livers. At Gause's, the Rother Igel, the Rathhauskeller, you may taste the wines of the country, rather too thin and shrewd for my palate; Vöslau, Gumpoldskirchen, Nussberg, Klosterneuberg, Retz, Pfaffstadt, Mailberg, and the heavier Dalmatian vintages. As I stuck to my favourite beverage, Pilsner, I can lay no claim to being an expert on the subject of the wines; furthermore, my pronounced taste for peppery, highly flavoured food is hardly a criterion for the milder palates of visitors from abroad. The big hotels know this, and there you get the "international" cooking, which prevails over all Europe, even in the dining-cars, a something that belongs to no nation, neither French, German, nor English — cosmopolitan, in a word. There are exceptions in Vienna; for example, at the Bristol, with its

French chef, you fancy yourself in Paris at Paillard's — that is to say, if you order a special dinner. Otherwise one hotel table d'hôte is like another: neither fish nor flesh, nor good red herring.

But the Pilsner in Vienna! That would need a complete chapter. While it is not so superlatively fine as at Prague, with that supernal touch which never can be elsewhere duplicated, it is wonderful enough, though I noted with dismay, as I noted in Stuttgart, Munich, Dresden, and Berlin, that the invasion of the American had been fatal in the matter of temperatures. The European now drinks his beer cold, even icy. In few spots could I find the precise degree of temperature at which Pilsner is at its bloomiest.

I do not think it necessary here to allude to the numerous beer restaurants, where all the world, his wife, mother-in-law, and the children eat daily and sip the almost non-alcoholic dark and light brews. I speak of certain semisacred houses where the ritual of beer-drinking is observed, where at prescribed hours fanatics meet and solemnly absorb the amber brew. Woe to the waiter if the foam is not of the creamiest! Woe to the host if any marked variation of temperature is felt!

In a little old house, which might be called "quaint," on a little street near a Greek church, is the Reichenberger or Grieschenbeisl. There the best-kept Pilsner in Vienna may be found.

There also many artists, actors, musicians assemble of nights, and a merry company it is. However, Vienna is not a "late" city, as is, for example, Berlin. At midnight the streets are deserted except at Carnival time or New Year's eve — last New Year's eve the crush was as bad as on Broadway.

In Berlin I have seen intoxicated persons, seldom in Vienna have I encountered one. The point is significant, as is the agreeable cooking of the city. Food plays a greater rôle in our psychology than our thin-skinned idealists will admit. Possibly our national cooking may be the bar sinister in our artistic productivity, for a country which is given over to fanatics and prudes — in the domain of eating and drinking — will never give birth to individual art.

II

The gayest city I have ever lived in is Vienna. Paris is feverish. Paris takes its pleasures very much as does New York, in a hurry, as if to snatch at the fugitive moment and like Faust cry: "Stay! Thou art so fair." Berlin, I found, was too self-conscious, too cultured to relax, while Munich is a trifle too soggy, too "wet." Vienna, for me, hits the medium of gaiety without hectic symptoms and leisure without Prussian stiffness. The elements of the Austrian race are heterogeneous; the Slavic counts, and counts the Magyar. The tongue is Germanic, the culture is, minus a heavy Teutonic quality, also Germanic; there is a lightness in the moral atmosphere that might be called Gallic.

The Viennese man is an optimist. He regards life not so steadily, or as a whole, but as a gay fragment. Clouds gather, the storm breaks, then the rain stops and the sun floats once more in the blue. Let to-morrow take care of itself, to-day we go to the Prater and watch the wheels go round. This irresponsibility is confined to no class. Whether all the folk you see in the restaurants, cafés, and gardens can afford to spend money as they indubitably do, I cannot pretend to know. They eat and drink the best, and, as a native said to me, if they were without a roof they would still go to the restaurants. Well fed, with good, flavoured food, therefore eupeptic, not dyspeptic, the Viennese are seemingly contented; they look so, and they are always cheerful.

Their tobacco is better than the tobacco of France or Germany — it is both odorous and cheap. Coffee is the magnet late in the afternoon, and it is difficult to get a seat after five o'clock in any of the numerous places. I remember one café, on the Kärntnerstrasse, which is appropriately called the Guckfenster, from the windows of which you may stare at the passing show. Every afternoon I went there early so as to secure my favourite seat, and there I sipped and stared and stared and sipped, and in the dolce far niente I marvelled over the futility of life, especially the futility of American life, its hurry, bustle, money-making. In six months I told myself I would be transformed into a joyous looker-on in Vienna, quite oblivious to the ambitions of the Western world.

Oh, how mistaken I was! No one works harder than the Vienna business man and woman; their hours are at least a third longer than the hours of an American, yet they contrive so to space them that they appear to have limitless leisure. How do they do it? The climate is soft, which allows of open-air life; the women work more than the men; the piety of the people at large is pronounced — the churches Sunday morning are as crowded as are the cafés Sunday afternoon — there is unmistakable poverty, nevertheless the mercurial spirit prevails everywhere.

It gives Vienna its primal charm, it hums in the air. No wonder Johann Strauss composed his music; no wonder the otherwise ponderous Johannes Brahms preferred this spot to his birthplace, Hamburg; no wonder Beethoven here wrote the scherzi of his symphonies. Vienna inspired these composers, as it inspired Mozart and Schubert. Some of these musicians cursed the frivolity of the capital, but her deep, abiding charm held them close to her.

The obverse of the medal is this same frivolity. But there is also an earnest intellectual and artistic life. In one week last winter I attended conferences by Gerhart Hauptmann, Georg

Brandes — the latter dealt with Goethe and Strindberg — and I heard Moriz Rosenthal, Eugen d'Albert, Godowsky, and the Rose quartet, and attended a performance by the greatest of orchestras, the Vienna Philharmonic, under the leadership of Felix Weingärtner, who gave a reading of the Brahms fourth symphony (in E minor), which, according to the interpretations of most conductors, is a grey-in-grey, crabbed pattern, instead of the glowing, luminous and eloquently expressive masterpiece it became under the hands of Weingärtner. Not a bad record, is it, for the city on the brown and turbid Danube?

Then there is the opera, there are the theatres, and, to jump to the other side of the scale, there are the medical schools and surgeons and physicians who have not their equal anywhere. And the university life.

I only know Vienna superficially, the inner social life not at all, but to my inexperienced masculine eyes the Vienna woman is the best dressed in the world after the American. (Paris is, of course, hors concours.) There, again, the touch is Gallic. The beauty of the Viennese women is proverbial. That gipsy-like colouring, hair, and eyes, the fresh complexions, the general style — best described as fesch — is to be found in no place but Vienna. The men dress like Londoners, are more particular than the Germans in the cut of their clothes, the colour of their ties, and the set of their silk hats. A prosperous, prodigal, vivacious population, hard as nails if driving a bargain, as hospitable as can be when business is over and the hour of recreation is at hand: l'heure exquise, not of absinthe, but of coffee. And then there is Vienna, the magnificent.

III

Vienna, the magnificent! I fear the approach of the dithyrambic. Vienna is truly the city of magnificent distances; not even Washington deserves the title as much. Every vista has its picture, either a church, a monument, a palace, or a park. You range and range and seemingly never exhaust the possibilities of the city. If you pick out the green shade of the Prater on a sunny day you presently find yourself in the thick of life at the Würstl Prater, or Venedig in Wien, a glorified Coney Island, Atlantic City, Crystal Palace, and Vincennes gingerbread fair, without either ocean or board walk. But gaiety prevails. If you are in the mood historical you have a field to work that is practically inexhaustible. Æsthetic cravings are satisfied by the superb architecture, the ceaseless music-making, the round of theatrical novelties — not to mention the artistic acting — and the royal museum, which houses so many old masters.

Of modern Viennese painting I can't say so much; however, tastes differ. I prefer the simplicities of Franz Defregger to the gorgeous arabesques of Hans Makart. The mixture of Celt, Roman, Slavic, and German in her veins has made Austria singularly sensitive to foreign influence. Under the Babenbergers she boasted a Walther von der Vogelweide, and such a dramatic poet as Grillparzer or Anzengruber can hardly be passed by. She almost starved Beethoven, and by her neglect helped Hugo Wolf, the composer, into madness. If you are interested in the modern there is a gallery of young talent, largely derivative, I admit, but interesting. Arthur Schnitzler — whose work has thus far not been adequately interpreted in English — Hermann Bahr, Richard Beer-Hoffman, the author of the drama Der Graf von Charolais, the clever novelist, Felix Salten, Hugo von Hofmannsthal (Loris), the poet and librettist of several Richard Strauss operas; Stefan George, poet, are a few names I recall; and then there are the poet J. J. David, the poet and dramatist Glücksmann of the Volkstheater, Karl Schoenherr, a Tyrolese, whose drama stirred all Austria (Glaube und Heimat), and many others. The special graciousness and charm that are characteristic of Vienna may be found best reflected in the writings of Arthur Schnitzler.

For the sake of curiosity, I made a computation of the number of fountains, parks, churches, etc., in Vienna. I discovered thirty-eight fountains, imposing ones, I need hardly remind you. The same figures cover the churches of every creed, and of monuments there are eighty, public parks thirty-nine, and I forget how many palaces. It is the gigantic scale on which the city is planned that impresses. London and Paris are at times stuffy, but the light and air of Vienna are so abundant that stuffiness is never experienced. I don't particularly admire the architecture of the residences; banal is the word that best describes these edifices, not always cheerful to gaze upon. There are too few first-class hotels; Berlin beats all Europe in its modern hotels, and Vienna is far behind Berlin in the matter of apartments. In the suburbs they are beginning to erect them. They are not as comfortable, as commodious, nor so cheap as in Berlin. In one I found that the steam heat never sent the thermometer above fifty degrees Fahrenheit, and despite the remonstrances of the tenants the landlord was obdurate in his refusal of more steam pressure. But chilly rooms, ill-lighted, are not confined to Vienna; London is as bad as Paris, and Berlin is the most comfortable in this respect. No doubt Vienna will march in the procession later.

In the parks and public squares you see statues erected to the memory of celebrated men: Beethoven (two), Brahms, Schubert, Bruckner, Anzengruber, Goethe, Grillparzer, Gutenberg, inventor of printing; Robert Hamerling, the poet; Josef Haydn, Theodore Körner, Lenau, poets; Makart, Schiller, Mozart, Strauss, and Lanner are represented, and with them an army of royal mediocrities and municipal celebrities. Think of the Central Cemetery, where is the empty grave of Mozart; where are the remains of Beethoven, Gluck, Franz Schubert, Johann Strauss, near his friend Brahms, and where lie such men as Von Suppe, Milloecker, Bruckner, Herbeck, Hugo Wolf, Makart, Clement, and the pedagogue Czerny! Vienna also honours Hebbel and Lenau in an appropriate manner. There is a Lisztgasse, named after the Hungarian composer, and it may be remembered that it was in Vienna that the youthful Chopin won his first triumphs outside of provincial Warsaw. There is a Beethovengang up on the Kahlenberg, outside of the city, a shady walk as you ascend by the Schreiberbach, in which Beethoven often strolled, hatless, singing to himself the motives he was weaving in his skull. The Viennese of his days pronounced him half mad. Perhaps he was, but he was also Beethoven. From the famous Karl Goldmark, the most venerable of Austrian composers (since dead, 1915), to the precocious composer, Erich Korngold, the chain of active musical effort is unbroken. Vienna is very musical, although I care less for its opera-house than I did in the days when Mahler and Weingärtner reigned.

Instead of beginning a chant royal of admiration for the cathedral, which is the "star" of the sacerdotal architecture in Vienna, I prefer to speak of the Karlskirche on the Karlsplatz, possibly because its pompous splendour and commanding position impress one more than the cathedral, too closely besieged by surrounding buildings. There can be no comparisons as to interiors — the miraculous altars and pulpits of the cathedral bear off all honours, and while the lace-like spires of the Votive Church are more attractive than the Karl's Church, the latter has an exotic semi-Asiatic exterior that fairly rivets the eye. It is named after its donor, the Emperor Charles VI, and is a notable example of German baroque. It was erected 1721–6, in commemoration of the extermination of the plague of 1716. There is an oval cupola; spiral-shaped columns flank the main façade. They are ornamented with basso-relievos and lantern-crowned. A lunar-shaped portico. The reliefs on the Trojan pillars show scenes from the life of St. Carlo Borromeo by Mader and Mattielli. An imperial circle crowns them. Low bell-towers terminate on either side of the façade, which form a vaulted entrance to the interior. There is a great marble altar with a statue of Borromeo. The frescoes are distinguished.

I am not in the least tempted by the desire to tell you that Vienna was founded before the Christian era and was known during the first century A. D. as Vindobona, or that Marcus Aurelius is said to have died there. Ah, these wise old guide-books! — but I may dare to intimate that the present Vienna owes most of its municipal magnificence to the present Hapsburg, the beloved Kaiser, who mounted the throne in 1848,

Franz Joseph I. (He at the present writing still smokes the long rat-tail cigars with a strong tang and drinks his glass of Pilsner daily.) He practically rebuilt the city.

In the Neuer Markt stands the old church of the Capuchins, Maria zu den Engeln, and its mortuary vaults hold much that is dear to the old Emperor: his murdered empress, Elizabeth; his ill-fated son, the Crown Prince Rodolph; the unfortunate Maximilian, once Emperor of Mexico, betrayed by the Emperor of the French, Napoleon III — in whose veins no Bonaparte blood flowed — also the tomb of the Duke of Reichstadt; a tablet to the memory of Peter Marcus Avenarius; and the sarcophagus of the Empress Maria Theresa. But tombs sadden; I prefer the light, and let us go out into the animated highways; let us go through the thriving Graben, the high-water mark of Viennese business streets, and if I pause before some brilliantly lighted café, arrested by the vision of pretty girls, the majority smoking innocuous cigarettes, don't blame me. All said and done, I am only an American avid of new sights and sounds, not to speak of new faces.

IV

And how about that famous walk? Isn't time to take it? Well, you start from the Stepphanplatz and you see the Stock im Eisen (a trunk of a tree studded with nails), said to mark the spot to which once upon a time the Vienna forest (Wiener Wald), extended; it is enclosed in a niche to which, so legend hath it, all journeymen locksmiths paid a visit before their Wanderjahre and drove a nail into the tree to spite the devil.

On our way we pass the Mozarthof, a building erected in 1848 on the site of the house where Mozart died. The glorious cathedral, celebrated in picture and prose, need not be here described. Nor the Graben. In the Hof are the War Office, the Credit Institute for Trade and Commerce, the Radetzky monument — do you remember in your childish years the stirring little Radetzky march, by the elder Strauss? It still tinkles in my ears to the tonality of D major. We see the palace of Count Harrach, the Scots Church, the fountain: then, through the Herrengasse, with its many public buildings, we achieve the imperial palace, the Hofburg — two monumental fountains, past the gateway to the Franzensplatz.

Another big monument. A military band is playing. A fine rain is falling, but the place is black with people. We see the Rathhaus, the museums, the House of Parliament; we go to the Maximilianplatz and admire the Votive Church; look at the monument and the Stock Exchange and the university; then we stand amazed before the majestic proportions of the Hofburg Theater, whose entrance and stairway are the finest in Europe; admire the spacious

Volksgarten, note the monument to the Empress Elizabeth, past the Volkstheater to the Burgring, with the pair of imperial museums, the Maria Theresa memorial, as far as the Opernring, on the right the Schillerplatz (Academy of Fine Arts, full of canvases); opposite the Goethe statue, a stout, mature gentleman in a badly fitting frock coat, and the opera-house, a very imposing structure. Continuing along the Kärntnerring through the Künstlergasse we pass the home of the Musikverein and the Künstlerhaus on the Karlsplatz, which also holds the Polytechnic School; the Brahms monument is worth while studying; then you go across the Schwarzenbergplatz, where stands the palace of that name, to the Kolowratring — Vienna topographically is like a circular saw — to the city park, with its numerous monuments, handsome Kursalon, and well-laid-out walks, back to the Kaiser Wilhelmring, where there are palaces, and on to the Stubenring, a museum of art and industry. As for the post-office, the Chamber of Commerce, the bridges crossing the arm of the Danube, the Tegetthoff monument, the Rotunda in the Prater, and the pleasant trip to the imperial palace of Schönbrunn — these are subjects that cannot be seen, much less discussed, in a day.

One thing is certain — the surroundings of Vienna are particularly beautiful, whether at Semmering or Baden, the Klosternburg or Grinzing, the Kahlenburg, Leopoldsburg, Mödling, Laxenburg at Franzenberg, or Mariazell. And how the town mice do visit their kinsmen in the country when the weather is fair! And the Prater has only one rival in Europe as a driving resort, the Bois de Boulogne. Among the private art collections, that of the Prince Liechtenstein is the most celebrated. There is a great Frans Hals, the portrait of Willem van Huythuysen, and Rubenses, Rembrandts, and Van Dycks of prime quality. Count Harrach has an excellent collection; also Count Schöborn, and in Count Czernin's palace I found the greatest Vermeer, said to be the painter's atelier with the portrait of his wife and himself.

In the Albertina, the library of Archduke Albert, there are fifty thousand volumes, an extraordinary collection of drawings and engravings (autograph drawings by Dürer and Raphael, the Green Passion by the Nuremberg master), and two hundred thousand copperplates, in which is the finest work of Marc Antonio Raimondi. I only mention these treasures, not to emulate the catalogues but because I saw them and admired. In the modern gallery I didn't find much that I liked, except a grand Van Gogh. There are complete collections of Egyptian antiquities and the Imperial Art History Museum. They must detain us. Also a Museum of Weapons and Armour.

In the picture-gallery of the Imperial Museum there are nine authentic canvases by Velasquez, a Madonna by Raphael (his Florentine period), numerous early Italian masters, Giorgione's Geometricians, Dürer's masterpiece The Trinity, and some of the best Holbeins I ever saw (portrait of Derick Tybis); the Cranachs are distinguished, while Rubens and Van Dyck are abundantly represented. The old masters of the Netherlands, Italy, and elsewhere are of the best quality. If you made a trip to Vienna only to see its art treasures you would not be wasting your time. For me Count Czernin's Vermeer will ever prove a lodestone.

I have only skimmed the surface. Instead of spending all your vacation in Berlin or Paris or London, take the Oriental express to Vienna and enjoy that glorious city. Besides, Budapest is but five hours down the Danube, and while I never met a Viennese who was enthusiastic over Hungary, its capital deserves a visit. Of all the European cities (after New York, if I may be permitted to perpetrate a mild Celtic bull, for New York is becoming more European than Europe) I best like Vienna, the magnificent.

II

PRAGUE

When the Bohemian composer, the late Dr. Antonin Dvořák, with the much-accented name, was director of the National Conservatory two decades ago, I often talked with him about his native land; above all, of its music. For Dvořák there was a musical god, and he was Bedrich Smetana; Bohemia's greatest musician, the composer of the opera Dalibor, of the string quartet Aus Meinem Leben, of many songs and symphonies.

One work of his had always piqued my admiration, a symphonic poem, with several sections, one called Vltava — the Bohemian name for the river Moldau, which winds its shining length through the city of Prague; another Vysehrad, the name of the ancient fortress in the same place.

But Vltava caught my ear. I remember asking Dr. Dvořák to pronounce it for me, which he willingly did, as he disliked his beloved river to bear the heavy Teutonic appellation of Moldau. Like the majority of his countrymen, the composer of the New World Symphony was not enthusiastic on the subject of the Germans. There is a reason for this antipathy, as we shall later see.

The music of Smetana for me was merged in that blessed word Vltava, surely as blessed as the old lady's Mesopotamia, or as was the Susquehanna for Robert Louis Stevenson.

And from sounding Vltava to myself I longed to see the precious river and the historical city of Prague, built on both its banks. I often sought a verbal setting for Prague: Prague, the picturesque; poetic Prague; but after I had lived there I found the precise combination — Prague, the dramatic.

Prague is the most original city in Europe, not perhaps so startling or so melodramatic as Toledo in Spain, yet more original; and that it has preserved this originality is remarkable, if you consider that pretty, placid, modern Dresden is only four hours away, and farther down the map lies Vienna.

Now, Toledo is isolated. Many travellers go to Madrid and Seville, but do not dream of visiting the town perched high over the Tagus, whereas Prague is a stopping-off spot, the Slavic city farthest west, the gateway to the Slavic lands. Cosmopolitan, nevertheless it has preserved its proud individual profile.

The first time I passed it I was en route for Vienna and Budapest. In my ears the musical sequence of words reproachfully hummed:

Vltava, Vysehrad, Vysehrad, Vltava! and I grew indignant when the railway guard pointed out the "Moldau." The cathedral and castles grouped on the hill made a fascinating silhouette against the sky-line; yet I stayed in the train, from sheer inertia, I suppose, and it was several years after that I paid the city my initial visit. I could not forget the alluring prospect of wood, of noble architecture; above all, of the sanguinary pages of its history. Arthur Symons put it well when he wrote that to a Bohemian "Prague is still the epitome of the history of his country; he sees it as a man sees the woman he loves, with her first beauty, and he loves it, as a man loves a woman, more for what she has suffered." It was love at first sight when I peeped at Prague from a moving train.

Who hasn't heard of the Bridge of Prague (the Karlsbrücke), and who of the older generation cannot recall that thunderous pianoforte piece known as The Battle of Prague? It even smote upon the tender ears of Thackeray. To-day I haven't the remotest notion of its composer, nor do I care to know his name; such music, The Maiden's Prayer included, is immortal. But I always puzzled over the particular battle this particular morceau is supposed to musically illustrate. Probably the fierce one of 1757, and a bloody battle it was, with the Germans.

I also made the astounding discovery that Prague is spelled "Praha" by the natives, pronounced Prah, and that the famous Prager Schinken (Prague ham) is not so good in the city from which it takes its name; also that Pilsen, a few hours away, is spelled Plzen, and that its magic amber brew tastes better in Prague. Verily, you may exclaim with George Borrow: "Those who wish to regale on good Cheshire cheese must not come to Chester, no more than those who wish first-rate coffee must go to Mocha."

Tossing the proverbial advice of guides over my left shoulder for luck, I left the Blauer Stern on the Hybernska Ulice — the words begin to blister your eyes — went through the powder tower opposite the hotel, and by the Celetana place reached the Rathhaus, or Town Hall, passed the historic Tein (or Tyn) Church; also the old Jewish cemetery, and presently found myself on the river's edge at the Cech Bridge, a modern affair, quite wide, flanked by tall columns at both ends and leading to the delectable territory which I had earlier viewed from afar. It was only the night before that I had arrived from Vienna, and I was too tired to rove about; besides, Prague is not a brilliant night city. The Graben, or main thoroughfare, is not wonderfully illuminated, and the inhabitants retire early, or seem to; at all events, I preferred a good rest to noctambulistic prowlings.

The morning proved cloudy. Rain was imminent. And, not in too high feather, I was on the point of crossing the bridge when a polite official held out his hand for a tiny toll. At this juncture, and as I searched for small change, the sun stabbed through the mist high on the hills the imperial palace and the Hradschin, or capitol (on the Hradcany), the pinnacles of St. Vitus's Cathedral (Veitdom), the four Ottokar towers, and two towers of St. George swam gloriously in the air above me, a miracle of tender rose and marble white with golden spots of sunshine that would have made envious Claude Monet.

The spectacle was of brief duration, for the day cleared, and as I mounted the broad road leading to the pile of masonry I could note the solidity of what was once ancient Prague, its impregnability in case of siege, and its extraordinary romantic beauty.

It is the lodestar of the city. No matter your position, your eye finally rests on the Hradcany. I went to the Schloss Belvedere, and from its terrace I had another view of the cathedral. Close by it is more wonderful, especially the apses. From the Karl's Bridge you see it in profile; from the Marienschanz it is not so effective. But always it dominates the city, it is the leitmotif in an architectural symphony; yet never has it since showed for me such supernal beauty as that first morning when the sun had decomposed its massive lengths and transformed its masonry into a many-hued opalescent vision.

I confess that I was rather disappointed with the celebrated Chapel of St. Wenceslas (Wenzel) in the cathedral. It was built about 1360, and there is a display of Bohemian jewels that make a garish impression. The frescoes are dim, and the little picture depicting the murder of the saint — his amiable brother, Boleslay, was the assassin — is said to be of Cranach's school, but it is mediocre. A ring in the door was grasped by Wenceslas when he was slain.

The church is crammed with the bones of buried kings. The shrine of St. Nepomuc (St. John Nepomucane) is of more interest. It is composed of nearly two tons of silver. Modern iconoclasts deny the existence of Nepomuc, but there is his tomb, and, if my memory serves me right, I think there are relics of his in Philadelphia, where they are said to have worked miracles.

However, I was not sorry to leave the cathedral after vespers, for the air within was heavy. I descended by way of the Mala Strana (Kleinseite), enjoyed the view of the Hasenburg, with its lofty tower, then crossed the Karlsbrücke, counted its many stone saints and heroes, and finally reached the Town Hall (Rathhaus) in time to see the old and curious clock of the Erkeskapelle perform its little play for the benefit of a throng of peasants and others.

It was made in 1490 by a patient, pious, and ingenious person called Magister Hanus. It announces the hours and the rising and setting of sun and moon. Over the clock is a little window, in which the figures of Christ and his apostles appear when the hour strikes. The best part of the show was, of course, the people who with serious expression watched for the clockmaker's puppets as if assisting at a solemn service. I told myself that the age of faith is not dead; that whether Hussitek or Catholic, the Bohemians always were, and still are, of a religious nature. On Sunday the churches are packed, and if the citizen and his family enjoy themselves in the afternoon, vespers show no falling off in attendance; indeed, the favourite promenade after the midday dinner and before the afternoon coffee is up the Hradcany Hill, there to visit either Sankt Veit's Cathedral or St. George and attend the vespers service. Along the river bank is another favourite promenade, or up to the Star Hunting Lodge, where in 1620 was fought the battle of the White Mountain.

These same people, despite the Germanic strain, are as Slavic as the Hungarians are Magyar. Since the revival of the national tongue, in the early part of the nineteenth century, the speech is preferably Czech (or Cech, as they spell it), German not being so universal as it was. All the storekeepers speak German, English, and French, but interrogate the average man or woman in the streets and you will seldom be answered in anything but Czech. This is a gratifying evidence of reviving patriotism.

It must not be forgotten that Prague, as

Count Lützow has pointed out in his valuable books on Bohemia, "is now an Austrian provincial town, though Bohemia has always been officially described as a kingdom, not as a province." Reserved to the point of reticence even when you are made free of their homes and welcomed with unaffected hospitality, the Bohemian is persistently Slav. He speaks with affection of the aged Emperor Joseph, but he does not in his heart of hearts love Austria.

Centuries of warfare have made him both hardy and suspicious. He will fight at the drop of the handkerchief, but will hold his tongue if you mention the Tripartite Kingdom, which is as it should be. The Hungarians are less prudent.

I walked much in Prague town, old and new. I never saw so many pretty girls elsewhere, either in Vienna or Budapest, which is saying a lot. Now, since the Bohemian emigration to the United States is considerable, the peculiar type of beauty may be familiar in our coast cities. Not always brunette, though, as a rule, these young girls, chiefly of the peasant and poorest classes, are noted for their brilliant colouring, eyes as magnificent as those of Tuscan belles, strong, well-knit figures, and in bearing extremely proud. Splendid, is the comment you make as at eve or early in the morning hundreds and hundreds of these healthy creatures pass you to and from work. Saturday evening the Graben is crowded with them shopping, coquetting in anything but a subtle fashion, gossiping, and thoroughly enjoying their holiday.

The hotels in Prague are second-class, the cafés, with one exception, not of the sort you have so regretfully left in Vienna, but there are compensations. The cuisine, while its chief ingredients are Austrian, is Bohemian. There is a Czechic nuance in the pastry and I have seldom tasted such apple tarts, muffins stuffed with poppy-seed jam, dumplings of cream cheese, crumpets unparalleled, ham, egg, cream, and apricot jam. A Bohemian cook "cuts up a bird, spices its liver in a casserole, boils its back and serves it with rice, spices its breast and bakes it, and makes a brown stew of its giblets and feet." I quote from a well-known authority. And I have enjoyed just such "gollygubs" as the little Bohemian Hungry Henriettas would call their titbits at the Blue Star, where, frankly speaking, the cooking is better than any I tasted at Berlin in vaunted restaurants.

As for the Pilsen Urquell — and you can't go to Prague without drinking its chief beverage — I can only say as a humble admirer of the liquid that makes pleased the palate but does not fatten, that not in Pilsen, its home, is the brew so artfully presented.

One night I went down — or up — the Graben to a narrow street, well-nigh an alley, called the Brentgasse, there to find a restaurant consisting of several small rooms, the ceilings low, the tables bare of linen, a huge stove in a corner producing the necessary heat, and the ventilation not very good. I gave my order and it took exactly eight minutes for me to get what I had asked for. But it was worth waiting for a year. At a table hard by sat a group — three officers, two clergymen, and one civilian. They spoke low and earnestly. I suppose they took at least an hour to empty one glass, yet that glass of Pilsen looked as if it were newly born. As they conversed in Bohemian, of which I understand one word, "Plzen," I never enjoyed a pleasanter hour.

Sensible people, temperate in eating and drinking, are the people of Prague.

The newly built Representatives House, next to the powder tower, is a gorgeous building, with flaring lights, thronged with coffee drinkers between five and seven in the evening, and containing an excellent restaurant, the best outside of the Blauer Stern. I should like to print a specimen menu card for your edification, but I fear printers and proof-readers would rebel. I had an Omleta royal, a Fogos fish, a Telec filet specarky, and Ledovy crême, ending with an Americky compot, and, of course, some Austrian light wine.

Oh, the joy of roaming at night in a dark, strange city! I often found myself in quiet, mean streets, the windows and doors of the houses as if sealed, the silence of death about all. However, I believe I did overhear snoring on more than one occasion, a hint that I did not fail to take.

Once in my hotel I disdained the snail-like "lift" and went to the second floor, perhaps not without panting, but happy when I could find my room. Fancy about a mile of dimly lit corridors, freakish twists and turns, sudden little staircases that lead to sprained ankles or else blasphemous ejaculations; then another vista of doors, with boots, secret-looking, sinister boots, in front of them; comes a familiar curve, and you are not at home, though in a hallway large enough to hold your trunks and a horse and carriage besides, but in a safe harbour at last.

The old-fashioned bathroom, with a tub as deep as a well, as big as the Giant's Causeway, tells you that you are not in America but in the land — meaning Europe — where bathtubs are not taken seriously, where, indeed, no man in love with art will sell his spiritual birthright for the sake of a bathtub; where — and then you fall asleep to dream the battle of Prague and its cannonading.

But there are plenty of sights left for the soft daylight. If you should happen to be in the mood antiquarian or ethnographical there is the oldest Jewish synagogue in Prague, built, so tradition hath it, by the first fugitives from Jerusalem after its destruction. Certainly it is known to have been rebuilt in 1338, a date sufficiently far off to gladden the heart of the lover of mould.

A large flag testifies to the bravery of the Jews during the siege of Prague by the Swedes in 1648 and was presented by Ferdinand III. The Jewish burial-ground near by is a quaint spot. It has not been used for over a century. There are literally thousands of tombs covered with vegetation, many of which bear either the names of the occupants in Jewish script or else the symbol of the tribe to which the deceased belonged. A strange and not too cheerful place.

The view from the Palacky Quay (named after the great Bohemian statesman) is picturesque; bridges, palaces, and churches lie in the perspective.

The Bohemian National Theatre is pleasantly situated. The theatrical performances are high class. Sometimes Dalibor is a favourite — Dalibor, after whom is named the Daliborka town, was a knight who was in revolt, imprisoned, and beheaded. He was a violinist and became the theme of many romantic tales. He is also the hero of a novel by Wenceslas Vlcek.

At a concert in the Representatives House I heard a programme consisting of a scherzo by Dvořák, a symphony by Smetana, a new symphonic poem entitled Prague by Josef Suk, one of the most gifted of contemporary Bohemian composers, and a work by Sdenko Fibich (a much-neglected composer in America). Truly a feast for patriots as well as the musical.

I may say without fear of denial that the Bohemians are musical to the pitch of exaltation. They dearly love a good fiddler. And wasn't Prague the very hub of violin playing, for there the pedagogue Sevcik has turned out such pupils as the faulty faultless Kubelik, Kocian, and how many others? The Sevcik school is in Vienna at the present.

And now I approach the more serious, nay, tragic, side of my little recital: the history of the religious wars which for so many years ravaged the fair land of Bohemia — a more romantic-appearing land does not exist, not even Ireland — spilled cataracts of blood divided father and son, daughter from mother, put a curse on progress, and all this devastating misery for what? For something that to-day has as much interest or value as certain mediæval scholastic discussions regarding the number of devils that dance on the head of a needle.

What a waste of human life for naught! I remember once some one saying to me: "Religion is made for mankind, not mankind for religion," which very liberal opinion coming from the mouth of a wise and pious person caused me to stare. I have thought of this remark each time I read the history of Prague, and I have wondered what would have been its history if the Huss embroilment had been left out by the gods, on whose laps are shaped the destiny of nations. But such a thought is worse than futile.

When Kaiser Franz Joseph visited Prague as a young archduke he said: "It is impossible to conceive a history of Bohemia from which the Hussite wars are excluded." He was right. Like the Irish, the Bohemian is a theological man. He loves the knotty discussions that lead nowhere, or else to the battle-field; he is stubborn, without the natural fund of humour the Celt possesses, but he is as quarrelsome, and no quarrel is as attractive as one over doctrinal issues.

I said just now that the Huss-Wycliffe-Catholic-Church controversy seems futile in the light of modern reason, but some centuries ago it was the very bone and sinew of the Bohemian race. For John Huss or against John Huss; that was the question, and the theme that stirred so mightily an entire race then is bound to stir us now. Every dog has its day. John Huss, who set Prague by the ears, was not even born there, nor did he die there. Betrayed by the lying promises of King Sigismund, he was burned at the stake in Constance (November, 1414).

I found the speech of the Austrian Emperor quoted above in Count Lützow's exceedingly readable book about Prague. Not only a patriotic Bohemian, Lützow, who writes English as if it were his mother tongue, he is also a member of an old and noble family (you surely remember the legend of Lützow's Wild Hunt), distinguished in the history of his race. He has, therefore, written with sympathy and an intimate knowledge peculiarly valuable to those foreigners for whom the larger works on the subject are naturally inaccessible.

He tells us in his story of Bohemia of the legendary Libussa, who succeeded her father Krok, or Crosus, on the throne, although she was the youngest daughter. Finding her task as a ruler difficult, she decided to call in the aid of a husband, and to accomplish this she prophesied to her malcontent councillors. Pointing to a distant hill, she said: "Behind these hills is a small river called Belina, and on its bank a farm named Stadic. Near that farm is a field, and in that field your future ruler is ploughing with two oxen marked with various spots. His name is Premsyl and his descendants will rule over you for ever. Take my horse and follow him; he will lead you to the spot."

This beats the story of Cincinnatus. But the lady prophesied truly. Premsyl was found (what he thought of the affair has never been told) and crowned, and later his queen built Prague on the hill called Hradcany. (So Prague may be claimed as a petticoat creation.)

If a political party grew too powerful or too odious in the old days, its principal members were usually enticed into the palace chamber in the hill under the pretext of an important council and then suddenly thrown from a window to the moat or ditch below. This is called defenestration — which sounds better than it is.

In the Hradcany castle on May 23, 1618, several royal officials were pitched through the window. Oddly enough they were not killed, and their escape was pronounced a miracle by their pious adherents.

But let us return to a pleasanter theme. I visited the Clementinum, occupied by the Jesuit fathers, which is rich in manuscripts and possesses a library of nearly two hundred and fifty thousand volumes; and I visited the Rudolphinum, a stately structure built in 1884. It contains two concert rooms, a conservatory of music, and a picture-gallery, the latter housing much mediocre art, also a few excellent examples by Rembrandt, Rubens, Terburg, Watteau, Holbein.

Bohemians wonder why their rarely beautiful city is not visited by more Americans. The Germans overflow the town, as do the Austrians. Arthur Symons discovered it for the English in his exquisite epitome of travel, Cities, but Americans prefer the blandishments of Berlin, Paris, or London.

I think I can give one reason for this avoidance of a spot that is both a sacred shrine of history and a living witness to the magic of natural beauty. It is this: To reach Prague you must, if you come from America, travel viạ Berlin, Dresden, over Bodenbach, and the train service, according to our latter-day demands, is not up to the average. Stuffy carriages, whether first or second class, poor restaurant cars, no de luxe trains, and every one a crawler.

PRAGUE

Some day I hope the German and Austrian railway officials will realise what a jewel they are neglecting, and that we may go from Berlin to Prague in five hours instead of seven, and in new coaches with a decent dining-car attached. But in any case Prague is worth the bother getting there.

III

LITTLE HOLLAND

I

ROTTERDAM

It is raining in Rotterdam. But you are not melancholy. From a balcony at the rear of the old hotel you view with joy a wide canal. On it float two or three flat-bottomed boats. You have been surfeited for days with the ocean, with the round cupped horizon; here is water again, but civilised and restrained by the arts of man. Therefore the rain matters little. It is not a heavy downpour, only a misty, pervasive wet that adds to the intimate quality of the cityscape. One of the canal-boats has just discharged a cargo of peat-bog; not a clean job. The bargemen have gone away; the fiery-tempered little dog of the man and woman who live on board barks at canine passers-by, and the flat brick façades of the warehouses opposite recall certain streets in old Philadelphia. The architecture is the same: the dull dark brick picked out with marble, the low stoop of stone or marble, the air of exaggerated cleanliness, and the homelike atmosphere. You could swear you were walking along the wharfs of the Delaware River as they must have looked about 1850. But the odour is different. It is not at all Pennsylvanian. The moment the Hook of Holland is sighted from your steamer the specific Dutch smell begins. It is tarry, fishy, swampy, and not without acerbity. When you walk along some antique gracht (canal) the odour becomes malodorous. But we shall later return to this ever-present question. Let us look at the boats.

The man is preparing for Sunday. While he sluices the deck with water drawn from the canal by bucket, his wife hangs out the family wash to dry. It is not large. She has dipped it into some yellow stuff and it is as white as snow that has been trampled on. No sympathy need be wasted upon this stout, good-natured Dutch woman. No cohort of suffragettes could ever convince her that a woman's duty was aught else but to cook and wash for her husband and to bear him children. He works eighteen hours out of the twenty-four; why shouldn't she? There is no woman question in Holland. There is only the baby question. Large families abound, and if wages were higher and gin dearer happiness would be universal. As it is, the poorer class seems content. This particular boatman and his wife had a crew of children with them, tow-headed youngsters, boys and girls who when ranged on deck for the midday soup looked like a row of organ-pipes. Little wonder the rain could not spoil the picture for the pilgrim.

It is a pity that so many Americans entering Holland by the Holland-American Line do not remain longer at Rotterdam. There are many sights, many beautiful views from the top of the White House, and the enormous vitality of the city life impresses one as nowhere else in Holland, not in Amsterdam itself. Indeed, as a port, Rotterdam has quite outdistanced the mother capital and is causing Antwerp to look sharply after its own business. The White House is the tallest building in the country and was built on the profits of American oil. Ten stories high, its foundations are necessarily deep, for the soil is treacherous and swallows up wooden piles like quicksand. From the top you may see The Hague, only a half-hour away, Hook of Holland, Dordrecht, Gouda — where the meadow cows still wear coverings as noted by Carlyle in Sartor Resartus — Delft, and about half of Holland. But the most inspiring spectacle is the river Maas winding its silvery way to the sea, bearing every variety of craft from a steel steamship to the tiniest fisherman's coracle; above all, American petroleum tank steamers. By no means as grandiose as New York Harbour, the Rotterdam haven, with its bridges, its network of canals, its shipping; and the ceaseless play of light and shade on the many-coloured objects, the vivid green of the islets, the low-lying, lazily moving fleecy cloud boulders, the bustle and hammering, shrieking of steam-whistles form a distinctive picture.

As for the churches, St. Lawrence leading in interest, the Stock Exchange (Beurs), the various public edifices, the private residences, and the historical monuments, these are matters best left to Baedeker. A first visit to this fascinating country should dispose of all such necessary though fatiguing attractions. Traversing mouldy palaces, churches, and other damp, disagreeable buildings has a charm for the newcomer. There is another Holland, however, the Holland of glorious pictures, the Holland of byways, odd corners, queer, unexpected alleys far from the noisy centres, where A. D. 1909 suddenly becomes 1609, where groups of industrious humans live and die without ever getting farther away from home than the zoological garden.

The much-talked-of native costume you seldom see in Rotterdam. The canal-boat people dress in sombre garments, sailors are the same the world over, and the business men are just what you expect. Holland can boast of long-legged men. The proverbial little Dutchman, thick as a hogshead, is not nearly so prevalent as you think. Tall, broad-shouldered men wearing on their small heads hats too small for harmony hurriedly pass by, swinging the inevitable cane. They are warmly clothed for September, but the late afternoon brings dampness, the evening coolness. Every one who wishes to see, or to be seen, sits at the tables in the café terraces. They drink beer, excellent imported Pilsner, Amstel, or Heineken. Yet one cannot call the Dutch a nation of beer drinkers. The climate does not invite the thirst of the Teuton. Just as their existence is a long battle with the invading sea, so the chill of the air, omnipresent the hottest days of July, must be battled with, and gin is the chief weapon. The juice of the juniper berry is popular. A Dutch American shook his fist as we passed Schiedam on the steamer, declaring that the city was the devil's distillery; but gin is not such a curse as has been asserted. The poor man who earns ten to fifteen florins a week, or the dock labourers who earn much more, drink their gin, too often on an empty stomach. Nevertheless, Holland is a fairly temperate nation. In Rotterdam we saw one drunken man in three days, and he was celebrating of a Saturday night. His wife, shamefaced at the public disgrace, supported him as he stumbled, cursed, and roared. A great crowd followed, jeering. We asked a café waiter if it was a common occurrence. He replied in the negative, but a companion waiter shook his head affirmatively. When doctors disagree it is well to strike a happy balance.

Amusing, and also sad, were the antics of a girl aged about six, who led a band of desperate babies in petticoats in a charge upon every stranger who sat on the café terrace. She might have stepped from either a Holbein or a

Hals canvas. The round head, the thick neck, ash-blond hair, cheeks loaded as if with patches of paint, sharp little beady eyes, with a stout body, strong hands and dirty — the rascal simply caught the eye and held it because of her health, humour, and audacity. She came fairly by her temperament, as her father had spent nearly thirty years of his forty in jail, not for thievery, but brutality and a too-ready knife. Strong as a buffalo, he saw red when a policeman passed. Gin was the mainspring. Ten myrmidons of the law it took to subdue him a few years ago, and he contrived against such odds to snatch a sword from one of them and to stab the man. This Hercules of the back alley has a pretty wife. He beats her, of course, and she adores him, for he is handsome and good-tempered when he isn't drinking. Only he drinks whenever he can. His daughter is promising. She begs, insults the folk that give her pennies, and makes faces at the diners. Her mother indolently follows her, but the brat always evades her. It is easy to predict her future.

Bumping the boompjes is a pleasing game in Rotterdam. These docks are imposing and picturesque, but if you ride you are shaken to your very centre. Only Dutch spines can endure without quailing these wheels without tires which rumble around the town. For the rubber tire you must hire a taxicab; there are plenty and at a cheap tariff. That stony-hearted mother. Oxford Street, so eloquently hailed by

De Quincey, is tenderer than the streets of Holland, which are better suited to the hoofs of oxen than to the heels of mankind. Belgian blocks are as asphalt in comparison. After an hour's ramble your head resounds like a hollow copper kettle; this is caused by the vibrations of your suffering toes. Until the pneumatic tire is adopted in the larger cities of Holland we refuse to believe them anything but provincial.

The Sabbath is observed in Rotterdam; that is, people go to church in the morning, walk in the afternoon, visit the theatres and cafés in the evening. Overwhelming gaiety there is none, yet no sign of the moroseness we have been taught to look for in the character of the Dutch. They are a sober, self-contained, hard-headed people in business, but they relax when that business is transacted. Pious they are, whether Roman Catholics, Protestants, or Hebrews. Their Sunday is by no means of the Glasgow or London sort, and might shock Sabbatarians, innocent as it is. The servant-girl in all her glory hangs on the arm of her soldier, or else sits in a Bodega drinking a little glass of cherry brandy. The air is full of bluish tobacco smoke; nowhere else are cigars so good or so cheap. The Dutch colonies supply Sumatra tobacco, and one may puff at a five-cent cigar (Dutch money; in ours two cents) without tasting a stogie or a German cabbage. Havana cigars are equally low in proportion. A Bock, a Henry Clay, an Upmann, the kind for which you pay twenty-five to forty cents apiece in the United States, you may enjoy at twelve, fifteen, or twenty cents, American money. All the men and boys smoke in Holland. Fancy a staid father sitting at a table in the park, he with a cigar, his boy of ten with a long clay pipe! The schoolboys use cigarettes as freely as the American boy his marbles. And the tobacco seems to agree with the Dutch chaps as do the schnapps and the smell of the brackish canal waters.

The Boysmans Museum is an amiable preparation for the great feast of pictures at The Hague, Haarlem, and Amsterdam. The usual Dutch artists figure in the catalogue. There are no startling masterpieces, though Roger van der Weyden's Apostle John is worth studying. Three Jacob Ruysdaels, two Hobbemas, a capital Van der Neer, some Mauves and modern landscapes, a Vermeer and Klinkenberg's view of the pretty Vijver at The Hague, and Jongkind's moonlight view make up, with the Maes and Van der Helsts and Flincks and many print and flower pieces, a pleasing if not distinguished collection. The portrait of his father by Rembrandt is a boyish essay of historical interest. Rembrandt's unfinished allegorical painting (probably begun in 1648) is not particularly striking.

The Dutch are not phlegmatic. This statement may be as trite as that the Dutch have captured Holland, yet it may be a novelty to many. Among the polders, out in the fishing islands, and the farther you go, Friesland, Zeeland, old Dutch characteristics may persist like the old dress, but in the towns and cities the modern Dutchman is far from being phlegmatic. He is rather vivacious. He moves rapidly, speaks rapidly, and indulges in gestures. He burns his own smoke better than the Italians, but he is not the morose, pipe-smoking, sententious individual you read of; and the women, who dress as modishly as they know how, they, too, are mobile, swift in gait and speech. Go into any of the principal cafés of Amsterdam between five and seven o'clock in the evening, into Krasnopolsky's or the American, you seem to be in Berlin or Munich. At the Café Riche it is more Parisian. The man of Amsterdam works too hard; his hours are long and his relaxations are few, for here commerce rules. Nervous diseases, a Dutch specialist told us, are on the increase. The business man takes his coffee or his consommation. A theatregoer, a lover of music, he is nevertheless a great home body. Tea drinking after dinner is the rule in Holland. Every one who has been lucky enough to get a glimpse of home life will tell you of the cordiality, the hospitality, the genuine interest with which a stranger from overseas is made welcome. They like the Americans. We are in their eyes their country's grown-up children. Pictures of the Half Moon and of New York harbour are displayed in numerous shops. The reciprocity is sincere.

II

THROUGH THE CANALS

If ever there will be such a social reconstruction as the United States of Europe, then surely The Hague ought to be the capital. It is both charming and cosmopolitan. It possesses the intimacy of a little Holland city and in it is sounded the note, though faintly, of a Weltstadt. It is a garden dotted with villas, and they say that every Hollander with means looks forward to dying in this delectable spot almost within sight and sound of the North Sea. It commands a position between Rotterdam and Amsterdam, and in atmosphere is different from both. The summer residence of the court, in name at least — Queen Wilhelmina prefers Het Loo palace near Apeldoorn, for years, the accredited capital, if not actually so—The Hague, with its parks, its forest, its stately houses on canals seldom troubled by commerce, and its excellent hotels, is the least Dutch city in the country and one in which life goes upon oiled wheels except in the noisy business district. To summer there in one of the walled-in villas along the old road to Scheveningen, take a daily swim at that pretty seaside resort, and sleep under the immemorial elms undisturbed by anything but the diabolical baker boy in the early morning slamming the lid of the wooden bread box — wooden oaths with a vengeance — is a dream of many Americans. Dignity, order, moderation are cardinal virtues of the Dutch. They may be best observed in this city.

The happy disposition on the map of Holland of The Hague makes it a pivotal point for many excursions to such little cities as Delft, Haarlem, Leyden, and Utrecht. The express-trains stop at almost every station and move slowly; if they went at a rapid rate they would soon run into the sea or into Belgium, and the road-bed will not permit high speed. We recall with a sinking feeling a damp Sunday, September 13, 1903, when the Amsterdam-Berlin express jumped the rails somewhere between Barneveld and Apeldoorn, and the results thereof. Luckily a train can't run far astray in this land of sand and canals, and our Pullman landed in a sand-bank; but several of the other coaches were not so fortunate and there were casualties. This tale has always been received with polite incredulity by Dutchmen, for accidents are rare. Nevertheless, an American enjoyed his first railroad accident out among the dikes and ditches of Holland.

Leyden, when we reached it, after an easy jaunt of thirty minutes, was sunny and comfortably warm. The pictures of this grave and venerable university town did not attract. We knew that it had to be seen, and after that there was the inviting trip on the Carsjens line of steamers out on the narrow canals past the polders, over the lakes, and far away; so around Leyden we went, hobbling and analysing the odours of its various canals, hoping to discover their differences from those of Delft, of Rotterdam, and of The Hague; but they were plain, old-fashioned bilge-water smells, not necessarily unhealthy, though never pleasant. The atmosphere of the place suggests hoary wisdom. The dogs are dignified, men walk slow, and the women lower their voices when calling the children. The miserable four-wheelers, with cast-iron wheels (seemingly), alone break the Sabbath peace. Nevertheless, Leyden is far from being a cheerless spot, and it is picturesque. The view of the fish market from the canal, with the steeple of the Hooglandsche, or St. Pancras Church, is very striking. The old city hall on the Galgewater boasts an early seventeenth-century stepped gable, and in the Lakenhall (cloth hall) there are pictures by Lucas van Leyden, Van Goyen, Engelbrechtzen, Rembrandt (a study of a head), some Jan Steens, and others, all in various stages of decay. The Steens are the freshest. This place was the birthplace of Rembrandt van Rhyn (they pretend to show you out somewhere on the Old Rhine, so called, the windmill of the painter's father), of Lucas, Jan van Goyen, Gerritt Dou, Gabriel Metsu, Frans van Mieris, Jan Steen — surely honour enough for one town. At the municipal museum there are several fine altar-pieces by another son of Leyden, Cornelis Engelbrechtzen, and there is a chimney decoration at the town hall by Ferdinand Bol. The university, the buildings of which are scattered about, was founded in 1575 and harboured many lights of learning.

The cloth-weaving industry did not interest us, and after a hurried visit to the Peter's Church we returned by way of an old canal to the cattle market (Veemarkt), more determined than ever to avoid the National Museum of Antiquities (Indian, Roman, Egyptian, Dutch, of the Carolingian period) and to adhere to our original programme—see Holland out-of-doors and Holland painted. Like the late Dr. Syntax, we were in search of the picturesque, not of prosaic historical details. We even forgot to visit the grave of Spinoza at The Hague.

The Carsjens excursion is the most charming in Holland. If it were not for fear of abusing that overworked word intimate, we should apply it definitively to this steam around the country. Amsterdam affords various trips, but they do not seem to be in the heart of little Holland. The Zuyder Zee is large, the North Sea is not far away, the canals are broader than in the territory where move the Carsjens. At noon the boat leaves — a small, comfortable craft with an enclosed saloon through the windows of which you may study the country if the wind is too raw on deck. Through a canal we move as far as the Old Rhine, sadly shrunk from its noble proportions in Germany. Farmhouses, always in the shade of trees; brick and tile yards; meadows with cows, horses, sheep, pigs, chickens, windmills, whose wings look like razorblades; a low, serene sky-line, water everywhere; clouds that roll together and separate as sharp shafts of sunshine emerge and touch the earth. Van Goyen, Cuyp, Hobbema, Ruysdael painted these views many times. It all seems so familiar, so homelike, with the church spire emerging from a clump of trees and the kitchen windows of a brick house wide open as we pass. We can smell what is cooking. The dogs bark at our one sailor, and the stewards throw bread-crumbs to the myriad ducks that haunt these waters. Their outcry recalls the scream of the gulls as the ocean steamship enters Rotterdam — or Hamburg, Plymouth, Cherbourg, or New York. You grow hungry yourself. The air is delicately inviting in its coolness. "Steward!" A brief consultation. Not so bad as you expected. Omelet, beefsteak, compote. Wine or beer. The price is sixty cents, American money. But hang the cost! As you eat you stare across a flat, beautiful land and recall Sir Seymour Haden's remark that some French landscapes are immoral. If this is so, then the Dutch landscape is eminently moral. The lines are formal; there is no suggestion of the exotic. Every meadow has been a battle-field where man fought the water by miles. Every dike is a lesson. Holland is not lyric, as is Venice; hers is a sober prose; coloured, yet never lush. The only lush thing is the walking in the country. What fat glebeland! What black loam! Is it any wonder that the salads are so green, the vegetables so abundant, the flowers so blooming, the cattle so beefy, the sheep so muttony, the women so fat, and the men so tall?

The Rembrandt windmill is passed; passed, too, the miller's bridge; and then the steamer has reached the Heimanswetering. Woubrugge, with its tiny brick houses on either side of the wake, is in view. A few children regard with lazy eyes our noble ship. Grown-up folk give us no attention. As we stop nowhere there is nothing to be gained by looking at us. The Dutch are time-saving, and we are a thrice-told tale signifying no profit. The stream widens and we have the sensation of going out to sea. It is the Brassemeer, broad and calm, with plenty of pleasure and fishing boats on its placid bosom. Steam-yachts are no novelty. The channel then narrows as we enter the Old Wetering; we arrive at the circular canal around the Haarlemer meerpolder, one of the great polders of Holland. The old Haarlem Lake is larger than the Brassemeer, having an area of one hundred and ninety-three square kilometers. Farms, tilled land, roads, storehouses, and pumping-stations may be seen. The windmill is more ornamental nowadays, steam superseding it in the serious task of keeping the plains from flooding. You easily understand, after looking at this polder, the history of the brave people who were capable of cutting away the dikes when invaded by the enemy.

Presently the Kaager Lake is attained; the village of Kaag is in the middle distance, then the Zeil, and soon Leyden looms before you. It is 4:30, and you feel as if your voyage of discovery had just begun. Only the hymn-singing of a pack of geese who came on board in native costume marred an almost perfect excursion — certainly more characteristic than the Marken, Volendam, and Zaandam trips. Best of all, you never leave the boat; you are not persecuted by guides or children crying "Penny, lady! Penny, gentleman!" yet you are so near land that you can step ashore, and there are no annoying, time-wasting locks.

But in the end, so feeble and infirm of purpose is man, you tire of the eternal flatland; tire of innumerable views of somewhere, by God knows whom; become excited at the sight of the distant dunes, which seem like hills on the sky-line. At the mere thought of the Palisades a vision of Himalayas is evoked. The softness of the atmosphere is marked, the light is pervasive; just as set forth by any Holland master. The modern men have been particularly happy in rendering this atmosphere. Jakob Maris, Willem Maris, Mesdag, Weissenbruch, De Bock give in their canvases the effect of mist, of flat perspectives, of churches that stand out from their foundation-stones to their spire with startling clearness, yet are miles distant.

Auguste Rodin loves Holland for its slowness. It is in his sense a "slow" country. The landscapes are slow, to an andante tempo; slow, but thorough. Outside of Rotterdam and Amsterdam no one is in a hurry. A land of long nights, big, deep beds, heavy feeding, heavy drinking, every movement calculated, every penny accounted for — and remember that the Dutch two-and-a-halfpenny piece is worth our American cent; they think here in cents and florins. The florin contains one hundred pennies. It is the Dutchman's dollar.

III

HOLLAND EN FÊTE

(1813–1913)

When Henry James visited his native land a few years ago he was invited to a meeting of the publishers, or was it book agents? He sat through a long dinner punctuated by much talk, and when some rising young author, Bill Liverpool or Mat Manchester, I've forgotten which, asked the father of What Masie Knew whether he didn't think the affair altogether an interesting one, he ironically answered:

"Abysmally so."

And abysmally interesting for me were the formal proceedings which opened the Palace of Peace at The Hague, in September, 1913. It was a great day for Mr. Andrew Carnegie and the hopeful persons who believe war is to be abolished by sentiment, but it was severe for those who had to sit still while official wheels went round slowly in the newly opened building out on the old road to Scheveningen (I dare you to pronounce this as the Dutch do). No doubt it was a thrilling sight for the chief actors, but I thought of Mr. James and his fatal phrase. De profundis! I said to my neighbour more than once, for Dutch pomp and ceremony go on leaden feet. The tempo, as they say in music, was andante throughout this lovely land of slow landscapes and lazy silhouettes.

Royalty was gracious, Mr. Carnegie smiling, and solemn gentlemen sonorously rumbled. The verbiage was interminable. But there is no gainsaying the magnificence of the palace. When its utter futility is finally demonstrated I think it will make one of the handsomest restaurants and cafés in all Europe. As such it will be useful and provocative of peace.

The *Paris Figaro* achieved the feat, without parallel as far as I know, of printing the story of a special correspondent in which the name of Carnegie did not occur; nor was this done with malice prepense, for the cost of the palace is given, and the fact is mentioned that because of the huge outlay a small admission is charged. But of Mr. Carnegie's benefaction not a word. I relate this well-nigh incredible anecdote simply to throw into high relief the almost universal knowledge of the Carnegie idea in Europe. In every city and hamlet of Holland his portrait is shown. American flags decorated the streets of The Hague and adorned in company with the Dutch colours every motor-car. I saw them at Groningen, Friesland, and at Arnhem, in the village of Zeist, and at Amsterdam. There is a distinct wave of popular sympathy for America and the Americans. And this is very pleasant.

In a certain sense all large cities bear a strong family resemblance; it is in the small towns that the curious traveller finds innumerable differences. Delft has its own physiognomy, so Utrecht. Zandvoort as a bathing resort is distinctly different from Scheveningen, as Ostend is different from Blankenberghe. At Haarlem you see Frans Halses, or wander in the famous Haarlem wood. At Leyden, after you have exhausted the learned town, you go off on one of the Carsjens boats through the canals, patrol the flat Harlemmer-meer, see the polders, or at Amsterdam you will visit the island of Marken, not failing to notice the picturesque humbuggery of the peasants in full costume for the benefit of the tourists who believe in that sort of theatrical nonsense.

But I confess that the conventional Holland of the painters and holiday seekers is beginning to pall. Canals and dikes, spotless villages like Broek, the low horizons and miles of melancholy dunes no longer interest me as do the people, the flowers, the magnificent woods, and the life of the little cities—the Holland not known to the average visitor, because he hasn't the time.

The magic of sails mysteriously gliding through walls of green trees is, however, ever fresh.

At The Hague, cosmopolitan as Paris and London are not, the Mauritshuis is the chief magnet. There the Vermeers are wonderful, more wonderful than the Rembrandts, though the multitude prefer that wooden-legged bull of Paul Potter. In 1909 I saw the two new additions, the Diana and the allegory of the New Testament, but the view of Delft is for me more fascinating than either. I have written elsewhere at length on the art of Holland. I need hardly add that the international exhibition of sporting requisites at The Hague did not long detain me. Far more attractive was the ship exhibition (E. N. T. O. S.) at Amsterdam. This was well worth a visit. The development of ships from the Middle Ages down to the newest achievements in battle cruisers and ocean steam palaces were to be seen. A comprehensive show. On either side of a canal was a historical reconstruction of old Amsterdam houses. There was a Luna Park, modelled after Coney Island, with shooting the chutes and many other familiar diversions for the delectation of grown-up children. At night the electric display was gay.

Amsterdam, more than any other Dutch city, has ill-smelling canals, because the water is stagnant; and it has more than its share of nuisances. A special chapter could be written on the noises of Holland. Certain of them are indigenous to the soil. At 6 A. M. you are awakened by the banging of bakers' and butchers' wagons; they slam the lids of these little carts after they have delivered their orders. It is like the continual popping of rifles; then the dogs begin to bark. Their name is legion. All sympathy is due them for their arduous toil — they are strapped under the various vehicles both for draught and protection purposes. They growl at every passer-by, probably from a sense of duty, and they get the nervous visitor out of bed an hour earlier than is his custom.

Worse remains, the beating of rugs and carpets in the streets and open squares. Holland is the cleanest country in the world — though Berlin West is cleaner than Amsterdam — that no one will deny, nevertheless not the most hygienic country; otherwise this intolerable stirring up of dust would not be permitted. It is the custom of centuries, and when you complain a surprised look is the usual answer. I asked a distinguished scientific man why Amsterdam, with its numerous hospitals, sanitariums, and the like, could endure not only the noise, which is distracting, day and night (the long roll of artillery is the nearest approach to this appalling racket made by vigorous blue-eyed, blond-haired maids), but the clouds of dust which fill your nostrils and eyes if you venture abroad. He shrugged his shoulders. Carpet-cleaning establishments and vacuum cleaners were suggested as being less destructive and healthier. I saw that I was talking in vain.

Hollanders possess nerves of iron, and ages after mankind has definitely conquered the air the good people of Holland will maltreat their rugs with rattan paddles, and likewise the ears of their visitors.

But say these things and you say all that is disagreeable in this miniature land. Sober, serious, industrious, the people relax in a natural manner, enjoying themselves heartily on Sundays and holidays from Dordrecht to Leeuwarden. Except on state occasions, such as historic pageants, the national costume in all its variety is seldom seen. More's the pity, for it is very becoming to the robust girls, who look, somehow, queer in modern attire.

The artistic life is satisfying, and also the intellectual. With such a world-renowned genius as Hugo de Vries at Amsterdam, and such a brilliant neurologist as Dr. C. U. Ariens Kappers of the Central Institute of Brain Research (Amsterdam), or Dubois, who discovered in Java the so-called missing link (Pithecanthropus Erectus) at Amsterdam, to mention but three names with which I am familiar, Holland is far from singing small at any international congress of scientists. Advanced ideas in sociology are the rule.

Among the younger painters I found gratifying evidences of individual talent. The younger Israels will never make us forget his great father Jozef (whose masterpiece is in the Rijks Gallery), but he is an ambitious artist. There are many men who pattern after the Maris palettes, Jakob and Willem, without compassing the rich colour effects of either. Yet you feel that Holland will not lose her reputation as a colourist in their hands. My favourite etcher among the younger artists is Marius Bauer. Naturally, Vincent van Gogh is the master of the new school, the greatest Dutchman of them all. How regrettable is his premature taking-off you feel when you see his self-portrait at the Royal Museum in Amsterdam. For other modern artists one must go to the Municipal Museum.

As for music, I've seldom listened to a better band than the Concert Gebouw, conducted by the fiery and versatile Mengelberg (not dead). The Amsterdam choir, mixed voices, is a sterling body principally devoted to Bach. Otherwise, despite the sporadic visits of German operatic organisations, and the presence all summer at Scheveningen of either the Berlin Philharmonic or the Lamoureux Orchestra of Paris, Holland is more than fond of Sousa marches (a Dutchman by the way) and Yankee ragtime. Recently I heard nothing but one tune, a famous Tenderloin tune, whistled by the urchins, howled at night by the populace, and hummed by women. Its title I don't know, but it's simply entrancing! Thus does America repay Holland for its imported "old masters" (manufactured yesterday), which are spread over America since the new art tariff went into effect.

De Vrouw was the name of the exhibition

devoted to woman's achievement through the ages. To say it was pitiful would be beside the mark — the show robs the achievement — and the buildings erected by mere man were equally flimsy. The pictures were amateurish, the sculpture not much better. One of America's women art exhibitions would be ashamed to put out such work as representative. You long for Cecilia Beaux or Mary Cassatt. In the book section Ella Wheeler Wilcox and Bernard Shaw were the principal "feminine" authors in evidence. Next to the exhibition was the big Amsterdam ballast works. Was this intentional irony?

More satisfying was the concert given under Willem Mengelberg, in which such women composers as Cornelie van Oosterzee, Anna Lasubrechts Vos, and Elizabeth Kuypers were heard. The cleverness, learning, and natural talents of this trio were admirable. Van Oosterzee's symphony will make its way. It is the most "important" musical composition from the pen of a woman that I have thus far heard, and I don't believe the composer has ever set a torch to a hen-house, slapped a cabinet minister, or blown up a church.

The Dutch tongue is comparatively easy to one acquainted with German and English, but it is far from melodious. When spoken by the veteran actor Louis Bouwmeester, in parts like Shylock or Julius Cæsar, it has a certain harmony. Herman Heijermans, whose Good Hope is known to English playgoers, is now the manager of two Amsterdam theatres. I enjoyed under his direction Allerzielen (All Souls) and Ghetto. I also heard a Dutch version of Clyde Fitch's The Woman in the Case (De Vrouw in 't Spel). Shaw's Doctor's Dilemma was announced for production. Leonard van Noppen, Professor of the chair of Dutch Literature, Columbia University, has done much to make the English-reading world familiar with the great epic of Von Vondel, Luzifer (with which Milton was evidently familiar when he wrote Paradise Lost), and the prose of Douwes Dekker (better known as Multatuli).

The younger Dutchmen are unavowedly influenced by the newer French writers; also by Wilde and Shaw. For the latter they cherish an affection, but when a body of Leyden students wrote him inviting him to visit their venerable university and lecture he tartly answered that never would he go to a country that plundered him of his plays, or words to that effect. Since then the eminent altruist gets his regular royalties, as there is now a copyright law in operation.

A word could be added about this polyglot speech of the Hollanders, whose English is excellent. After the Russians they are possibly, because of the difficulty of their own language, the most accomplished linguists in Europe. Everywhere you will find men and women who answer your questions in idiomatic English.

The Dutch cuisine is richer and more full-flavoured than the German. Never go to Holland to "reduce." The wines imported from France, a few hours away, are cheap and sound.

The race itself runs to tall men and women. The girls are "daughters of the gods, divinely fair," strapping Alices in Wonderland, though the promise of good looks in youth is seldom fulfilled in maturity. Corpulence is not a common characteristic. Active, seldom phlegmatic, the men are more vivacious than the Teuton. And while much "schnapps" is drunk by a certain class of workmen, wine, not beer, is the national beverage. Living, especially house rentals, is much cheaper than in America. Everywhere the residences are of brick or stone. The bath-room is yet to become universal, but for comfort and economy the little cities of Holland are without equal. The moral climate of The Hague and Amsterdam is less torrid and frivolous than that of Paris or Berlin.

From Amsterdam to Haarlem is only a half-hour by railway; to Zandvoort on the North Sea fifteen minutes more. There is more fun, natural and undisguised, at Zandvoort than at the mundane Scheveningen. The "plain people" go out on the beach and dance to the accompaniment of a genuine Hoboken brass band (yellow-dog clarinets and all), and drink under a tent on the dunes. Approaching this resort, you fancy yourself in a sort of Holland Switzerland; the sand-hills are sometimes one hundred and fifty feet high. The bathing is beyond criticism, the beach shelving, with firm sand and quite safe.

In Haarlem Louis Robert continues to give his biweekly organ recitals in the Cathedral of Sint Bavorek, playing upon the mellow-toned instrument with skill and sympathy. I heard one programme of Bach, Mendelssohn, and Guilmant. Nothing will convince me that moving the Frans Hals portraits from the old Town Hall has improved them. I visited a half dozen times the new museum, and an appropriately built house it is, yet the lighting is not as direct as at the former quarters. Consequently the Regent groups do not come out so brilliantly. The new Frans Hals statue is placed in a pretty park.

After Haarlem, Utrecht. There all was peace (barring the inevitable rug-hammering), and if there were few pictures, and no music-making (excepting the eternal whistling, a trait of Hollanders, young and old), there was a little city of exceeding charm quite its own. The antiquarian will find in the twelfth-century cathedral and the numerous additions a perfect compendium of Gothic art, and for the student of science there are several seats of learning. For the flâneur, the writer, the scholar, the world forgetting by the world forgot, there is a tranquil existence beyond compare, and if he has the lust of the eye for the things pictorial then he can gratify it at his very elbow. The old canal, with its houses underneath; the new canal and its rows of dignified dwellings; the walk under broad avenues of foliage; the Malieban; Wilhelmina Park and its umbrageous attractions, not to speak of the suburbs; green is everywhere, flowers everywhere, and at every turn a vista that makes you envious of such municipal government that has transformed a town into a park. There is only one modern hotel, the Pays-Bas.

Utrecht is not, for some reason, included in the ordinary itinerary of the tourist, though only thirty-five minutes from Amsterdam. If you wish to go farther afield, there are Zeist and Baarn, both leafy paradises and only thirty minutes away by train or tram. At Baarn are a number of villas, owned by wealthy people, which seem ideal. No mosquitoes or grachten (canals) smells annoy you at Utrecht. Your nerves soon quiet down. You sleep the sleep of the unjust (the soundest of all) and wonder as you doze off why people visiting Holland rave over windmills and canals instead of the magnificent woods and flower-beds. Ah, the processional forests of Holland!

I attended a cricket-match (almost as soporific a game as golf — true sport for somnambulists), and I saw young, handsome, well-set-up chaps pulling in single shells with sliding seats up the Katharina Singel (a broad canal). Football, too — they call it voetbal — is a pastime much admired. Bicycles are omnipresent, the roads for motoring almost faultless.

The festal event of the season at Utrecht was the exhibition of North Netherland art previous to 1575. It was a profoundly significant gathering. Such masters as Lucas van Leyden (in black and white as well as in colour), Jan van Scorel, Engelbrechtzen, Jacob Cornelisz, and a flock of unknown painters, beginning with the master of the Death of Mary, were represented. Archaic in technique, these ancient panels and canvases contained a wealth of sentiment, religious feeling, and sincerity in the delineation of nature. You see, not without wonder, how the new men of yesterday and to-day, the Neo-Impressionists and Cubists, have boldly pilfered the technical procedure of these old fellows and have vainly endeavoured to trap the emotion and recover their "innocence of the eye." So many Scorels I never saw assembled. I have long since registered my admiration for this painter's Mary Magdalen, which formerly hung in the Town Hall, Haarlem, but is now in the Rijks Museum.

A note made reminds me that Jan van Scorel was born at Schoorel, near Alkmaar, in the year 1493. He studied under Jacob Cornelisz at Amsterdam and with Jean de Maubeuge at Utrecht. He died in that place, 1562. He visited Albrecht Dürer at Nuremberg and resided for a time in Italy. His portraits are undoubtedly Italianate in expression, and the portrait of Bishop George van Egmont in the Utrecht Gallery is no exception. It is a panel picture and cracked, but otherwise in fair condition. The Lucas van Leydens were the glory of the exhibition.

I forgot to say that the clangorous chimes of the cathedral in Utrecht are so out of tune that they remind me of castor-oil in buttermilk.

No great composer has yet emerged from Holland, but her instrumentalists are celebrated. As befits the grave diapason of national feeling, the violoncello is sedulously studied. We need only recall the elemental power of Fritz Giese and the astounding virtuosity of Anton Hekking (is it necessary to mention the sonorous Josef Hollman?); Dutch 'cellists in the modern orchestra are as indispensable as Belgian woodwind players.

A word might not be amiss about the high average of culture; the Dutch are omnivorous readers in a half dozen languages, and, thanks to their proximity to Brussels, Berlin, Paris, and London, not to mention their newspapers, are a well-informed people in matters contemporary.

It was a warm September Saturday morning when in company with Dr. Kappers I met that truly great scientist and most modest man, Hugo de Vries, and in his own "experimental garden" at the Amsterdam Botanic Garden (Hortus Siccus, is the legend over the gates). Professor de Vries — he is professor at the University of Amsterdam — looked very well after his long visit to America, where in New York he was invited by President Butler to join the teaching faculty of Columbia College. He wisely declined the honour, notwithstanding the horticultural temptations of Bronx Park. But, being a canny Dutchman, he hammered this offer into the heads of the Dutch authorities and was given a new and more commodious building in which to work out his now-famous doctrine of the mutation of plant and flower life. He admires Luther Burbank and thus sums up the difference in their respective experiments: "Burbank crosses species, I seek to create new ones." He does create new species, does this benevolent-looking Klingsor with the flowers in his magic garden. But it is white, not black, magic. He lets nature follow her capricious way, giving her from time to time a gentle hint; a sort of floral eugenics. I saw eight-leaved clovers and was told that many more leaves may bud, as the clover was originally a stalk full of leaves. For the superstitiously inclined there are three, four, five, six, and seven leaved varieties. The evening primrose (Æonthera lamarckiana) is at present the object of Professor de Vries's experiments. Certainly this yellow flower means more to him than it did to Wordsworth's Peter. He ties up its petals in tiny bags and, protected from marauding birds and bees, and no doubt being bored by its solitude (though pistil and stamen remain), it begins to put forth a new species. With my own eyes I witnessed the miracle of a half dozen flowers in the world that were not in existence a year ago. That is creating life, indeed, and even Sir Oliver Lodge must give his assent to the statement. The new flower is a "constant," it goes on reproducing itself, but at times the back of a leaf shows a struggle to revert to its old pupillaceous state. Darwin taught that evolution is orderly, progressive, slow, without jumps — nature never leaps; there are no sudden miracles. De Vries proves the reverse — the miracle had taken place overnight in his experiments; nature strikes out swiftly, blindly, apparently without selection. The age of miracles is not past. I saw what he called a rosette, a green plant-like production, and was told that it was a new birth of the commonplace primrose — in Alabama he gathered his parent flowers. Really you think of the "Dr. Moreau" of H. G. Wells (his most arresting book), and wonder if such things could be possible in the human order. De Vries is the most significant figure in the history of science since Darwin.

He has just published a big volume concerning his travels and experiments while in America. His great work on Mutation was translated long ago, but it is principally for students. I can recommend, however, a pamphlet of thirty-seven pages, entitled Afstammings en Mutatis — Leer (published in the Levensvragen series at Baarn, near Utrecht, Holland), as containing in crystallised form the doctrine of mutation, set forth by its author with a wealth of argument and in his usual clarity of style. Professor de Vries speaks and writes English fluently and idiomatically, but he is too immersed in his work to translate his prose into our language.

I was loath to leave the presence of this man who, in the Indian summer of his life, looks like a bard and philosopher, summoning strange and beautiful flowers from the vasty deep of nature. He is an exalted member of the most honourable profession in the world, a gentle gardener of genius.

IV

BELGIAN ETCHINGS

I

BRUSSELS

THE man who first called Brussels le petit Paris must have been imbibing many bottles of the fiery Burgundy for which the city is renowned. Brussels is only a mock-turtle Paris. The cookery is more savoury, less sophisticated and oilier than in Paris. Naturally we allude to the Flemish cuisine, not to the imitation Parisian restaurants that flourish in all the leading hotels. Stews, hotchpotches, meats smothered in onions, soups so thick that a spoon will stand upright in them, sauerkraut, hot salads, sea food cooked with plenty of butter are Brussels specialties. Birds abound in season and out, and as to the quality of the wine there is no doubt. Clarets and Burgundies of authentic vintage are to be had at moderate prices in certain tavernes and restaurants, but not at the hotels or in resorts frequented by tourists. The difference between Holland and Belgium, if one were cynical, would be to note that in the latter country they never serve fish after the meat. That is a Dutch custom which is still a mystery to us. But the Belgian kitchen is richer than the Hollandish, and the wines better and cheaper. On the other hand, the cafés are not as comfortable. Those long reading-tables with student-lamps, which so humanise a café, are all through Holland; in Brussels the café is rather cheerless. The majority of hotels are old palaces and mansions altered into very uncomfortable rooms, where a bathroom is buried in a wall as if bathing were some forbidden luxury. What these houses are like in the bleak, rainy winter one may imagine. The horrors of hotel life must be experienced here to the full. And that "M. the director," who seems to eat, drink, and sleep in his frock coat and beard — has his bland smile a parallel on the Continent?

The fact is Brussels caters largely to English people. It always has been a favourite city. And as the English are stubborn in their adherence to antiquated customs, Brussels hotel keepers consider themselves very à la mode because the majority of their guests are from Great Britain. Americans come here in throngs, but they are birds of passage, their season is brief, while the English matron with her daughters winters at the pensions and hotels, for the price of living is cheap. The English are better liked, better understood; they don't grumble as do the Americans over the cruel dampness and the unsanitary conditions of the hotels and pensions. They know. They come from England and they have eaten its soggy cookery.

But Brussels is gay. Narrow and provincial and noisy as it is, it enjoys itself, whether in the lower town crowded with cafés or in the upper with its broad avenues, tree-lined, vast squares, palaces, and museums. The cafés are the social barometers of the place. At seven o'clock it is difficult to get a seat for your consommation, and in the restaurants there is a waiting list. Again we may remark that the food is capital. A glutton of renown once drew up an itinerary for a week — a grub route which, while it makes the mouth water, would be apt to produce a formidable indigestion. For some reason, presumably climatic, one is hungrier than in New York. Two hours after a heavy dinner you will see people swallowing sandwiches. Perhaps the wine and beer aid the metabolic processes. Chicken, so much cheaper in Holland, is very good in Belgium. Fresh mushrooms are in vogue, but Brussels sprouts we did not see except the comical little ones on the chins of pale young men — all smoking the deadly Belgian tobacco.

The Brussels woman runs to waist. Good cheer and the admiration of the men for ladies of generous proportions have much to do with their size and weight. They dress a shade more exaggerated than in Paris. If Paris wears big hats, Brussels sports cart-wheels. At the present time the edict as to the suppression of the monster head-gear has evidently not reached the ears of Brussels dames and daughters. They are all hat and feathers and shoulders. The Rubens woman rules. The very men you rub shoulders with might have stepped from a Jacob Jordaens canvas. Women's rights here? Why, every woman has the right of way in the street, in the cafés, and in conversation. A pleasing sight it is to see the portly mother, the undersized husband (meek but thirsty), the flock of children, the family friend enter a restaurant of a Sunday night. The function begins with due solemnity. The waiter is summoned and submits to a cross-fire of questions. Sunday only comes once a week and there must be no hitches on the programme. Soup, fish, meat, vegetables, salad, dessert, and wines are considered as if a national crisis were impending. Then the overture sounds, the curtain rises, and the play begins. It is a jolly comedy. Good humour, laughter, hearty appetites rule. A dyspeptic American is filled with dismay or consumed with envy. They go to their homes, these worthy people, and sleep the sleep of the overfed.

The children are without exaggeration very pretty, curly, blond, stout, with cheeks blazing with colour. They play in the streets, roll in front of honking automobiles, dodge tram-cars, splash in the fountains, and make more noise than the rug beaters of Rotterdam. (Rugs are not abused in Belgium, nor are there many bicycles, the motor-car is sovereign.) Brussels is not clean; that is, not as clean as Holland, nor are the inhabitants as spruce as the Dutch. They are in a civic sense conceited. Too many tourists have spoiled the broth of their politeness. They are anxious to do you a service for a slight remuneration. Beggars are more plentiful than in Holland; unquestionably there is more poverty. The shops are small, but cheap is shopping, so womankind says. Gloves, perfume, millinery are sought after by strangers.

When a big fire automobile whizzed by containing something that looked like a douche, an honest gentleman asked us with ill-stifled pride if New York could show any such miracle. For answer we went to the fire, a piffling cigarette affair, and witnessed the Flemish temperament working at top speed. The spectacle was impressive. Not apparently as excitable as the Gallic race, the Brussels men and women chanted at fullest lung power a sort of mixed choral, with crazy Flemish counterpart for one thousand voices da capo. The vocal sounds were the outpouring of admiration from overheated hearts for the pompiers. When the Spritze — we can think of no better title — sent forth a garden-hose stream, joy was unconfined. There was more enthusiasm than on a wet Sunday in Versailles when the fountains begin to spurt and the band to play. Unappeased, our Belgian acquaintance asked for further information.

The New York Fire Department was evidently a myth manufactured at the moment, the population figures pure lying. Good old soul, within his bosom beat true patriotism. They stand in the streets here in deep water watching the cinematograph advertisements as did their fathers the Punch-and-Judy shows.

The bells are not so insistent as those of Antwerp and Bruges. But they may be heard. One church rings the hours on the half and repeats the number when the regular hour is reached. Why? Aren't we galloping to eternity fast enough? Why should eight-thirty sound nine, and nine be sounded over again at the real hour? Sunday is the best day to see the people in gala. There is dancing in the open in some quarters of the town during the Kermesse — as is the case at Antwerp. In the Grande Place opposite the magnificent Hôtel de Ville — one of the greatest squares in Europe — on Sunday mornings there is a bird-and-flower market until midday. From narrow side streets comes the atrocious singing of the café chantants. Hobnailed shoes clatter over the stones, parrots scream, women chaffer, and across the way is the noble façade of the old building. At the Théâtre de la Monnaie we heard a mediocre performance of Massenet's Manon. Second-rate singers and an excellent orchestra.

The parks are pleasant and the view from the upper town inspiring, while the first glimpse of the Palace of Justice evokes erratic architecture. It is one of the largest and most imposing buildings in the world. The Cathedral, Sts. Michel and Gudule, is a fine thirteenth-century Gothic structure. It is not a bad plan to stop at Malines on the way down from Antwerp. The old schedule of fifty minutes has been reduced to thirty-six minutes by the trein-block. Malines or Mechlin is not far from Brussels, and the paintings of Rubens in the churches of St. Jean and Notre Dame make the trip a notable one, setting aside the picturesqueness of the town and its famous lace-making industry.

Flowers are plentiful and there is no danger of conversation perishing. As a fine art here we cannot pretend to judge. We believe that the American woman's speaking voice has been too much criticised, not only by Henry James but also by genuine Americans. The Flemish and Walloon voice is loud, is often raised to screaming with the women, and noisy in the case of men. As for the dogs, poor overworked animals (the Belgians are not so kind to animals as the Dutch), dogs here haul heavy burdens; we often wished their recurrent nerve could be severed, so as to still their continual barking.

The general aspect of the street is animated. Life does not run at slow tempo in Brussels. It is gay and it is not a little Paris. But the large army of domino-playing shopkeepers and bourgeois give it a philistine aspect on holidays.

As one American remarked on a hot Sunday: "Come now, doesn't all Europe remind one of East Grand Street on a Saturday night?"

II

LITTLE CITIES AND THE BEACHES

The staid old Flemish town of Malines, better known to Americans as Mechlin, where they make the lace, has been pluming itself on an exposition which opened in August and lasted months. The affair bears the following title: Exposition des anciens métiers d'art Malinois, d'art religieux de la province d'Anvers et de folklore local. It is exactly what it pretends to be, an exhibition devoted to old pictures, sculpture, tapestry, embroidery, jewellery, pewter ware, iron ware, bronze, brass, clocks, bells, gilded leather, lace, ecclesiastical vestments, sacred vessels, manuscripts, apothecary's mortars and what-not. A more fascinating collection we never viewed, not even at the Bruges exposition of 1900. This exposition at Malines is under royal patronage; also churchly, his Eminence Cardinal Archbishop Mercier representing the latter. There are about forty-five old paintings, some on panels, though none of magisterial importance. Brabant once occupied an important position in the history of the fine arts, beginning with Jean de Woluwe in the fourteenth century. There are Bruges, Ghent, and Tournai with the Van Eycks and Robert Campin, called the Master of Flémalle; Brussels with Bernard van Orley and Roger van der Weyden (De la Pasture); Louvain with Thierry Bouts; Antwerp with Quentin Matsys — not to mention Rubens or Van Dyck — and Malines with Master Vrancke van Lint and the Van Battele.

There is a panel in the Malines show attributed to Robert Campin and a Descent from the Cross given to Van der Weyden. Also a striking triptych, The Legend of St. Anne, of the Antwerp school, sixteenth century. Michel Coxcie is here, also a J. Patinir, the latter with his characteristic blues. A Bernard van Orley (?) represents Man Under the Reigns of Law and Grace. There are several Francks. Velvet Breughel is present, and a Virgin with the Infant, by Giovanni Bellini. This Italian panel is, to say the least, rather questionable. The sculpture is for the most part in wood and is marvellous. There are rooms arranged as at the Metropolitan Museum so as to show the precise manner of living at the period. There is no mistaking the Flemish kitchen or the dining-room, with their massive tables capable of holding barons of beef and the huge tankards of the mighty drinkers. The finest tapestry on a large scale is sixteenth-century Brussels make, depicting episodes in the life of St. Elizabeth of Hungary.

Just off the lace room we saw an old woman

sitting near a window making lace. She must have been one hundred years old, though her eyes were youthful and her hands, instead of skinny claws, were plump and looked like those of a piano virtuoso. She was very industrious with her bobbins, her fingers working with nervous agility; in a doorway a painter had planted his easel and was painting her. You fancied yourself in the Middle Ages, with die Meistersinger around the corner serenading mine host of De Goude Kroone. But if you walked away and then happened to enter the low-ceilinged room from another side you would find, as we did, the gay old lady with her venerable hands in her lap and conversing with the painter, who was quite idle. A bit of a disappointment, yet not without its compensation from the picturesque view-point. The carefully prepared mise en scène is one of the features of the show.

Malines has become hopelessly commercial, therefore thriving. But apart from the fine Van Dyck, the altar-piece at St. Rombold's, it is no longer as interesting as it was. Bruges beats it to a standstill when it comes to a question of atmosphere. There are canals enough, forsooth, though they are prosaic and muddy. When we reached the train that took us back to Antwerp, a matter of twenty minutes, the official thermometer registered ninety-two degrees. No wonder the waiter of a near-by café slept calmly in the boskage. No wonder the beer was hot and placid. No wonder we were glad to escape. The fields in Belgium are burned up by the too-fervent sun of last summer. The trees are grey and dusty looking; no silver gleams from the network of canals. As for Antwerp, it was with genuine dismay that the pilgrims from America found a weltering heat and, horrible to relate, mosquitoes of the true-blue New Jersey breed. They sang and stung with an avid earnestness that betrayed their origin. No doubt they came over on the steamships from New York. All Europe is suffering from them and another superstition is vanished, that there are no mosquitoes in Europe. The Europeans now know the luxuries of an American August. At Antwerp they say the pests came from Asia; but they probably breed out in the mud-flats of the Scheldt and thence overspread the country like a new plague from Egypt.

There is no denying the fact that Antwerp is a noisy city, with its cathedral chimes at first an attraction and after twenty-four hours a nuisance. Bells that ring every seven minutes soon become intolerable to modern ears. Besides, these chimes play secular music, arranged for them by two well-known Belgian composers, Jan Blockx and Peter Benoit, not exactly good material. We recall one maddening sequence, a run in double chromatic sixths, not one bell in tune with another, a nightmare when heard in the small hours. Bruges suffers from the same dire noises. In the old times bells not only summoned the faithful to worship but warded off tempests, exorcised demons and succubi, and announced to the fugitive that sanctuary was nigh. But in this century their tintinnabulation gets on the nerves. The natives have no nerves; neither have the hardy Britons, who prowl the curved streets of Bruges or peep and botanise in the churchyards. It is the semineurasthenic American who is the sufferer, and after being aurally bombarded by the monsters of the Bruges belfry he cannot help remembering that the Chinese torture political prisoners by placing them bound under a big bell and literally tolling them to death. If Edgar Poe had lived in Bruges he would have added this line to his jingling Bells: O the binging and the banging of the hellsbells of Bruges.

We heard the celebrated Tony Nauwelaerts, champion bell player of Belgium, play the chimes at Bruges. As music it was horrible for sensitive ears, but as an exhibition of athletic skill it was excellent. Mendelssohn's Spring Song taken at a funereal tempo was one piece and later came the inevitable Chimes of Normandy. It was odd to hear a tune from Traviata and a few bars of what seemed intended for Put Down One and Carry Two from Victor Herbert's operetta Babes in Toyland at Bruges. You can endure the solemn tolling of the hours between now and eternity, but latter-day tunes are a synchronism.

We saw a little Kermesse one hot Sunday afternoon at Hoboken, a suburb of Antwerp. The joyous creaking carousel, the hokey-pokey ice-cream man, a small army of children yelling and dancing evoked a picture of Coney Island, a few thousand miles away. Some men in velveteens overcome by slumber and gin lay in the middle of the road; the dogs sniffed them and went their way; the tram engineers merely smiled. Yet drunkenness is by no means as prevalent in Belgium as it was ten years ago. A determined effort on the part of the church has, comparatively speaking, driven out the schnapps or gin drinkers. Sunday is a day of piety, followed by harmless recreation. People flock to the churchyards, for the cult of the dead is sedulously practised, or to the New Park in Antwerp, a vast tract of uncultivated meadows and trees. The summer proved disastrous to the foliage, and the walks are thick with dust. The most attractive spot in all Antwerp for an afternoon's outing is unquestionably the zoological gardens, behind the Central Station. The actual territory is small in comparison with the Bronx zoo, but it is agreeably laid out, and much is made of scanty resources. A new aquarium adds to the interest, although it cannot be compared with the one on the Marina at Naples. The band plays; people walk or sit sipping coffee; the air is cooler as dusk approaches, and you feel at peace with the world despite the mosquitoes.

The working man, the street labourer, for example, earns about a dollar a day. We watched a group from our window on the Place Verte lay down some rails for the tram-cars, and the amount of time consumed in proportion to the work performed was masterly. Here in practice was to be seen the prime concept of socialism, half a day's work for a whole day's wages. You won't find this set down so baldly in Marx or in the pamphlets of his followers, but that is what socialism, with its protean forms, amounts to; a sort of temporal sabotage, in which one man aids the other in wasting the minutes of his employers. They idly swept the tracks or laid down at an interval of ten minutes a Belgian block. It was positively exhilarating to see these blond giants stare at the neat, fresh-coloured servant-girls and pretend to labour. Occasionally one stole away and returned wiping his lips. Beer, sweet brown beer, is very cheap in Belgium. The country is honeycombed with socialism, and its results are far from assuring. Perhaps there is also a woman question; but we doubt it, as the women are the whole shooting-match here — the women and the dogs. Little wonder the men have gracefully resigned all cares of business into the hands of the women, who are marvels at petty swindling the green tourist on shopping bent, and also a great aid to the dogs in pushing or pulling wagons. The poor dogs suffer for want of water, otherwise are lusty and always barking.

We were held up on the railroad between Ghent and Bruges the other evening for three and a half hours. Usually the trip takes only forty minutes by the express. We had visited the Cathedral of St. Bavon in Ghent, had seen where as a boy Maurice Maeterlinck played pussy-cat with the late Georges Rodenbach; had seen the magnificent Adoration of the Pascal Lamb by the Van Eycks, and only regretted that old Mottez had died and that his once-celebrated restaurant on the Place d'Armes had disappeared; nevertheless we felt that the day had not been wasted, when the annoyance of spending several hours on the rails outside of Bruges came as a reminder that accidents will happen in the best regulated of systems. A passenger express from Ostend had overturned three freight cars of the usual match-wood variety common to these parts in the Bruges station. The excitement was terrific. An accident had never before occurred in this town; that is, in the memory of the oldest inhabitant. The station force was demoralised. Not a thing was done for half an hour. An eye-witness relates that for at least that length of time the head man and his assistants ran about like decapitated chickens, waving ineffectual wings, or arms, and exclaiming mightily. Then it occurred to some bright person that trains were being held up, fast trains from and to Brussels and Antwerp and Paris, from Ostend. If a few soldiers had been sent for from the city garrison the rails would have been clear in an hour. About nine o'clock, five hours after the mishap, the ways were free. About two hundred and fifty trains a day pass through the cramped station. Luckily they are building a larger one outside the town. We wished to get out of our train and walk in from Oostcamp, but the conductor said no; such a procedure, simple as it seemed, would have upset the entire system from Brussels to Bruges. Did we not have to surrender our tickets to an official at the latter place? There is red tape for you. At last twenty-five trains were halted within sight of the lights of Bruges, and not a human escaped.

The old town is as charming as ever, with its walks under the immemorial trees of the ramparts fringed by sombre canals, the scum on whose surface is a pistachio green. There is more noise than formerly and the city sadly suffers for the want of a first-rate hotel. There are several glorified boarding-houses with more or less indifferent imitations of a French cuisine; whereas the real Flemish cooking is preferable with its rich soups and sauces, its hochepot gantois — a sort of celestial hotchpot — and the still richer Burgundies. But you get none of these things at the hotels. The average visitors prefer tepid flavours and are correspondingly catered to; in the local restaurants you secure what you want, though the note of elegance is missing. The death of the venerable Van den Berghe, once a cook of unrivalled skill, is a great loss. The only two hotels that count are active rivals. Does the one set up an automobile, the other announces a lift, although there are but two low stories to the building; then the first puts a big flower vase electrically illuminated in its courtyard; you assist nightly at the incantation scene from Faust, without music; that operatic coup starts the second hotel into the extravagance of a private coach with a monogram, not to speak of a haughty coachman got up in the English mode. And so it goes. If only there were less bell-ringing and more native cookery Bruges would be still more desirable than it is — and we find it the most desirable spot in Europe for a summer or fall vacation. And with the exceptions of Prague, Toledo, Venice, it has no rival in picturesqueness. Every turn of an alley or waterway is a pure ravishment for the eye. We purposely refrain from again dilating upon the art of Memling, Van Eyck, and Gherard David, who may be studied here in all their efflorescence. If since Johann Sebastian Bach nothing new has been created in music, then no original painting has appeared since the magnificent work of Jan Van Eyck. His is indeed a lost art.

Another attraction in Bruges is its position as a summer city. In twenty minutes by express you may reach Ostend, Blankenberghe, Heyst (Heist), or Knocke, where the beaches, the vast stone piers, the huge hotels, and the high prices — that is at Ostend — fill the visitor with awe and admiration. Blankenberghe is rather too noisy, Knocke is cheap, Heyst is pretty and not too dear. At Ostend we paid sixty cents for two cups of poor coffee. At Duinberg, near Heyst, they play tennis behind dunes as big as cathedrals, play with a stretched tape instead of a net. They think it is very English. The sea is as wet and tumbling as at our beaches, and people enjoy themselves even as we do. There is much of a muchness even at these pretty Belgian bathing resorts. If you don't wish to go to Heyst or Knocke by the regular trains, steam tram-cars that start from the Bruges station and snort ferociously will carry you through a lovely region of meadows intersected by canals; by alleys of processional poplars you dream of Hobbema and his Mittelharnais alley or of Ruysdael as you pass a sudden silvery waterfall. Even the sunlight seems of silver as it glances through the white clouds, and the sight of a windmill revolving at a lenten pace reminds one that over here the rhythm of life if not exciting is at least conducive to content, which is the true equivalent of happiness.

You can't blame the Brugeois, who is a veritable burgher, for not becoming excited over Georges Rodenbach's Bruges la morte. The dead poet delicately scarified the gossiping inhabitants, mocked at their superstitions and called attention to their inquisitiveness, as evidenced by their telltale mirrors attached to so many windows. But they were right according to their lights. Bruges is a rattling, wide-awake, sparkling little city, not a dead one. If you want the poetic, albeit morbid, Bruges come over here in November when the mist hangs white scarfs of nebulosity on the Minnewater, where the black swans move like phantoms over the phlegmatic surface. Then Bruges la morte is to be seen, and after you have caught a nice cold you go to your inn through the dense fog to the accompaniment of the metallic clangour of the bells, bells, bells, and the next day you escape to Brussels. We prefer Bruges, the cheerful.

V

MADRID

SPAIN is not always sunny. Spain is not lyrically charming, as is Italy. Italy is a beautiful, coquettish woman; Spain is epical and sternly masculine. The barbers in Seville are not Figaros, and nowadays they dip their razors in antiseptic fluid. There are no bandits; the only bandits are the beggars. Spain is rapidly becoming modernised. Hotels of excellent quality may be found, railroad trains are seldom more than two hours behindhand, and the people do not dress like toreadors or gipsies; that is, on the streets. No romance left? Plenty of it; but not of the operatic sort. The Spain of the Cid, of Théophile Gautier and of Prosper Mérimée has vanished; it is now the Spain of Emilia Pardo Bazan, Blasco Ibañez, of Zuloaga; and, let it be added, it is as fascinating a Spain as in the days of Cervantes.

Nevertheless Spain is only partially civilised; she is still semibarbaric. For which fact travellers with a spoonful of imagination ought to be grateful. Spain is a laggard in the procession of the nations; yet she is still in the procession. And she is not decadent. The Moors left their impress on Spanish culture, but perhaps their importance has been exaggerated. Moorish architecture with its lace-like fioritura in ornamentation is marvellous to behold. The Alhambra is an Arabian Nights dream, though its fantastic beauty is outweighed by Spanish Gothic; the cathedral at Seville is infinitely more inspiring. It has been the good luck or the misfortune of Spain that her arts came to her from the outside: Flemings, Italians, French, and Moors. Even El Greco, who is more Spanish than Velasquez, was not a Spaniard. Ribera, despite his powerful personality, derived from Caravaggio; while Velasquez, half Portuguese, is the glory of Spain, the glory of the world.

The best Spanish dancing is not to be found in Spain to-day. You must go to Paris for Otero and Carmencita. Nor is the most characteristic cookery in Spain; at least, not in Madrid. The greatest Spanish opera was composed by the Frenchman Bizet. Mérimée has given the world veracious Spanish types. What does it matter if they are operatic? Carmen could not have been a gipsy, and Señora Bazan has proved that the cigarette girls of Seville are moral and hard-working; but the Carmen legend persists, it will always persist. Madrid is not the city to spear beloved and familiar Spanish character. Nor is Seville, for that matter; Seville out of season. During Easter week, when the city is masquerading, your taste for the footlights is gratified. Seville is then more Spanish than Spain. It is Toledo, only a few hours from Madrid, or, indeed, any of the small towns off the main travelled highways, that gives you a taste of real Spain. Granada is now a commonplace commercial community. Its charm has vanished. It needs summer moonlight to recreate the magic of the Alhambra.

To tear one's self away from beloved Paris when on the threshold of the season is a painful experience, for in the Louvre is the art of all lands — even if the Velasquezes have been reduced to that solitary and superb portrait of the Infanta Margarita. But a sure way to accelerate your departure is to go to the Opéra and hear a performance of Die Walküre. This we did, and longed for Spain — or New York. Dear old Delmas as a goatlike Wotan, Mother Grandjean as Brünnhilde (it is a toss-up who is shriller of lung, Bréval or Grandjean) and Journet as Hunding! The busy little director, Messager, conducted as if he had to catch a train for the suburbs. (He had.) Poor Wagner! One missed the millionaire Chauchard, who usually occupied that stage-box planted at the side of Hunding's hut. And one also missed Wagnerian atmosphere. Like the foolish father in Charpentier's Louise, you shake your fist at the opera-house, exclaiming "Oh, Paris!"

It was without regret, then, that we took our allotted seats in the southern express, bound for Madrid via Hendaye-Irun. It is the swiftest way to reach Spain; also the most expensive. You leave the Orléans station at 12:17 o'clock and ought to be in the Spanish capital twenty-six hours later. A noticeable slowing down after Irun and a slackness in the service remind you that you are on Spanish soil. But you miss a lot on this night trip. Bordeaux is viewed by daylight, Bayonne is not. Getting to Madrid in such short order has its renunciations. On the other hand, it is exhilarating to go to sleep at Irun — where you change cars, and see that your trunks accompany you — and awaken in staring sunshine and read the name of some station in the wildest region of rock and desert and mountain. Torquemada! You shiver and dream of the Inquisition, though Lea has partially dissipated its legend. But there it is — Torquemada. There are goats, too, and men a world too large for the donkeys they so lazily bestride. The scenery is volcanic; no trees, no water, no green. The sun blazes over these burnt-up stretches of stone and sand. How can life be supported in such a sterile land? Presently you are reminded of Mexico. Adobe huts, the same sort of humans, earrings, wide trousers, conical hats, and the inevitable donkey or mule. The few women are frowsy rather than picturesque. The stations are miserable affairs. It may be admitted that the first peep at Spain is not reassuring. What a different impression when one enters by way of Gibraltar-Algeciras. Southern Spain is entrancing.

The climate is mild and soothing to travel-worn nerves.

Madrid, a middle-class provincial city, is one that proved an agreeable disappointment. You hear so much of its dulness, its dirtiness, its high prices, its indifference toward strangers, and its lack of charm that when you have gone about for a few hours you exclaim against such slanders. High priced are the hotels on the Puerta del Sol and noisy. But no one who knows the ropes goes to them. As board and lodging are, as a rule, engaged at once, you may be asked one hundred pesetas or francs a day at a so-called fashionable house. Go, however, to a retired and admirable caravansary and a chamber with board for two will cost only fifty francs. Of course, almost every hotel has its drawbacks in Madrid. We looked out from the balcony (a national institution) on the noisy Calle del Principe and can vouch for the statement that many Spaniards never go to bed in the night-time. Such gabbling. Such smoking — the tobacco in Spain is strong, cheap, and of good flavour — such quarrelling and laughter. And from neighbouring balconies voices would join in the discussion. A mandolin was plucked and a voice hummed passionately and out of tune. The material for romance was close at hand, but we were too sleepy to appreciate it. The Ferrer affair was agitating all Spain that week — he was shot on October 13 — and the Puerta del Sol was jammed by sullen crowds.

We saw no overt acts of violence, but one could note that the temper of the populace was ugly. Perhaps it was because so much conversational steam was let off during the night that the Barcelona violence was not repeated at Madrid. We wisely held our peace on the subject; while the Spaniard is the politest person in the world, his politics must be respected. Quite as many approved of Ferrer's execution as execrated it; that is, in Madrid.

We said that the Spaniard is polite. It is true. He is sincere, in a grave, virile manner. His treatment of the Americans proves it. The bitterness still rankles, yet he talks frankly and tells you that Spain is well rid of Cuba and the Philippines. It is impossible to doubt him. Madrid is second-rate, no doubt, but it is a homelike town, where you are not stared to death, where no one is in a hurry, for the motto is still mañana; where the men are better looking than the women; one looks in vain for the slender Goya majas, with the saddleback, the dusky green eyes, the comb, mantilla, and fan; instead are mediocre imitations of Paris; numerous fat ladies, as many brown haired as black, rice powder on sallow skins, feminine moustaches, lace scarfs, fans, of course, no eyes of midnight hue, and no beauties. The cafés are comfortable, the beer is fair — a Spanish Pilsner — slightly sweet, brewed by the ubiquitous German. The beggars are a terrible nuisance, they are everywhere. And such cripples! Victor Hugo could have found new patterns for his Cour des Miracles in Madrid. Repulsive half-men jerk your coat tail, asking alms in the name of Christ. Goya-like hags and children afflicted with sores that revolt your senses supplicate. You sit at a café table. At once a blind family appears and a concert begins. Each member plays an instrument (the humble ocarina is in vogue here); or an orchestra of blind men makes hideous the afternoon. Not once do you hear a strain of Spanish music from these perambulating noise makers. But you give them something. Every one does. The temper of the Spanish is lenient toward its beggars.

In vain we sought the so-called Flamenca dancers; the dreariest dancing is in Madrid. Later, in Seville, we saw the genuine dances and were very much surprised. There is little excitement, beauty, character, in this capering of a half dozen sallow alleged gipsies who, when smiling, displayed a half inch of pink gums. Zuloaga has trapped the type to perfection, and in Spain, with its cruel, diffused light, you understand the patchwork of his colour, his use of primary tints. You meet his old women beggars and gipsies all over Spain.

The Madrileñian eschews the national dancing; he seems ashamed of it. The bull-fighting is going the same way, though it may not die out for a century. Our first bull-fight was a fizzle. We prefer an abattoir. To be frank, the sport is sillier than football, though not as cruel. The meanest feature is not the slaughter of mild old cattle but the occasional disembowelment of a horse. The toreadors, matadors, picadors are operatic creatures, more spoiled than Italian tenors and thrice as useless; otherwise the massed impression is gay and worth the trouble of gaining. As it is with the dancing so with the eating. Real Spanish cookery is only to be had in some humble restaurant. The noble garlic (ajo), so happy an ingredient in salad, is absent at hotel tables. Peppery dishes are missing; too much deference is paid to foreign palates. It is the same with sauerkraut in Germany, with macaroni in Italy, with frogs' legs in France. So much fun has been poked at national dishes that Señor Gomez told us the Spanish have become sensitive on the subject of garlic. But we had tortilla con jamon (omelet with ham), renones à la brochette (kidneys), pescado frito and puchero (pot au feu), with its garbanzos (white beans). Gaspacho we did not taste, nor the famous olla podrida.

Here is an average menu for luncheon: Entremeses: (olives, radishes, butter); ostras (small oysters, metallic in flavour); tortilla á la Francesca (omelet); entrecot á la bordelesa; denton salsa verde (a good fish); fiambres à l'aspic; pasteles variados (pastry); quesos y frutas (fruit), washed down with either a fiery Valdepeñas, a fiery Spanish Burgundy, or a smooth Rio Romay. This at the regular hotel table d'hôte at the Inglese. Nevertheless there is a little Spanish restaurant on the Rue du Helder, Paris, where the food is more national.

The street cries, never ending, are interesting. We heard one old woman with a voice like Scalchi's, when that singer had a quartet in her larynx. We confess, however, that the most Spanish looking woman we ever saw was not in Spain, but on the boards of the Metropolitan Opera House. Her name is Lilli Lehmann, and she sang the part of Donna Anna in Don Giovanni. Tall, grave, raven of hair, with eyes like stars, she was the Spanish aristocrat. She revealed race and character. Certainly none of the prognathic jawed Hapsburgs look so Spanish or so noble; which illustrates what Henry James once wrote in his tale The Real Thing. In this case truth was inferior to fiction.

The secular charm of Madrid is in its wide avenues, such as the Calle de Alcalá, its park, the walk through the Prado, its royal palace, a few churches, a few public buildings. The Prado is simply a boon on a hot day — and it's a fierce sun that beats on the city, treacherous as is its night air. Across the way a new hotel has been erected by the Ritz-Carlton Company. The prices are sufficiently exalted to make the hotel men on the Puerta del Sol open their ingenuous eyes in astonishment.

In conclusion, we warn the timid tourist that he is quite as apt to lose his baggage in Italy as in Spain; that travel is by no means a hardship, though there ought to be more corridor cars; that the railway restaurants are better than any of the same class in America; that the Spanish are kind-hearted, considerate, unfailingly courteous, ever optimistic, and anxious that the golden shower of foreign money be diverted from France and Italy to their own tremendously romantic land.

VI

DEAR OLD DUBLIN

I

After all, blood is thicker than water; in Ireland it is even thicker than whisky. I forgot the joys of Vienna, the trim existence of them that reside in Berlin on the River Spree, when, after a ride through the Happy Valley, Wales, I found myself on the Irish Sea, then on Irish soil at Kingstown. The reason I speak of blood is because I'm half Irish by descent and was brought up in the good old-fashioned beliefs: Ireland, the Isle of Saints; Ireland, oppressed by the Sassenach; Ireland, the land of the bravest men and best women; Ireland, the most beautiful country on God's footstool.

I had read and believed in the Ireland of Samuel Lover and Charles Lever, of Carlton and Dion Boucicault's Colleen Bawn, of Tom Moore, and Father Burke. The New Ireland, the Celtic Awakening, the new-fangled fairies of Yeats, the mystic music of A. E. (George Russell), the exquisite carolling of a younger choir, the bitter-sweet pathos and humour and dramatic power of John Synge — all these were not in existence when I was a lad; nor were Lady Gregory's gods and fighting men and the epical Cuchalain and Deirdre. Instead, I was fed upon splendid legends of Fenianism. My grandfather, James Gibbons, had been vice-president of the American organisation.

You may imagine what a different Ireland was unfolded when I read T. W. Rolleston's Anthology of Celtic Poetry. The "natural magic" of Matthew Arnold is not missing in the new men and women; the ancient and fascinating poetic potion of smiles, tears, and tenderness is as cunningly concocted as ever, for as long as there is a Celt on the rind of our planet there you will find sentiment and romance. All the busy professors of criticism cannot kill romance with their little metallic essays. Romance is out of fashion? Go to Ireland and see if it is.

"An' I wisht I was in Ireland the livelong day . . . Och! Corrymeela an' the blue sky over it." Well, I got there last June, and, while I didn't find Moira O'Neill's Corrymeela, I discovered Dublin; also discovered that the Irish of Ireland don't come over from Liverpool on cattle boats, as Bernard Shaw ingenuously suggested; nevertheless, the race is much more like the men and women of Synge, Yeats, Lady Gregory, Martyn, George Moore, Birmingham, Dr. Hyde, and Shaw than the stage Irishman of a past generation. (I even discovered that the Celtic Casanova and the Irish Ibsen were familiarly called Jarge Moore and Barney Shaw.) The modern Irishman is rather melancholy, a pessimist born, and his womenkind are the reverse: robust, hopeful, hard-working.

I've reached Kingstown. The trip across was ideal. The British fleet is in the harbour. Everywhere bunting, gaiety, and patriotic demonstrations. The Irishman at home is very English. In the general excitement I forgot to sphygmograph my feelings, and presently, after a brief, bumpy railway ride, found myself in a hotel on Sackville Street. The view either way was impressive. But if mighty London appears down at the heel after a sojourn in Berlin, then in a figurative sense Dublin is simply barefooted.

It is very dirty. There are too many beggars; beggary in Ireland is raised to the dignity of a sport. Buxom women with nursing children implore you for a penny, and if you refuse, smile at you so forgivingly that you double in your tracks to make speedy reparation. The Irish are good-humoured, and it must be their transplantation that makes them less so in America. That they are as humorous as witty I am not so sure. John Quinn contends that they are not, but he underwent the rigours of Irish Players' ructions in New York and Philadelphia, and the enormous imbecility of that affair was enough to make any one a sceptic on the subject.

I couldn't help thinking that the public buildings would be less mouldy after a house cleaning.

Ireland, like all Europe, is more in need of bath-tubs than armaments. Cleanliness there would be greater than godliness. A first-class hotel there is not in the place, though the national cookery is better than in London. The best roast beef in the British Isles is to be found in Dublin, but that fact is a thrice-told tale, like the excellence of the porter. There are few restaurants; one dines at his hotel, though there is an excellent French café and one spot at least where Pilsner is kept by a man with a Celtic name all wool and a yard wide.

As for home rule, Ulster's wooden oaths and wooden rifles, the revival of the spirit of Boyne Water, "Croppies lie down," and Ulsteria, I found few traces. Throughout the south there is but little enthusiasm for home rule, though no actual hostility. "What is home rule?" one Dublinite asked of me. "How can any one say what it will be like?" he continued. He was a good Catholic, but he had his misgivings about increasing the power of the Church in the land, and that is what is feared. George Moore is not the only Irish writer who sees through the hole in the millstone. The old faith is strong in the Ould Dart, but there is a growing scepticism as to the value of a political clergy; furthermore, there are too many able-bodied lads and lassies taking orders and filling convents when they ought to be better employed in fathering and mothering families. There are several ways of race suicide. Ireland is practically short of people, for, if the emigration has fallen off, so has the birth-rate, and a country peopled by saints would not be a country worth living in. Gerald (Jeremiah is the real name) O'Donovan's novel, Father Ralph, is conceded to contain wholesome truths. And it is by no means an indictment of religion, only of the creaking machinery of a certain Irish clericalism.

You see, I've reached Dublin, but I haven't left the hotel. Roast beef, Guinness's stouts, and politics kept me indoors, and, with no Baedeker to help, I was forced to be my own guide. (Herr Baedeker hasn't thus far condescended to include Ireland in his invaluable list of travel books, and, oddly enough, Dublin contains little literature on the subject.)

II

Thus spake the ancient Stanihurst:

"The seat of the citie is of all sides pleasant, comfortable, and wholesome. If you would traverse hills, they are not far off. If Champaign land, it lieth of all parts. If you would be delited with fresh water, the famous river called the Liffie, named of Ptolome Lybnium, runneth fast by. If you will take the view of the sea, it is at hand."

This chronicler did not exaggerate. The air in Dublin is charged with salt odours. You sniff the sea fish. My hereditary enthusiasms revived when I found myself in front of Trinity

College and the Bank of Ireland, and how charming the lake in Stephen's Green and the winding walks of this park! A more impressive building than that of the Law Courts is seldom seen, and to match it there is the Custom House. As for churches, there is no lack. St. Patrick's Cathedral is a noble pile, so is Christ Church Cathedral. The believer in the old faith must be saddened at the service in St. Patrick's — the Church of England and St. Patrick! — but for all that it is a noble place of preaching duly arresting.

I went over to the procathedral to an early mass and was touched by the fervid piety of the congregation and appalled by the abundant evidences of poverty. Outside of Spain no such poverty is to be found, and in many parts of the island it is worse, and with intemperance as an accompaniment. Why? Is it altogether the fault of the Sassenach, the hated but much-courted Saxon? Admiring the time-battered — scarred by the revengeful hands of patriots — statue of King William by Grinling Gibbons on the college green, I passed within the historical precincts of Trinity, passed the statues of Burke and Goldsmith, and, mindful of Bishop Berkeley, Dean Swift, Robert Emmet, Thomas Moore, the learned Ussher, Edmund Burke, not forgetting my friend, the late Professor Edward Dowden, I reached the trees in the park opposite the Kildare Club, at the corner of Nassau Street, and smoked the pipe of peace under a soft blue sky, through which wind-propelled white cloud-hummocks lazily passed.

This, I said to myself, is the real Ireland, not the too busy, commercial Belfast or the prosperous "far-down" of Donegal. I felt at home, as I never felt at home in Budapest. The two and three story houses across the park recalled my native city of Philadelphia; even the accent of the Dublin people was like music in my ears — streaked, as it was, with an insinuating brogue, but infinitely purer English than the grotesque cockney accent of London. To be sure, I had dined on wonderful mutton, washed it down with appropriate fluids, and was smoking good tobacco; therefore cheerfully disposed. In my hand I held a blackthorn. Afar came the sound of the tram-car on Nassau Street. I thought of the times when James van Gogh Gregg, better known as El Greggo, raised his mellifluous voice in the stadium, or when Dean Swift coined epigrams striking dismay in the heart of Delany of Delville; of Henry Grattan and Wolfe Tone; of Daniel O'Connell, and the night that Larry was stretched — "Oh, the hemp will be soon around my throttle and choke my poor windpipe to death!" — of Handel and his Messiah, sung in the old Music Hall centuries ago; of Samuel Lover and his famous grandson, Victor Herbert; of Harry Lorrequer; of unhappy Oscar O'Flaherty Wilde — a more unreal figure to-day than either Harry Lorrequer or Charles O'Malley — and of cabbages and kings.

Then the omnipresent guide begged me to visit the interior of the college, but for that day, at least, I refused. I dislike relics, muddy portraits; above all, I dislike inhuman documents. Day dreams and soothing tobacco were more in the Celtic key than futile rummaging in the coprolitic mud of antiquity. However, the guide was too decent a chap to insist — only Irish-Americans, so-called, are insistent — and he sat him down hard by and smoked his pipe. Then he fell to conversing.

"Why does that President of yours call himself an Irishman?" he asked. (My speech betrayed my nationality.) I was startled. Had Dr. Wilson been discovered? I put this to the guide. He in his turn was puzzled.

"Wilson," he retorted, "I don't know any President named Wilson in the States. I mean a man who calls himself Bryan, the real President, I take it, and not an Irishman, by the same token, for no Irishman would drop the 'O' from his name; no Irishman would drink grape juice; above all, no true Irishman would change his faith." And with that he left me to my thoughts.

An Irishman, I reflected, is either fiddling in the zenith with the archangels or he is wrangling in the nethermost hell with Satan and his spit and spawn. The Irish and the Poles are chips off the same temperamental block.

Naturally, I visited the Castle and a dozen buildings of historic interest, veritable treasure-troves for antiquarians; but I was held in the spell of the streets and the look in the faces of passers-by, or by the fair lawns of Phœnix Park. I know I should have been overcome by the prospect of Sackville Street, the Nelson Pillar, and the stately Post-Office, but I preferred the small and altogether attractive Zoological Garden, where the peacocks, cranes, and ducks troop after you crying for crackers and the lions roar like Irish sucking doves. It is not a large collection, this, but within its limits it is complete; the lions are numerous and the primates true natives. Far more real to me was Chapelizod, where Isod or Isolde of Malory's romance walked and talked in company with Brangaene. Nothing but a memory, not even a handful of stone marks the spot. In Dublin City there was at one time Izod's Tower on the walls, but for a sight of the living Isolde you must go to Gotham, when Olive Fremstad sings and Arturo Toscanini conducts. The Metropolitan Opera House is now the only Chapelizod.

You will like Grafton Street, and if you are a mere man, Duke near Grafton Street. (This is a secret like the pattern in the carpet of Henry James; but I don't mind telling you that Pilsner from Pilsen is very real at that spot.) What boots it to struggle in chill prose with descriptions of Bray Head, of Dalkey, or Killiney Bay, and Sorrento? Yes, an Irish Sorrento, with its cup of blue liquid and its shore an emerald green curve of trees. You remember

Walter Pater's slighting criticism of Alpine lakes as "pots of blue paint"? "The pots" are here, marvellously cerulean, as a background the Wicklow Mountains. No wonder you think of Sorrento, the Bay of Naples, even of Vesuvius, for here towers the peak of Sugarloaf. Beyond the Dublin and Wicklow Mountains is truly a sainted land, holy with beauty, Glendalough, the Vale of Ovoca, "the meeting of the waters," Powerscourt, and gardens that haunt the memory. You forget the blood-drenched history of the countryside, forget Donnybrook Fair, the Blarney Stone, and the jaunting-cars, and only enjoy this beauty; and soon the chords of patriotism sound and you feel proud to call yourself Irish, or even half Irish. The very soil is sacred with its bones of the martyred dead. I became so overwrought that to restore the balance I motored back to Dublin to see the Honourable Richard Croker of Crokersville, and a grand place Himself has, a show-place for every one that visits Dublin.

The little streets and dirty alleys are not to be missed. There, as in Naples, you come to grips with the population. Never once did I hear a solitary soul whistle The Valley Lay Smiling Before Me (to the tune of Pretty Girl Milking the Cow), or The Harp That Once Thro' Tara's Halls, or The Wearing of the Green; instead, ragtime and vulgar London music-hall ditties were sung or piped. In an ugly, crowded street full of Sunday-morning drunkards and leading to St. Patrick's Cathedral I saw a poster advertising breakfast food. A militant suffragette is depicted behind the bars in jail. She is emaciated from self-imposed starvation, but when shown the food by the keeper, what all the king's horses and all the king's men couldn't accomplish with this petticoated Humpty-Dumpty, the appetising food is supposed to do. She clamours for it, and the moral is irresistibly conveyed: even the most stubborn suffragette must eat our patent food! Great are the uses of advertisement.

My second visit to Dublin was not as pleasant as the first. I went over from Holland and landed in the very heat and disorder of the strike. Now, the striking Irishman is not a pleasant companion in New York; in Dublin he is far worse. Not for me to discuss the economical cause of the strike, but they tell a pretty story of starvation wages and exhausting labour hours. The employers have their side of the question. I never wish to see again the panic which occurred during the funeral of the unlucky James Nolan, whose skull had been battered in during a shindy with the police. It was terrifying, as much so to me in my hotel window facing on Sackville Street, near the Pillar, as to the mob that was "rushed" by the constabulary. If such treatment were accorded the public at one of our gatherings in the streets, vengeance would be swift. I quite agree with those who think the police were too brutal with their own people; not that the rioting Irishman is a pleasing spectacle, but in this case it was the women and children who were the sufferers. I heard, too, that Nolan was not the "I'm blue mouldy for want of a batin'" type of man. Mr. H. J. Howard in his book on Dublin quotes Giraldus Cambrensis: "Perchance it is the chastisement of God, whereby these lands are suffered to struggle continually one with the other, so that neither is England ever wholly victorious, nor Ireland thoroughly subdued." I suppose a thousand years hence there will still be an Irish question.

III

During his last pilgrimage to New England Henry James tells of the "emotion of recognition" he experienced when coming face to face with some specimens of Monet and other French impressionists in a most unexpected place. Evidently, for him Massachusetts and Monet did not effectively modulate. The anecdote threw much light on the artistic bias of the James temperament. I enjoyed the same sort of a thrill when I first visited the Municipal Gallery on Harcourt Street, although the primary reason of my presence in Dublin was the prospect of studying the collection of modern art gathered there through the efforts of Sir Hugh Lane. I was not disappointed. It is the finest assemblage of certain artists outside of the Luxembourg Gallery, Paris, and the Mesdag Gallery at The Hague. Not London, not New York can boast a better Edouard Manet than the large canvas, Eva Gonzalez, or the indescribably coloured Concert in the Tuileries Garden (with its dimly descried portrait of Charles Baudelaire).

There are several Claude Monets of various periods, all masterpieces. Renoir's Umbrellas is striking, while the names of J. E. Blanche, Pissarro, Vuillard, Degas, Le Sidaner, Mancini (too many to be effective), Corot, Barye (his oils), Troyon, Fantin-Latour, Fromentin, Courbet, Harpignies, Diaz, Gérôme, Bonvin, Rousseau, and a splendid study by Puvis de Chavannes, Boldini, Monticelli are not missing, nor is Daumier (a noble version of his Don Quixote and Sancho Panza); also Cottet, James Maris, Mauve, Alfred Stevens, Legros, Mesdag, and others may be seen. In the British section there are to be found the names of Brangwyn, Charles Conder, whose fame since his death has justly grown by leaps and bounds, also his posthumous prices, Gerald Festus Kelly (a discreet-toned portrait of a lovable Irish gentlewoman), Simeon Solomon, Watts, D. Y. Cameron, Wilson Steer, Charles Ricketts, John Constable, Sickert, Albert Moore, Whistler, Rothenstein, George Clausen, and C. H. Shannon (The brilliant Lady with the Green Fan).

The Irish section is well to the fore, as it should be. Nathaniel Hone, with his simple, sincere landscapes and marines; John Lavery, as ever, distinguished; George Russell, John Butler Yeats, Mark Fisher, J. J. Shannon, Osborne, Roche, Duffy, William Orpen, O'Meara, Roderick O'Conor. There are several rooms devoted to original drawings, the Millets coming out strong. The gallery of portraits is particularly interesting. Among the sculptures you will note the Age of Bronze, the Man with the Broken Nose, the Honourable George Wyndham, Bernard Shaw, Le Prêtre, Frère et Soeur, by Auguste Rodin, of which the Age of Bronze is the most important. The Shaw portrait bust is too "slicked up" for either Rodin or St. Bernard. Himself is neither so handsome nor so vapid looking. Rodin must have executed this marble in one of his perverse moods, possibly saying to himself: "Go to! I'll show the world that this Puck-like Irishman is in reality a conventional citizen." Certainly he has succeeded.

Barye's bronzes there are, and works by Furse, Lanteri, John Hughes, Paul Bartlett (New York), V. Rivière, Dalou, and the gifted Jacob Epstein (New York). I must not forget the names of John Sargent, Jongkind, Augustus John, a mural decoration, or a portrait of Daumier by Daubigny — an unusual combination. The Beheading of John the Baptist, by Puvis, is a large canvas. I prefer the reduced variation of the same theme by Puvis in the gallery of John Quinn, Esq., New York, as being richer in colour quality and more intense in conception. An amazing collection. An amazing experience, indeed, to find such art near the banks of the drab River Liffey. And what a tribute to the taste and generosity of the donor, Sir Hugh Lane. I hope some day to see the pictures housed in more commodious quarters. My abiding impressions of the various visits I made to Harcourt Street are the two Manets, especially the Concert.

A second artistic surprise was to find in the little known (that is in America) National Gallery of Ireland (of which Sir Hugh Lane is now the director) an array of canvases of prime quality, such as examples by Mantegna, Titian — the Disciples at Emmaus, otherwise known as the Tablecloth (not the original, but a variation?) — a beautiful Moroni, a fine Rembrandt, Jondarus, a lively little virgin and child by Adrian Ysenbrandt, a Van der Helst, a Frans Hals, a version of his Beach Boy at Antwerp, Botticelli's moving portrait of a violinist, Ruysdael, Ribera, Antonio da Solari, two Bonafazios, Carpaccio, Watteau, Reynolds, Jan Steen, Goya, Wilson, Cuyp, Raeburn, Thomas Lawrence (portrait of John Philpot Curran), Wouter Knyff, Gainsborough, Chardin, Coello, and in the National Portrait Gallery section characteristic heads of Jonathan Swift and several of Samuel Lover, one by Harwood, the other self-painted. A handsome old gentleman he must have been, and a versatile. He is Victor Herbert's grandfather — a title that alone gives him celebrity. Verily, you exclaim as you go out upon aristocratic Merrion Square, recalling in appearance both Washington Square and Rittenhouse Square (Philadelphia), verily, Dublin is the great unexplored for the majority of travellers.

VII

FIGHTING FAT AT MARIENBAD

Naturally, you must be fat, else a trip to northwestern Bohemia, where lies the charming little town of Marienbad, may result in the acquisition of avoirdupois, for, oh, brethren! Pilsen is only a few hours away — Pilsen, where the amber brew is beautifully brewed. Eating, too, is one of the seven arts. And once in Pilsen, farewell to shapes of slimness, farewell normal necks and wrists and waists. Jules Laforgue, that brilliant young Frenchman who was psychologist before poet, remarked upon the peculiar arrogance and imperturbability that large majestic women exhibit. His explanation of their attitude toward life proves his keen vision. "Cet avant de notre personne," he declares, surely breeds a feeling of superiority, leads to a pompous gait and a condescending manner. Wasn't it Dickens who compared women of certain weight to a ship of battle with all sails set? When you have achieved the eminence from which you gaze across your own bulk at your fellow beings, then it is time for a reduction cure at Marienbad. I had, some time ago, reached that interesting period when my friends didn't hesitate to poke me in the ribs — or where the ribs should have been — and advised me to join the fat men's club, any member of which must not weigh less than two hundred pounds, else be expelled from that paradise of clambakes and beefsteak dinners. So I went to Marienbad, and, incredible as it may sound, stopped at Pilsen only long enough to drink a glass of water. The water was not cold, though the heat was tropical, and it cost one penny for the glass. But I paid it. I had taken the first step in the steep path that leads up the mount of martyrdom.

Marienbad is not difficult of access. Five hours from Berlin on the fast express (there are slow ones in Germany), a day from Paris, and, if you happen to be at Karlsbad, you can go over in less than two hours. It may be that I am not a fanatic on the subject of fighting fat. Every train-load winding through the valleys and over the hills of Bohemia carries sceptics. Your reasonable objections are pooh-poohed out of court, and the fabulous tales are related of friends losing ten pounds a day for thirty days and then gaining thirty pounds in thirty hours — or some such rigmarole. The number of Germans I met after my arrival on the Kaiserstrasse, the main street, convinced me that the Lord loves a good liar, no matter his nationality. Two conspicuous things smote my consciousness when I had been ten minutes in Marienbad. One was the number of fat, healthy men and women; the other was the unusual display of food, whether in delicatessen shops, confectionery stores, bakeries; food — and drink — is the staple of the place. It took some time before I conjoined these two signs and the closeness of cause and effect. After a tour of the restaurants and cafés it burst upon me that the "cure" was only an incentive to hunger and thirst, that even if your particular hell was paved with good intentions, the temptations to gorge and guzzle were manifold. Where, this side of the fabled city in which roasted larks fall from the skies, can you find such a bewitching array of good things to eat as at Marienbad? The windows are stuffed to overflowing with fowl, game, fruit, and the toothsome cakes called oblaten. At dusk when you return from a thirteen-mile walk, footsore, thirsty, starving — you, being an obedient patient, have had cold ham, and, later, weak tea for dinner — the artful shopmen flaunt before your eyes a stupendous array of food and drink. You stand agape at the Tantalus vision, and then, if you are strong, you pass sadly on to more cold ham, more weak tea. I modified this first judgment later, for, in a collection of many thousand people, there are a few who are consistent, who adhere to the rules laid down by the doctors. However, the authorities shouldn't allow the weak-minded to be tempted. The shop-windows should be closed after dark, and the restaurants forced to hide their diners behind screens. An ascetic fresh from his Thebaid would shiver at the sight of all these well-fed persons stuffing meat — yes, and potatoes, too — and pouring down Pilsner from jugs fit for the throat of a giraffe. And further inviting the advances of old Uncle Uric (acid), as Acton Davies affectionately calls him.

Infinitely discouraged, then, during my first evening, because of these pagan-like evidences of revolt, I could not help thinking of Æsop and his choice fable, wherein the members rise up in rebellion against the stomach and are speedily quelled by that organ. The doctors, I reflected, may prescribe the strictest regimen; the waters may be religiously drunk every morning, but at eight o'clock in the evening that primal old rebel, that Lucifer among the bodily organs — the stomach — will exact due toll and homage for the hardships imposed upon it during the daytime. Wondering why I did not stop over at Pilsen, I fell asleep and dreamed of a brewery in which the waiters and guests were awful-appearing skeletons. The next day I sought a physician. Both an individual and a type, he regarded me with cynical, roguish eyes. "You Americans," he observed, "expect to bolt your meals, take no exercise except in express elevators, then come to Marienbad and lose five pounds a day without feeling nervous. I don't believe in taking off fat too fast." Slap number two was this, and straight between the eyes. A doctor in full practice at Marienbad who didn't believe in rapid reduction! He explained. I listened.

Then I became humble and determined to give the "cure" a working chance.

At six o'clock the next morning I was awakened by the solemn measures of a Bach choral played by the local orchestra, and as I dressed I listened to some excellent, old-fashioned overtures, seldom heard nowadays, from half-forgotten operas by Auber, Rossini, and Meyerbeer. They proved good company for the grey thoughts of the neophyte. Out upon the esplanade I fancied myself in fairy-land; it was the kind of operatic landscape one sees on the stage. The huge promenade was bustling with humans; men in silk hats and jackets; women in bath-robes, wearing diamonds; Galician Jews, with oily side-curls, their eyes bent on the earth, muttering prayers as they paraded; fat people and lean; fatter people than I ever saw before at a given point — and every one carrying graduated glasses, suggestively pharmaceutical — sipping, staring, chattering; above all, staring. Then there was a mad rush to a certain point; even the long line of those who patiently awaited their turn at the spring was broken. Somebody of eminence approached. Looking very much like a prosperous Hebraic Wall Street banker, the King of England went by with a remarkably spry gait for a man of his years. He was accompanied by his friend Captain Fitz Ponsonby and Sir Stanley Clark.

We looked after him with the rest, and, as we were very curious, joined the thronging crowd that doged his movements. King Edward VII was very popular. The poor Polish Jews fairly worshipped him, for he was sympathetic. As if the earth contained no bomb-throwing assassins, the King of Great Britain and Emperor of the Indies came down every morning of his two weeks' sojourn at seven o'clock precisely. His valet handed him a glass, a glass tube, and a red napkin. He drank, walked, talked, and if the day were fine, laughed. Such a hearty, unaffected laugh you do not hear often from the lungs of a young man. Everything amused him. He had forgotten affairs of state, forgotten, too, tedious ceremonial. He wore a loose-fitting flannel or tweed and sported an Alpine stalker upon his imperial brow. When he stopped, several thousand people stopped; when he paused to pay a pretty shop-girl in the Colonnade a compliment, a gratified murmur was heard in the vast mob. He had done a popular thing and that girl is marked for life. She will tell her grandchildren of the royal blue eyes and the perfect royal German accent. A few secret-service men kept close to the exalted visitor, but, as one old Bohemian said: "The King of England can do what the King of Austria cannot, even in his own realm!"

The day the King of Greece appeared and with Sir Arthur Goschen stood and gossiped with Edward VII, excitement ran so high that the next day the Burgomaster plastered the town with the announcement that such enthusiasm must be gently discouraged. Karlsbad, boiling over with envy, was in the seventh heaven. "Mobbed the King of England" was the head-line in the local newspapers. But when the King went over one afternoon to Karlsbad in a motor-car, he was literally forced to go indoors so persistent was the sightseeing crowd of that place.

However, kings and dukes, princesses and dames of high degree are so many bubbles on the surface of the tranquil Marienbad waters. We go there to be cured — or to get a new appetite, or bath; and while it is mildly exhilarating to rub shoulders with the mighty ones of the earth, it is far more important to secure a seat for breakfast.

Your water drunk, you go for your breakfast at Utscheg's. After many futile wanderings, climbing to Café Panorama or Café Egerlander for the first meal, I came to the conclusion that man may dispense with landscapes at dawn, if his coffee be near at hand. So to a modest chalet I repaired at eight o'clock, resolved to drink weak tea and eat but one soft-boiled egg. Alas! I always drank coffee and took two eggs. My doctor had said: "Do not starve yourself" — as he did not favour swift flesh reduction. After breakfast arose the important question of the day: which walk should one take? If you are not lucky enough to secure permission from your doctor to bathe at the Turkish or mud-baths there is nothing left for you but trotting. The walks of Marienbad! It is a proud municipal boast that not in Bohemia is there such a variety of shaded, romantic, and toilsome walks. This seems to be true. The hills are not so high as at Karlsbad; they are prettier, and the sweep of country you catch at the top of the Café Panorama or Café Rübezahl is most inspiring. The Bavarian mountains in the dim distance and the dense Bohemian forests; a country that rolls with green reverberations in the golden sunshine, a naturally romantic landscape trained by artistic gardeners; a mass of marble and granite structures, imposing in size, graceful in architectural line; all these framed by pine-trees and a melting southern sky — you feel as you fill your lungs with the pure, sweet-smelling air, that there are few such spots as Marienbad on our globe.

And the everlasting twistings and turnings of the forest paths; the mystic twilight of the wooded avenues; the sheer ascent to some remote peak where coffee and conversation crown your tired feet for a small fee! Then in some sudden secret glade which seems all your own, as you dream of St. Wenceslaus, the patron saint of Bohemia, of brave John Huss, or of the rustling melodies of Antonin Dvořák — you enjoy better in his native land his music — suddenly a ponderous figure bars your path. Mayhap you have heard it before you have seen it, an elephant crushing through the underbrake. It weighs at least three hundred, and smilingly attempts to pass. When fat meets fat then comes the tug of tact. Two hats are lifted as the weaker — the thinner — goes to the wall, or sits down, or cowers against the hillside. Thus is your dream disturbed a dozen times a day. As the monster puffs noisily from view you tentatively remark to your companion: "I hope I'm not as big as that animal," while the answer, though not consoling, is invariably the same: "No, but you soon will be if you don't obey the doctor." Yes, mild as are the injunctions of the doctor, he is not always obeyed. The spirit is willing but the flesh is ever athirst and ahungered. There are rainy days (and how it can rain in the land of the Czechs!), when the whole scheme of creation needs readjustment, not to mention this miserable little Marienbad. There are hot days when the thought of an ice-cream soda drives one almost delirious. There are sombre evenings, when, to see fat men drinking cool Pilsner — oh, why continue? These things happen to every one. They are not serious deterrents to the good cause. There are brave days when you walk fifteen miles, live on tea without milk or sugar, and spinach (doleful, gritty spinach), and the eternal ham; nevertheless, the scales tell you agreeable news, and your head feels as cool, as empty as a gourd in a cellar. You pityingly sneer at the fattest man — he weighs over four hundred, wears a red necktie, and is always eating candy or ices — and you know that life is worth while. The unhappy chap told me that formerly he was a chef at the royal palace, Potsdam, but champagne had been his ruin. The following season I was informed he died. One comical sight was the small peasant boy who followed him with a chair — he had to sit down every few minutes. He assured me that he had lost over one hundred pounds during the season.

On fine days you occupy, if so inclined, the rustic spot where Goethe rested — he was a visitor in 1821 — or else gaze upon the house where lived, in 1845, Richard Wagner. Chopin, too, was there in 1836. Then, after these sentimental pilgrimages, you become prosaic and have yourself weighed. You retire exultingly to a café, for you have lost ten pounds in ten days. How did it come about? Your doctor looks wise and tells you that the waters — Yes, the waters; rather not the waters, that is, no water at meals. The secret of Marienbad is yours when you have mastered this point. The waters are mild, almost tasteless; two or three glasses a day is all you are asked to consume. Glauber salts is the chief ingredient. At the Rudolfsquelle the relief from gouty pains is rapid. But are the waters everything at Marienbad? The answer is a decided negative. Remember that thousands are cured annually of various ills. Can it be done elsewhere? Yes. In twenty-two days I lost twenty-two pounds. Walking, dieting, early in bed, early rising, incomparably fresh air — all these make for health, for fat-destroying, for muscle-building, blood-purifying. Yet I affirm with all the solemnity of a man who won back his adipose tissue six months after his return to New York, that the secret of reduction is so simple that it usually escapes the attention of the patients who travel so many miles to find it. It is this: Don't drink with your meals — tea, coffee, water, wine, beer, vinegar, or poison — not a drop two hours before or after eating! All the mountain air, scenery, carbonic-acid waters avail not if you absorb liquids while you eat. This is the famous Schweniger cure that Bismarck found so beneficial. If you plumply put the question to your doctor — there are hundreds of medical men camped in and about Marienbad — he is apt to answer you enigmatically. The full force of the discovery dawns on you after you leave the town. In Central Park you can take the waters at the pavilion, walk from Fifty-ninth to One Hundred and Tenth Streets and back, go home, eat breakfast, avoid liquids at meals, and four weeks later you will have pulled off from ten to twenty pounds. I know this from experience. But there is the sea trip; there is the fair land of Bohemia; there is Marienbad, a white city of miniature palaces and castellated heights — during moonlight the Café Rübezahl is like a frozen fairy-tale — with its air, its freedom from the fashionable crowds of hill-hemmed Karlsbad, its romantic surroundings, its moderate tariff, and its perpetual eating and drinking (such cookery!), and its weighing machines. When you are tired of the music you get yourself weighed. When you are weary of walking you listen to the band. There are less interesting watering-places on the map than Marienbad — and there is always Pilsen forty miles away. So, if you would fight your fat pleasantly and distribute your Yankee dollars — go to Marienbad, and don't forget to close your eyes when you pass the confectionery shops or the cafés. That way fat lies.

PART III

SAND AND SENTIMENT

I

ATLANTIC CITY

WHEN in the course of human events it becomes necessary for a man to study his own people, let him select the excellent old summertime for such a purpose; let him go down to the sea in Pullmans or naphtha launches; let him, with observant and kindly eye, note the peculiarities of the nation in which he is an unimportant factor, and he may see things — many things undreamed of in his little European-saturated philosophy.

Let us pose a possible case. A traveller, restless because he has seen or fancied he has seen all Europe, resolves to stay on his native soil for one summer. From much globe-trotting he has not become blasé, he still emulates Dr. Syntax in his pursuit of the picturesque; but his conscience begins to ring accusatory alarm-bells. You know Sorrento, but do you know Cape May? You have patrolled the beach at Scheveningen, but do you know the delights of Atlantic City's Boardwalk? Can you offhand say whether Bailey's Beach has as good surf as Seabright? Newport vs. New Jersey. Do they sell you worse imitation Havanas at Southampton or at

Richfield Springs? Where is the most pessimistic beer served on the Atlantic coast? Can you answer one of these profoundly interesting questions?

Why? Because you don't know your own country. Because you don't know how it chooses to amuse itself during the heated term. Because you do know that it always rains in Salzburg; that it is always hot and high-priced in Paris; that you sit up too late in Berlin and retire too early in London. My possible case is not a representative American, though he is by no means a myth. You know him. I know him. And the sign whereby he may be recognised is this: his superior airs and his manner of calling a coloured waiter garçon or Kellner. Otherwise he couldn't tell the difference between a Da Vinci and a Carlo Dolci, a Bach fugue and a Nuremberg sausage. The gilt of his too rapidly acquired culture is apt to become blurred by ocean's rude breezes.

Consider me for the moment as one of those self-expatriated compatriots, but one of humble spirit, one willing to learn, and one to whom the great idea made a visit and a proposition. Suppose, said the tempter, you made the acquaintance of the Americans at play! Suppose you try to forget noisy New York for a day, a week, a month, and range boldly up and down seeking forth prey for your pen, recording daily what you see, imagining nothing but divining much. Suppose, in a word, you take a peep at the real world, not at a few hundred luxurious people, and endeavour to escape the obsession of those you fancy to be the elect in art and life and literature. What a "bath of multitude" you will give your convention-weary soul; how you will refresh your eyes, too long accustomed to Broadway and its brass bands!

I confess I listened to the voice of the tempter, and here am I, in Atlantic City, quite oblivious to Budapest or Copenhagen and positively absorbed in the novelty of the situation. For you it would be a thrice-told tale, signifying a summer outing. For me it is as if I had fallen asleep in Peru and awakened in Philadelphia — with a difference. Consider me, then, as consulting time-tables, as discussing various routes to the sea. It was terra-nova for me. I saw with the eye of the newly born — at least, I hope I did. I confused the man in the office by asking for a first-class ticket for Atlantic City. He jeered. Then I remembered I was in the land of equality, where a man could make himself superior to his fellow beings and also uncomfortable by paying for seats in a parlor coach.

The psychology of Atlantic City! It is a bold man who will attempt its elucidation. It has no moral landscape, though it boasts the finest of seascapes. If there were already invented, as there will be some day, a psychical cinematograph, then, perhaps, a complete picture could be presented of this fascinating and vulgar resort — for vulgar in the sense of popularity it is, monumentally vulgar, epically vulgar — epical — that is the word. There is a sweep of colour, a breeziness of space, a riot of sound, and a chaos of movement that appal by their amplitude. All creation seems out-of-doors. You jostle elbows with the man from Hindustan, the man from Newark, the man from London, and the man from California. Black, white, yellow, red, and brown races mingle on the Boardwalk in that never-ending promenade from the Inlet to the new pier. Between the Pickle pier and the Marlborough-Blenheim the course of humanity takes its way. In that section it is thickest. You use the short-arm jolt at every other step, and you wonder, if it is so bad at the beginning of the season, what it will be next week. In fifteen minutes you long for the comparative ease of the rush hour on the Brooklyn Bridge.

But how to "decompose" this swirling kaleidoscope into the semblance of a picture? You may have come over from idyllic Cape May, where the locust clicks at noon and the cricket twitches a duet with the booming frogs after sundown. You may have come from Ocean City by boat to Longport, thence by trolley to your hotel. Confused by the change, looking vainly for old landmarks, a prey to various apprehensions — hotel prices, the rapacity of porters and hackmen, the insolence of waiters — you fall into the nearest house and wish you hadn't five minutes later. However, you are on the beach, and as you remove your dripping linen you sigh for New York. But that is because Atlantic City has not begun to work its deadly spell. As a rule, the first ten minutes in a strange place is a period of disenchantment. To orient one's self takes at least an hour. The barber and a cooling cup of tea (I said "tea"!) are great aids to the shy spirit of man. If you have not to formulate your impressions on paper, then, lucky one, fear nothing except the occasional mosquito. After the paucity of ideas aroused by such a simple spot as Cape May, the visions, complex, multitudinous, that pour in upon your sensorium at Atlantic City are very disturbing. Where to begin! Where to end! Doubtless the best way would be to describe the Boardwalk by day and by night, then trot about the hotels, make a short dash to the Inlet, another to Longport, and — home. But you would not have compassed even the superficies of the island. There is a different Atlantic City every hour. To register accurately its shifting moods of the moment would need the combined pens of Gautier, Zola, and Mark Twain.

When our gifted gang of young fiction miners are quite through imitating Bret Harte and Buffalo Bill in the depiction of a Wild West that never existed, when they have finished currying the national mane, let them turn to Atlantic City as a more fruitful theme. It's broad avenue of wood by the sea will be supplanted by concrete in time. The medley of life, the roaring of megaphones instead of newspapers, the frantic rush and indescribable gabble of a Babel-like chorus, the dazzling single line of booths, stores, divans, holes-in-the-wall hotels, cafés, carousels, soda-fountains, shows; the buzzing of children, the shouting newsboys, the appeals of fakers, the quick glance of her eye, the scowl of beach hawks and the innocent mien of bucolics — a Walt Whitman catalogue would not exhaust this new metropolis by the sea, this paradise of "powerful, uneducated persons," patricians, millionaires, and mendicants. In the foreground a brilliant sea with its "husky haughty lips"; as a background against a limpid western sky-line is set a row of hotels, some palaces, some breath-catching, many commonplace. And the piers — the Steel pier, the Auditorium, Young's, Heinz's, and the new million-dollar steel-and-concrete pier of John Young, completed some time; another city, a second Atlantic City, on steel and iron stilts extending a half-mile into the water, containing a half-hundred diversions — what shall we say to these piers? They may recall the evolution from the lake-dwellers of central Europe, whose lacustrine deposits we marvel over, just as huge structures, reared in the air, the modern hotels are the highly developed habitat of the cliff-dwellers. Doubtless five thousand years hence ardent geologists will rummage into the deposits of Atlantic City and erect systems on the strange shapes discovered, the combs, corsets, shovels, hairpins, flasks, and other "kitchen midden" of our days that will have been buried.

Atlantic City is a queer cosmopolis, and a cosmopolis that may perish easily in a giant inundation, so closely does it crowd the rim of the sea. I called it vulgar. It is, and ugly, too, with that absorbing ugliness of modern life; but it is also many other things. Not Ostend, not Dieppe, not Brighton (England), not Trouville, not Scheveningen, not Boulogne, nor Etretat, Abbazia, nor Cuxhaven, Naples, nor the Riviera rival its infinite variety. Yet if you wish to loaf and invite your soul, Cape May is preferable. Atlantic City is not a retreat for the introspective; it is all on the surface; it is hard, glittering, unspeakably cacophonous, and it never sleeps at all. Three days and you crave the comparative solitude of Broadway and Thirty-fourth Street; a week and you may die of insomnia.

There is in reality no type of American girlhood. When you hear of the summer girl you may be sure that the phrase was invented by the same lazy-minded male who created the matinée girl. Both exist only on paper. A stroll along the Boardwalk will prove this. Every variety of girl passes you. She is dark haired and red, blond, and brunette. Her nose is long and thin, thick, Grecian, or upturned like the petal of a rose. But she is pretty in her undistinguished way. Pretty girls are really as thick as politicians. The interesting girl is rare. They all dress with admirable taste, possibly not without an overaccentuation of colour — a tropical profuseness, one might add. However, it is hot weather, and — one thing we forget — America is the tropics during July and August. In the genuine tropics they dress accordingly; we do not. We wear abominable linen and leather and woolen; therefore a little latitude in the cut and hue of women's dress is pardonable. I never saw such a forest of bare arms before, arms held slightly in rear of the body, not in bathing costume, but street dress. And such shapely arms! A Mahometan would turn his head the other way if he spied them. This display of flesh and muscle, coupled with the towering head-dress à la Pompadour, gave me an impression of the barbaric. And when I saw a brace of dusky belles with their frizzly locks puffed up in the same extravagant fashion, the illusion was still more complete. These descendants of Lybian queens are nearer the soil than their white sisters, but the "pull" of their sex made them all row in the same boat. Such costly dressing, such huge bowknots on their low sleeves, such palimpsests of veils — the more you peel off the farther you are from the face, like those trick boxes of conjurers! I am free to confess that the American girls I saw were more imposing than their male escorts. They did, indeed, lack a certain distinction, and the English you heard fall from their mouths was often dreadful — not dreadful alone because of its slang but because the intonation, pronunciation, and enunciation were so careless, so slipshod, so deadly common. These are sins overheard in most cities. In Atlantic City they salute you with painful emphasis. But what a carriage, what light-footed elegance, what perpetual chewing of gum, what a mixture of twangs!

The young men resolve themselves more easily into a type because they persist in dressing alike. The peg-top trousers, the flaring cut of the sack coat, the flat felt hat, the gaudy shirts and ties seem from the same shops. You notice with grateful eyes that the tinted waist sash has disappeared and that hosiery is less voluptuous in design. The man who wears naughty socks is a man lost to a higher purpose. His is an essentially trivial mind; for him Emerson hath no charm; a yellow primrose is an ever-yellow primrose in his clockwork-haunted eyes. The notion the stranger gleans of these young fellows is that they are a well-meaning, sturdy, and slightly hard-featured lot. They shave clean. The square jaw, blue-grey eyes, and short nose betray Celtic or Germanic traces. Their forebears were Irish or Teuton, and the whole mass is leavened by a generous infusion of the Eastern; you see, too, the olive skin, the deep-cupped eyes, crisp locks, and brilliant colouring of the Oriental. Among the women the Semitic is often encountered, and invariably the ensemble is harmonious, the figure in particular attracting attention by its richer and more generous curves. Of the purely exotic one never fails in Atlantic City; Syrians, Turks, Indians, Gipsies, Armenians, Russians, Chinese, Siamese, Japanese — the beach swarms with all manner and conditions of outlanders. The costumes are correspondingly picturesque.

If our native girls seem to copy in carriage and general style a combination of Ethel Barrymore and Maude Adams, the young men affect the rich and careless collegian attitude. They would have us believe that they have just escaped the university. It is when the inevitable African brother appears that comparisons are ludicrous; the same pancake grey felt, the same baggy trousers, the same belt and tie, the same stride and "stolid demeanour." It is a time for discreet smiles. Imitation is not always the most agreeable form of flattery.

Away from the ceaseless patter of feet and the humming of many tongues you escape to the beach. It is the hour of the most sacred function of Atlantic City — the hour of the bath. Apart from the absence of the little bathing-houses so familiar in Europe, from which you descend solo into the water, there is not a marked difference nowadays between the customs and costumes here and on the Continent. A decade ago American bathing suits were denounced by Europeans as wholly wicked. At Trouville to-day it is the American who will be shocked. To be sure, our mermaids are beginning to discard stockings; the effect of the glancing sunshine is rather disquieting. After all, Atlantic City is devoted to the ocean for itself; there are many beach-combers — the girls who let their hair down to dry while they make living sculpture on the sand and beam on their favoured young man browning himself at their feet; but the main business of these folk is to get wet and enjoy themselves in the breakers; also to fight out in a pleasant spot the never-ending duel of the sexes. There she goes, tall, alert, plunging in recklessly, riding the curling waves, a Galatea in silk.

The beach is a noble one for swimming, though not so perfect as the strand at Cape May. No table d'hôte salutes you as you breast the water — the coast is free from sewage. It is a pity that Atlantic City has become such a big town. There is no trolley on the beach; instead it runs from the Inlet through Atlantic Avenue, which is very businesslike, as far as Albany Avenue before the ocean is seen, but after that there is a superb vista until you reach Longport, not missing the elephant on the way. Nine miles and more is the distance you may travel on this trolley-line. The great number of hotels and cottages have robbed the place of all its old rustic al fresco charm. Even Brigantine Beach has succumbed to the superior magnetism of the larger city and to-day is moribund. There are railroads, hotels, steamboat service on this once-famous resort across the Inlet, but, notwithstanding the large sums of money expended, it has gone into a decadence, let us hope a temporary one. Too thickly populated in summertime, Atlantic City, when a land breeze blows, is as hot as any inland town — I was about to say hotter. The sun beats down upon your head with brassy splendour. There is no shade excepting the piers and piazzas. The hotels are stuffy, and at the end of the piers the thermometers range high. In the water is the only comfort to be had. Luckily such heat is infrequent and does not long endure.

Music assails your ears every few feet. From the howling of some hideous talking-machine to the loud, confident blaring of the orchestra of the wooden horses and wooden rabbits in the carousel you can't escape noise. Curiously enough, Wagner is the favourite composer. At Longport, where you drink cherry-bounce, I heard an orchestrion play the prelude to Die Meistersinger, and the carousel amazed me with its shrill performance of the Valkyrie's Ride. Lohengrin, poor, peerless knight, is hacked at by mechanical pianos and steam-organs. Various bands, brass and wood-wind predominating, attack Wagner in piecemeal. To hear an Italian orchestra playing the andante from the Fifth Symphony of Beethoven on the pier is to hear a wonderful misplacement of accents and expression. Never mind; it's better than ragtime. People whistle Wagner. He will end by becoming the most popular composer in the world — a horrible fate for a great man. To add to this overwhelming symphonic olla podrida the automobiles and their tritone whistles bring dismay to your ears with melancholy, blood-curdling wails like those of a banshee on the night when Larry was stretched.

You can fish in the Inlet, sail in the open. I had the Bluebird out for a memorable morning. Rockfish, I was informed by a facetious person, are caught daily and of great size at the Inlet. It proved to be my merry friend's witticism over the efforts of enthusiastic, misguided men, whose hooks became entangled in the rocks, when, thinking they had a bite, they attempted to uproot the bottom of the bay. To vary the monotony of a hot afternoon I attended a game of baseball at the Inlet. It was my first. I do not understand the game, but I understand the instinct that has survived from the bloody spectacle of the antique circus and is reincarnated in the national game. Is it not a refined form of cruelty to force full-grown men to rush about in the fiercest sun's rays after a contemptibly small ball, tumbling in their eagerness to please their tyrants in the grand-stand and on the bleachers? What is it all about? I saw a fat man wearing a life-preserver on his chest, a wire mask on his face and shouting signals while dodging the wooden club with which the ball is attacked — that is, when it isn't missed. Men sprawl in the gravel, men scream angry oaths, men are abused with vast vociferousness by the spectators. All this in the open air, with the heat furnace-like, and for the sake of a pitiable ball. Childhood's game of tag seems more sensible; golf is positively intellectual by comparison. And the cruelty of it! I only know one other form of diversion more cruel, and that is a piano recital wherein a pianist plays a list of twenty compositions from Bach to Tschaikowsky. I must confess, however, that this particular game had its humorous compensations. It was waged between the Philadelphia Giants, a coloured organisation, and the Cuban Stars, real natives of the Pearl of the Antilles. As the score was three to one at the close, I presume the Giants walloped the Cubans. A husky giant, black as a solar eclipse and on third base, kept us cool by chanting at intervals the sad story of his bet on a horse named Hydrant, a horse which is still running. This Solomon lent to the afternoon an air of distinction. But I was as thirsty as a rainbow before the affair was concluded, and you know a rainbow is double-ended.

At a hotel I saw a dozen women, their fingers covered with opals, emeralds, and sapphires, eating green corn on the cob. How this sight would have pleased the tempestuous fancy of M. Paul Adam, who has written a book about America! The dozen mouths opened simultaneously, pink and pearly traps; there was a snapping of dentals, a gnashing of corn. The diamonds flashed, the emeralds blazed with their sinister green, and the troubled milky fire of the opals matched at times the colour of the slaughtered vegetables. Surely no other could enjoy such a scintillating death at the teeth of a dozen pretty overdressed matrons and maids.

I have seen old men, whose teeth were worn away by many years of frozen punch, call for three kinds of dessert — the summer hotel dinner is a terrific thing. There is too much to choose from, and one eats far more than is good for him. You don't have to swallow everything, but the average sensual man when he pays five dollars a day usually tries to get even with the landlord. And the prices are on the upward move. For a room with bath you pay everywhere five dollars and extra for board. Nor am I disposed to wax patriotic over American hotels. Europe is no longer the place where comfortable, well-lighted rooms with bath are a rarity. You may grumble at paying twenty marks a day for your room at the Hotel Bristol, Berlin, but you are given a big marble bath sunk in the floor and a reception as well as a bed room. And this at the most expensive hotel in Prussia. Compare this with the rooms you are shown throughout America for the same price. I have done so throughout this little pilgrimage of mine and have been astonished by the inferiority of first-class hotels in the provinces to first-class establishments in Europe. The service and the cooking are on a much lower scale, for the native American doesn't care for the nuance in his food, in his art, in his literature. He likes them all flavourless. He gobbles everything in a hurry, and quantity is more telling than quality. This also applies to the manner in which he accumulates money; but there he has the better of the European.

Are pianos ever tuned at summer hotels? Better the mechanical eloquence of the mechanical piano than the cracked tintinnabulations of Chopin played by a young woman with a lawn-tennis touch. And we are as crude musically as in other things. The length of the land wretched music reigns. You may miss it in the city, but you are a helpless victim when vacation days find you on the countryside. A nation is no better than the music it makes; its music is its touchstone. Let us mitigate the rigour of this statement, else should we stand shamefaced before the world, so vile, so vulgar, so clatteringly empty is our popular music-making — with a few honourable exceptions. Don't fancy I yearn for the classics or Wagner during the dog-days. Better are the old so-called "darky" tunes of Stephen Foster as compared to the shrill insolence of the degrading ragtime, the snorting marches, and back-alley two-steps that fill the spaces of our hotels with their impertinent, shallow sonorities. How can a country aspire to artistic grandeur that tolerates such musical monstrosities! Better a toneless land than such parodies. No wonder we grow Comstocks instead of Mozarts!

Ah! If America would only stick to American cookery we should not be a nation of dyspeptics. There is better, because plainer, cooking in many farmhouses than at our hotels. The curse of imitation hangs over the menu — imitating the names of French dishes, it seldom comes nearer than the name. Why should we be poisoned by these wretched attempts at the Gallic. Everywhere the order of the French dinner — rather say the Parisian — is attempted. But we get watery soups, fish with mediocre sauce, the roast seldom rare and neither English nor French, the entrées ridiculous and chilled, while the unhappy vegetables are marshalled in like a fleet of porcelain scows surrounding the flag-ship — a plate of overdone beef floating in thin gravy. We have the best material in the world — meats, fowl, vegetables, fruits — and in America the cooking is the worst in the world. Why? Simply because we pattern at a deplorable distance after a foreign model. The real American home cooking sets your memory jubilating.

But Atlantic City at night! It is a picture for such different painters as Whistler or Toulouse-Lautrec, and it is a sight not duplicated on earth. Miles of glittering electric lamps light the Boardwalk. Even the dark spaces above the Pickle pier are now festooned with lace-like fire. It is a carnival of flame. You may start from the spot where in letters of fire you read, "Will you marry me?" near the Heinz pier, and with a book slowly walk for miles, perusing it all the while until you have passed the lower end of the walk, which recalls Coney Island, and finally touch the last wooden rail. Or, if you prefer riding, take one of those comfortable sedan-chairs and be wheeled by a dark lad for a small sum. The enormous amount of electricity consumed seems to make the air vital. Through these garlands of light moves a mob of well-behaved humans. The women are more mysterious than in the daytime. Everywhere you encounter the glances of countless eyes if you are still youthful. Evening toilets of the most dazzling kind assault your nerves. Wealth fairly envelops you. There is apparently no such thing as poverty or sickness in existence; the optimistic exuberance of the American woman and man is seen here at its ripest. There is a suggestion of the overblown, of the snobbish, in this display, but I was not looking for the fly in the ointment, and so I enjoyed the picture as I should have enjoyed some gorgeous tableau in Aïda or Salammbô. It was as real. The love-birds kept up their whirring as from the lighthouse to the new pier the procession bubbled and boiled. No wonder Sarah Bernhardt exclaimed in her effusive manner that Atlantic City is unique. And she saw it in the winter-time.

On the Steel pier they were giving a children's ball. I had wearied of vaudeville, of the roller-skating, of the thousand and two shows to be viewed, scattered over the various piers. A child's ball would be a genuine novelty. Children rule at this city. I saw so few at Cape May that babies appear to rain from the skies here. They roll about the sand like little animals, and when they should be in bed, dreaming of candy angels, they are togged in festal raiment and allowed to dance their tender legs off till midnight. The huge dancing-hall of the pier was filled with happy and proud parents. A band played with vicious precision a march as a half-mile of children and tots of three or four slowly paced the slippery floor. A master of ceremonies with a cool head solemnly guided the manœuvres of this juvenile army. Two by two, boy and girl, they moved to the music with shining, evening faces, all vainly dressed, all eager and joyous. They were each given a prize. The effect was indescribable. Nearly half a thousand children, preparing for the great, good game of life, some of them with matured faces, the majority wearing that wonderful expression of expectancy, as if the curtain were about to be lifted and the glorious secret of life revealed to their ravished gaze. I could not help recalling Thackeray and his moist spectacles when he heard the charity children sing at St. Paul's. I tried to weep, but the music was too excruciating, and a child slipped on the polished parquet and — drat that youngster! she dropped sand in my shoe when I was getting my handkerchief ready!

ATLANTIC CITY

They have a hyphenated hotel on the beach. The architecture of one section is so extraordinary that I gasped when I saw it. I haven't the remotest notion of the architect's name, nor did I go into the hotel, fearing the usual perfection of modern appliances and all the rest of the useful things that are driving romance away from our age. It was the exterior that glued my feet to the Boardwalk. If Coleridge, in Kubla Khan, or Poe, in The Domain of Arnheim, had described such a fantastic structure we should have understood, for they were men of imagination. But in the chilly, æsthetic air of our country, where utility leads beauty by the nose, to see a man giving rein to his fancy as has the man who conceived this exotic pile is delightfully refreshing. William Beckford, the author of Vathek, would have wished for nothing richer. The architecture might be Byzantine. It suggests St. Marco's at Venice, St. Sophia at Constantinople, or a Hindu palace, with its crouching dome, its operatic façade, and its two dominating monoliths with blunt tops. Built of concrete, the exterior decoration is a luxurious exfoliation in hues, turquoise and fawn. I did not venture near the building for fear some Atlantic City Flip would cry out: "Wake up! You are at Winslow Junction!" If ever I go to the place again it will be to see this dream architecture, with its strange evocations of Asiatic colour and music.

II

NEWPORT

At Newport I tasted sour grapes. In the heart of Newport I became a snob. Newport saw me fall from grace, social, not sinful. Worse remains — at Newport I took my maiden voyage in a motor-car. I am still giddy from the swiftly shifting experiences of the week spent at the Queen of Summer Resorts — as the real-estate agents call this little Rhode Island town. I had reached Boston, only to miss the one comfortable afternoon train to Newport. And the night of horror I spent in that congeries of crooked streets I endured as a penance for my frequent complaints against New York. We are noisy, but Boston caps us at the game. Their elevated railroad sounds like the thunderous approach of a tornado; to sleep within a mile of it is out of the question, particularly as they close the drug stores at eleven o'clock. What man said that he would rather be a policeman in Harlem than a poet in Boston? Although I do not know his name, I wave him a friendly salute.

Naturally I arrived at Newport the next day in a bad humour. The weather did not improve my temper. It was muggy. It weighed upon one like the folds of a deflated balloon. You felt heavier, older, more serious. This, then, I thought, is the nerve-soothing climate I have read so much about! Give me Saratoga. Give me the Berkshires. In a depressing mood I sauntered through the town, which was lively enough, preparations for the carnival being in progress. But I found it dull, not quaintly dull, as did Henry James, but provincially so. The old court-house, Touro Park, Morton Park, the Hebrew cemetery, the queer little streets with queer little houses on them, the narrow sidewalks — all these, with their historical memories, did not elicit from me the mental spark we call interest. My historic sense failed me when most I needed it. I did not feel the thrill patriotic when I saw Uncle Sam's sailors rolling about the place loaded to the gunwales with fire-water. Nor did I go out of my way to look at the Perry Monument or Fort Adams. In a word, I was a disgruntled human, suffering from the humidity, annoyed by the proximity of much inutile bustle, and selfishly absorbed in himself. Perhaps I was suffering from that minor malady peculiar to socialists called "sour grapes." I had asked several policemen to point me out an aristocrat, a millionaire; but my request had in all cases been received with suspicious glances. I had seen French and English aristocrats and had been greatly impressed by their disengagement from the quotidian things of life. They had sauntered, they had lolled, they had looked bored. Would the American aristo saunter, loll, and look bored? Finally a man who was reading Thoreau near the Old Mill advised me to hire a carriage and see the ocean driveway.

As soon as we entered Bellevue Avenue, what I had been searching for commenced to make its presence apprehended; the thrice-distilled, the precious atmosphere of Newport gently smote my dejected consciousness. I sat up and began to take notice. The driver was an old resident, a bluff person, middle-aged, shrewd, and not given to mincing his language. He called a millionaire a millionaire. Before I had reached the Spouting Rock I had made the acquaintance of the largest and most select closet of family skeletons outside of an anatomical museum. How they dangled before my eyes! How they beckoned with bony beckonings! How they leered from their empty eye sockets! How they wagged their shining skulls! It was a Danse Macabre this coachman set moving for my benefit. And what a catalogue of misery, sin, unhappiness, sordid vulgarity, even crime, was unrolled! Suicide, embezzlement, dishonoured homes, disgrace, and all manner of follies had happened within the sacred precincts of this billion-dollar paradise. Anecdote piled on anecdote; scandal trailed after scandal; no one was spared. In despair I asked this dealer in fractured decalogues if he took me for a newspaper man. He replied, without an appearance of surprise, that he knew I was a clergyman.

"Then drive to the nearest church," I sternly admonished him, "or else stop talking!" He swallowed the hint and we drove on. But I still suffered. What! this angelic retreat concealed such vile and pitiful histories? Of what value is great wealth if it cannot smooth away all the rough places, heal all the sores? This modern philosopher's stone for which we all struggle, this magic medium which occupies the foreground of our waking and dreaming thoughts our lives long — is it not the real solvent of evil? May it be in reality evil itself?

"Over yonder," said the driver, breaking my profound meditations, "is The Breakers." The mist encircled it and it looked like a mediæval fortress, full of torture chambers.

Many other wonderful houses I saw, veritable palaces, surrounded by magnificent gardens, embowered densely in flowers, beautiful beyond the dream of poets, and framed by rich vegetation and trees of heroic growth. All that has been said in praise of Newport you may safely set down as an understatement. It is more formal than you may expect — I mean in the rectitude of its wide avenues on the Hill and in the controlled efflorescence of its horticulture. Design, taste, even fantasy, are everywhere visible. There are explosions of hydrangeas of almost every hue, in company with the looming and floral flight of tall hollyhocks. I saw some gardens that recalled England, others that transported me to Italy — but Italy in the spring-tide, before the lustre of summer has robbed the hills of their delicate contours, the flowers of their virginal pose. If Newport should ever change its commonplace name it could be re-christened Hydrangea without doing violence either to fact or imagination.

The Cliff Walk is three miles and a half of the pure picturesque. From Easton's Beach to Land's End there is a series of surprises; not alone in the villas, but in the coy turns of the walk, the unexpected change of marine physiognomy, and then the sheer romance of the entire coast. Unlike Mr. James, I came to Newport unburdened by memories. It was my first visit. I saw it with eyes not haunted by ghosts of dead youth; nor did I fetch with me prejudices.

If society folk can't always catch the glint of gold on a canvas of Monticelli, or the harmonies in a Ballade by Chopin, or the ethereal tones of Shelley, or the marmoreal splendours of Milton, or the tortured music of a Rodin group, why, it is their loss. As compensation they may dine and wine — not things to be despised — dress and gamble, waste or win; above all, feel to their finger-tips a sense of power. And the last may be best. Things balance in this universe, notwithstanding our cry against the injustice of the cosmos. I should probably be a very unhappy man were I wealthy; yet I understand the pleasures wealth confers. So do not let us despise the multimillionaire. Often has his wealth been thrust upon him. Often it irks its owner, who seeks to get rid of the burden by opening his windows and throwing his money into the streets. We speak of such as dissipated; in reality it is nature striving to attain its accustomed mediocrity. Let us applaud spendthrifts and them that go down to the market-place, there to fribble away their inheritance. And let us also put an end to this useless moralising and continue our tale.

I had viewed all Newport from the outside. I had been to the Casino playground looking for my American aristocrat, instead seeing a nice set of young chaps with brawny, sun-spotted arms all playing tennis; I had lunched at Berger's, walked through Love Lane — alas! — alone; had glanced at General Prescott's headquarters in 1776, at the home of William Ellery, a signer of the Declaration of Independence; at the old Trinity Church, the Channing House, built in 1720; the New York Yacht Club, the Windmill, even had I gone to Lawton's Valley; I knew the Parade by heart, and I disliked the brittle noise of Thames Street, disliked its crowds, its ugly shops. At Mile End I found solitude; and I viewed Gooseberry Island — its seclusion — that tiny islet where poker is played to the swash of the waves, where jack-pots of fabulous sums are opened by the sporting old bucks who go over in launches and return often with empty pockets. When I passed Rochambeau's headquarters during the Revolution I tried to conjure up a thrill, but a baby playing on the door-step with a kitten was better to my eyes than all the musty, dusty memories. I saw Bailey's Beach, where the swells bathe in perfumed salt water; Easton's Beach, where the water is common salt for the plain people.

This same drive was under a slaty grey sky. The ocean was leaden in hue, and across the bay the clouds hung like those "white elephants" Henry James saw on the Cliff Walk. The world was drab for me. I met a few people driving. Otherwise Newport seemed unpeopled. The Addicks mansion, the "gas house," looked dreary on its dreary perch. And then something happened. A voice I well knew called out:

"You plumber, you! What comet shook you from its tail into Newport?" It was Clarence, the only son and graceless heir of a chewing-gum emperor, in his sixty-horse-power car puffing and blowing on the narrows and I sitting in a hired vehicle watching him with amazed eyes. My driver had also astonished eyes. He appeared downcast. He was evidently pondering his list of skeletons!

"You chump, get out of that trap and come into my boiler-shop. I call this machine of mine mangeur de poulets, it eats up the chickens so beautifully." I stretched my cramped legs and responded to Clarence's invitation slowly. For one thing, I didn't like the look of his piratical craft. I hated to admit it — I had never been in an automobile before. Clarence laughed.

"Don't let that worry you — you won't contract seasickness; and please call it a motor-car. They say 'automobiles' in New York. This is Newport." I grinned. Then I asked my man what I owed him. He calculated audibly. "You're not keeping to your contract," he blandly observed, "and so it will cost you a dollar extra."

"But, you old undertaker of live reputations," I hotly answered, "I'm saving you a farther ride." "I'm here and I've got to take the team home," he doggedly maintained. And so I paid him, greatly wondering at Rhode Island arithmetic.

"Serves you right," added Clarence, "for not letting me know you were here. Jump in. Hold on to your teeth. Let her go!" We flew homeward. We flew heavenward. I saw sky rush down to sea and meet in rough embrace. Houses looked like trees and trees like toothpicks. I remembered my past and I saw my future; the present was merely a humming bridge between. Clarence, still smiling, tooted masterfully. From Bailey's Beach to Easton's we ran in thirty-three seconds — at least that is what he said. Later I discovered that he had been boasting.

But the ride had other results. A psychical transformation was going on within me. My subliminal self was slowly pushing into the map of my consciousness a new Me. Suddenly I became a snob. A full-fledged snob sat in the place occupied before by a modest, middle-aged, stout person, full of the vapours. What had happened? Alas, I was become a snob! I meanly admired mean things. I admired myself. I admired the auto — the motor-car. I admired Clarence. Above all, I looked down on the world afoot. What black magic had emanated from the petrol of this fugacious machine that so changed a man into a snob! Mark the consequences.

"Clarence," I said, endeavouring to appear haughty, "Clarence, what are those creatures in the surf?" Clarence, still wearing that damnable smile of his, responded:

"Those are the common people bathing."

"Ah, you mean hoi polloi." I chuckled at my wit.

"Odi profanum vulgus," he quickly retorted. When bad Greek meets worse Latin, then comes the tug of tongues! Our chauffeur — I say "our" — who sat in the garage, or the panneau, or some part of the locomotive, was a New Zealander disguised as a man from Brittany. He was versed in all the moves of the social checker-board. As we turned toward the town he blew a whistle.

"I made him do that," remarked Clarence languidly, "to remind me of my engagements." The idea tickled my fancy.

"Why not employ flappers, as they did in Swift's Laputa?"

"Howdye do, Reggie?" called out Clarence to a young fellow in a red-wheeled bucking bronco.

The name sounded familiar. Reggie and Newport! Ay, ay, of course, said I to myself, remembering my blue book.

"Howdye do, Harry?" I sat up, displaying pardonable curiosity.

"The Harry?"

"Of course," replied Clarence pettishly. "And, old man, please don't wear your ignorance on your sleeve, I'll post you later. I'm ashamed if Armance, my chauffeur, hears you. Remember — not a word about chewing-gum down here. They won't stand for it. I'm the son of a sugar sultan, not, as you so stupidly call it, a chewing-gum potentate. And please don't make so much fun of the girls who chew gum in America. My father has already asked me to cross you off my visiting list. All American girls chew gum. Also — in the house of the hangman no one speaks of the rope!"

"And in Newport?" I hazarded. He pulled up his machine.

"Newport is not America — put that in your social pipe and smoke it. Newport is an island surrounded by Americans. All the smart Americans are working twenty-five hours a day to get here; their wives are driving them to it. And if work won't get them here they rob banks, plunder insurance companies, water railroad stock, milk the public generally so as to land here." He paused.

"And what do they do when they do get here?" I said, as if in a dream. I was still a snob. I still saw myself hugely silhouetted against the social horizon, with my friends at my boot heels. Oh, automobile — I mean, motor-car — what sins may be laid to thy account! Thou art the modern Mephisto who tempts the poor little Fausts that earn a handful of dollars every week!

"Do?" replied Clarence, calmly handing a cigarette to the hairy Armance, "why, work like the rest of the social convicts on this island of golden castaways." I roared. Clarence could be witty. But he regarded me sourly.

"Don't be a bromide!" he tartly commanded. Ever since he had met Gelett Burgess at a dolls' dance Clarence fancied himself a sulphite. But he wasn't. I knew it. I laughed again, loudly and, I fear, vacantly.

"There you go," he exclaimed. "You are like the rest of the rank outsiders. You come down here and go to the Casino or to the club, and because you see some people lounging you talk about the idle rich. But there are no idle rich at Newport. They are the busy rich. They work harder than a motorman. They are nearly all motormen. Mechanics, jockeys, athletes, gourmands — if they can't work their muscles they can their teeth — pedestrians, gymnasts, swimmers, sailors, butlers, dancers, polo players, bar mixers, lawn-tennis virtuosi, aeronauts, locomotive drivers, horse trainers, billiardists — why, the list might be stretched from here to the harbour. Idle? These people? They work harder than draught horses from morning to midnight. They toil as toils no sailor doing his daily stint. And they put their soul into their work. And the women are quite as devoted in this self-abnegation. Just watch Willie Dubbs — you know, the son of old Dubbs, who was painted by Sargent. Don't you remember that picture at the society's exhibition, No. 23, Portrait of a Gentlemanly Ass? Well, watch Willie mix a cocktail. No artist at the Waldorf can touch him. No, my poor old chap, you don't know this crowd as I do. Their money is not like that of Midas. Everything they touch turns them to work. If they can't work they die — die of indigestion or of ennui. And a healthier, handsomer set of men and women you won't see in all America. They all look as if Gibson and Dick Davis designed them. Go any Thursday night to Freebody Park, where they give a vaudeville show. Well, you'll find the boxes crowded with the best set. There is little difference, after all, between the poor American man and the American aristocrat. Both have the same tastes. Both eat, drink, smoke, and slang as much as they can. Both work hard, both enjoy vaudeville shows, both like pretty women, both" — I interrupted him.

"And how about poetry, art, music? How about the old-fashioned leisure and dignity?"

"Rot! Nowadays we haven't time to be polite. We're hustlers."

"Bravo, monsieur!" It was the voice of Armance. Clarence was touched.

"But as to Harry? What does he work?" I persisted.

"Oh, Harry! He makes epigrams. Here. Armance, take the wheel. Watch the compass. Keep her headed N. by N. E. We go to Reggie's festival." I was appalled. I wore plain clothes. My tie was Bromidian, even though my soul was snobbish. But Clarence would take no refusal. He pulled a note-book from his buff velvet jacket and began reading from it at the top of his lungs.

"Here is a batch of the cleverest things Harry got off at the Wormwoods' dance last Friday. I thought the Missus would die of smiles. Listen — and don't give me away: 'The first to holler is the first to collar.' Great, isn't it? 'Bridge is hell!' 'Faint nerve never won a full hand.' 'Who said fizz?' They always shriek at that one. 'Après moi — le poisson.' 'There's as good fish in the sea as ever came out of the Stuyvesant pond.' 'A live monkey is better than a dead leader.' 'What's the difference between Newport and the Pier?'" Clarence impatiently awaited my answer. I regarded him blankly. "Well?" "Isn't it because Brander Matthews stops at the Pier?"

"You're the limit," he coarsely said. "No, it's because at Narragansett the bathing is better." I moaned. Then I stretched my arms skyward.

"Oh, Clyde Fitch, where are you that I may make my apologies for having attacked your stage pictures of this life? You didn't make it half strong enough — no, not by a half."

"Stop your critical yapping; these are really mine, not Harry's. Here we are." We dismounted. There were about five thousand people, rich, poor, shabby relatives, parasites, social molluscs, and farmers, all trying to get in at once. It was a few miles from Newport. The affair was for a laudable benefit — I forget now just which one. I think few present knew. How the snobbery of these people sickened me! Not one-tenth of them knew their hosts by sight, yet they chatted of them like old friends. So did I to Clarence. I said "Reggie" a dozen times; and how they stared at the prettily garbed and beautiful society women serving ice-cream and lemonade! So did I. But I fancy I did it less rudely. Oh, snobs, snobs, snobs! And I among them all, admiring the display of wealth, the wonderful training-ring, the wonderful horses, the marvellous women. I saw all the fashionable people whose names were printed next morning in the papers. The trouble was that they didn't see me. I expressed this idea to Clarence, but he was busily engaged talking to a girl with turquoise-coloured eyes who spoke slang with a heavenly intonation. Oh, snobs, snobs, snobs!

I was about to address Mrs. Arthur Pompadour, when Clarence, holding me by the elbow, led me to his chicken-slaying chariot. Once ensconced therein he huskily asked: "Where?" "Armance, home for this social aspirant." Away we bowled. I was in the swim. So was Clarence. But Clarence was rich and I was poor. At last I dozed off, only to be overtaken by a nightmare, in which I found myself sweating as I tunnelled my way into the safe of the Chemical Bank. I must have money, money for Newport. Help! Help! I awoke. It was day. Es war ein traum. Alas, poor snob!

That afternoon we cut the dust on the way to Narragansett Pier. We took one of the ferries to Jamestown, crossed the island at a clip, rolled on another boat and, once ashore, rushed our gait until we stood puffing and clanking before the Casino. After some of Sherry's cooking we went about and I saw the place once beloved of Edgar Saltus and celebrated in his brilliant prose. Sherry's chef pleased me as much as anything I encountered at the Pier, even the ocean walk. There is a look of faded splendour about the place despite its wealth and its air of fashion. I have been told by Clarence that I am all wrong, that only now is the Pier taking on new life.

"Consider, reflect if you can," he proceeded. "You lunch at Berger's, over in Newport, and then you leave early and by hard steaming you may get over here and lunch at the Casino. Yet you say our set doesn't do a day's work."

The carnival week, with its glitter, colour,

bustle, gaiety, its crowds, yachts, and war-ships, soldiers, sailors, and numberless girls, left on me a brighter impression of the brave old town. Lovely, auriferous Newport, who shall pluck out the heart of thy melancholy mystery? Under what sinister sand-bank have the jealous gods hidden the proofs of thy family skeletons. If in New York money makes the mare go, in Newport it is wheels that turn the brain. My brain did not regain its average gait until I passed over the gang-plank of the Priscilla, which swam in that harbour that looks so English; and before we reached New York I had shed my snobskin completely.

Newport, thou pactolian city by the sea, before whom so many women of America immolate themselves, Newport, I adore thee, but I shall never look upon thy fair face again — that is, unless Clarence invites me to Villa Confiture. Then by train or balloon I shall storm thy adamantine social wall. Do not leave me, an adipose Peri, at the gates of thy paradise. At Newport I tasted sour grapes. Oh, snobs, snobs, snobs!

www.ingramcontent.com/pod-product-compliance
Lightning Source LLC
LaVergne TN
LVHW010154110826
845151LV00002B/515

* 9 7 8 1 4 2 5 5 3 8 1 2 5 *